BUILDING AND DETAILING
SCALE COMMERCIAL AIRCRAFT

Revell
CONCORDE
1:144
Plastik-Modellbausatz
Plastic model kit
Modèle réduit
Modelbouwdoos
43,3 cm
17,5 cm
BRITISH AIRWAYS
Original-Foto
Photograph of original
Photo: Originale
Foto van het origineel
04257

British airways

BUILDING AND DETAILING SCALE COMMERCIAL AIRCRAFT

MARK STANTON

THE CROWOOD PRESS

First published in 2012 by
The Crowood Press Ltd
Ramsbury, Marlborough
Wiltshire SN8 2HR

www.crowood.com

British Library Cataloguing-in-Publication Data
A catalogue record for this book is available from the British Library.

ISBN 978 1 84797 428 0

Dedication

Dedicated to Daniel, Aimée and Oliver, my co-pilots! Also to my Dad, Graham, who spent many hours taking me to 'watch the aeroplanes' and inspired my love of aviation.

And to Zuzana, thank you for your patience, support and encouragement and for your help 'putting the stickers on!'

Designed and typeset by Guy Croton
Printed and bound in Singapore by Craft Print International Ltd

CONTENTS

FOREWORD

As a Research and Development Engineer for Airfix for over twenty years, I had all sorts of tasks to perform in the course of my duties. However, I have to admit that I did not work on many airliner subjects, as we never had a great deal of money to spend in this area.

The Airfix SkyKing Series of 1/144th scale airliners started in the early sixties with the de Havilland Comet and carried on until the Douglas DC-10 of 1978. I did not personally get involved with Airfix until 1986, when it was purchased by Humbrol, and so was not involved with the tooling of these products. Subsequent to the initial release of these kits, the only changes we made were to the liveries and this was not always easy, as some airlines would not allow their old schemes to be used, only allowing us to release the up-to-date liveries for which we did not have the right aircraft!

There were in fact some very good choices of subject matter, and some of the smaller aircraft appeared in the 1/72nd scale ranges. Heller, when we were 'in bed' with them, did tool some large models that included the Concorde, for which I can claim no credit or, on the other hand, no blame! The nearest you might say I got to designing an airliner kit was the Nimrod, but this could not really be turned back into a Comet on which the original aircraft was based; I would certainly not attempt a conversion of that magnitude!

The good news is, now that Airfix is owned by Hornby, there is the possibility that we could see some new airliner moulds in the future and it will be interesting to see what types will be chosen and in which scale.

I certainly hope you will enjoy reading this book and that it will help you to produce a better model, something which, regardless of subject matter and scale, we are all trying to achieve within the hobby.

Best wishes,

Trevor Snowden
Airfix

OPPOSITE: ***Just a small selection from the very many and varied civil aircraft types released by Airfix over the years.***

BRITTEN NORMAN ISLANDER / DEFENDE
AIRFIX
www.AIRFIX.com
03067
1:72
AIRFIX
Boeing
727-200
SPECIAL
EDITION
03183
PAN AM
CONSTRUCTION KIT SERIES 6
LOCKHEED TRISTAR 144TH SCALE
AIRFIX
No. 06171-9
MADE IN ENGLAND
AIRBUS A300B
Lufthansa
RFIX

INTRODUCTION

Growing up in England during the 1970s, a visit to the airports of south-east England with my Dad was a real treat! Not just to the London airports of Heathrow and Gatwick, but the smaller, regional airports of Lydd, Manston and Lympne, near Ashford. These were all places where, as a young child, I could watch the DC-3 Dakotas, the Bristol Superfreighters, the turbo-prop Vickers Viscounts and Vanguards and the early jet powered airliners, the de Havilland Comet, Hawker Siddeley Trident and the Boeing 707, come and go. Long before the advent of budget air travel, where flying is no longer seen as the luxury it once was, these classic airliners would be carrying some lucky holiday-makers to faraway, exotic destinations.

I can still clearly remember the sight of cars being driven up the ramp into the cavernous 'mouth' of the Bristol Superfreighters. I recall the ear-splitting noise of the early jet aircraft, which made me jump out of my skin and the strong smell of burnt kerosene that seemed to hang in the air around the airports and, to this day, still provokes happy memories. The inspiration I received from these visits was instrumental in shaping my whole life, and my passion for commercial aviation continues to this day.

During my informative years, Airfix was the brand most commonly associated with plastic model kits and their range of military aircraft and vehicles adorned many other young boys' bedrooms, as well as mine! But the company did not cater exclusively for the demands of the military modeller. The civilian vehicle modeller was also looked after with such incredibly diverse model kits as: the SRN-4 hovercraft, the Dennis fire engine, various motor cars and motor bikes, both road and racing machines, scale model steam trains and spacecraft were also all kitted at some point.

At a time when there were visitor areas at every airport, scenes such as this were common: enthusiasts viewing the aircraft on a Sunday afternoon with a picnic! Here a Bristol Superfreighter at Lydd Airport is loaded for the Channel crossing.

The Bristol Superfreighter again, but beautifully presented in model form. This photograph was taken at ScaleModelWorld, the IPMS Nationals Show, at Telford in 2009. Sadly I cannot claim any credit for this build, but memories of airport visits in the late 1960s and early 1970s came flooding back!

Of course it should not be forgotten that the company's first injected scale model kit was actually of a Ferguson Tractor! This was produced as a promotional item in 1948, followed by the company's first commercially available model kit of Sir Francis Drake's ship, the Golden Hind. This small ship was just the start of a range of small model sailing ships that were the forerunners to a series of larger scale, early sailing ships. Even ocean liners were not immune from the grasp of Airfix's intentions to model all things in plastic! But despite the varied subject matter, the company is probably best known for its range of model aircraft and 1953 saw the first model aeroplane with the release of the 1/72nd scale Spitfire 'BT-K'. (N.B. Incidentally, this little classic kit was recently re-released, complete with the original card header and moulded, as per the initial release, in light blue plastic!)

As aircraft became more and more a central theme to the Airfix catalogue, a new range of 1/144th scale airliners were produced, collectively known as the SkyKing range: and what other way was there to build a Vickers VC-10, Boeing 747 or Airbus A300, but from this series? These kits were not the most detailed, neither were they dimensionally spot on, but the fact remained that the keen civilian aircraft modeller now had a canvas to work with and the range grew to incorporate almost every classic airliner of the 1960s and 1970s until the last airliner in the series was produced, the McDonnell Douglas DC-10.

It seems that, in recent years, the German company Revell has taken up the task of keeping civilian aircraft modellers happy and has been responsible for excellent model kits of some of the more modern civilian types such as: the Airbus A330 and A340, along with the smaller, single-aisle A320 family and, in 2006, the company released the first 1/144th injection-moulded kit of the Airbus 'Super-Jumbo' A380. The American company Minicraft has also released a variety of modern and classic airliners in the 'standard' scale of 1/144th. Not surprisingly, these have mostly been of American aircraft and include: the Boeing B707 and B727, along with many of the early Douglas, piston-engined airliners. If you

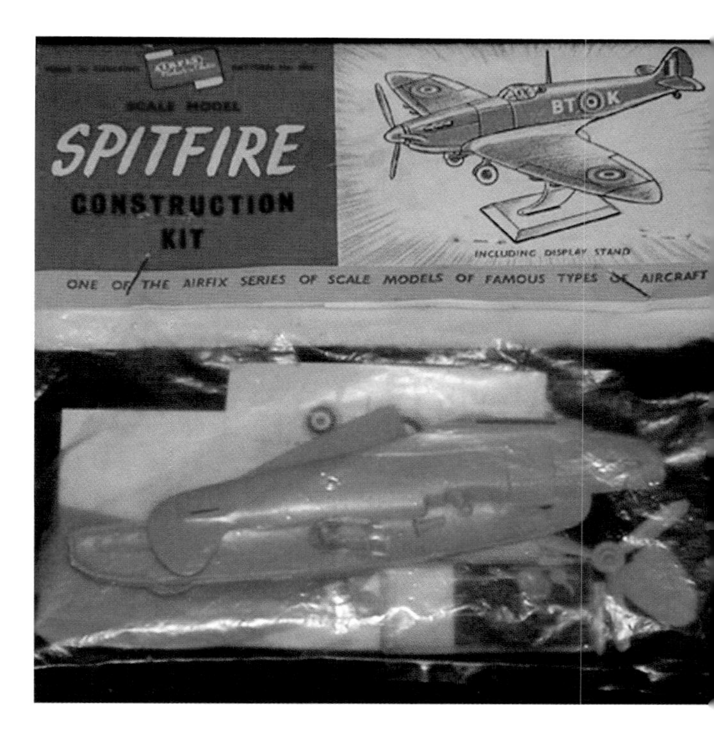

Although not the first Airfix kit, the Spitfire 'BT-K' was the first model aircraft kit produced by the British company.

The Airfix 'SkyKing' model of the VC10 was first produced in 1964; the kit was still available in the Royal Air Force Tanker variant until fairly recently.

know where to look, you can also find some less well-known companies such as Zvezda, who produce several very nice injected plastic kits of Russian airliners, as well as the best kit on the market so far of the Boeing B767-300. Boeing has also now directly licensed them; to produce the first injected plastic model kit of the B787 Dreamliner.

A2Zee, Gremlin Models, Welsh Models, S&M Models, F-RSIN and Authentic Airliners are all companies that currently produce model kits of commercial aircraft and these are all worth seeking out for the less common types and, in some cases, the most accurate representation of a type already manufactured by one of the larger companies: modelling is certainly one hobby where the major companies cannot always be relied upon to be the best! It is not always the case that the larger companies make the most precise representation of your chosen subject, so a little research is worthwhile should you want to depict a subject as accurately as possible.

There are literally hundreds of airline liveries and most have been available at some point in decal form.

The list of airlines, past and present, is far too extensive for this book but the decal manufacturers have certainly not left the catalogue of airline schemes alone and many current and long forgotten airline liveries are available from specialist manufacturers. These can, in some cases, produce an almost unique model for your display and who's to say you have to stay within the confines of the truth? After all, with the decals and many suitable kits available, you could start a 'what if?' themed build and here your imagination is the only limitation: a Virgin Atlantic Concorde perhaps, or maybe a Pan American Airways Vickers Viscount? The list is, of course, endless!

Detailing these kits, over and above what is provided in the box, used to be primarily down to scratch-building skills, and great results can be had with some basic knowledge of the methods used, in order to represent details that are missing from the kit. To help further enhance the model kits, there are now many companies that produce etched metal and resin parts, which can either add further detail to a kit or, perhaps, convert the original kit to another sub-type. In most cases, these after-market parts are better in detail and dimension than the kit parts that they replace: this book will show you not only how to use these parts, but also how to scratch-build some of you own simple parts to ensure greater realism.

Developing the idea of detailing your kit further, one company, BraZ Models, has even started to rep-

The commercial aircraft modeller is no longer being left behind by the after-market companies, with resin and etched metal detail sets now becoming available.

A good selection of reference material is readily available and can provide the inspiration for that next model.

ScaleModelWorld: the annual IPMS (UK) show has more and more model commercial aircraft on display every year.

licate the ground handling equipment and cargo load containers seen surrounding airliners on their stands, allowing the modeller the possibility of creating realistic dioramas. Bearing all the above in mind, it must be said that there has never been a better time for the airliner modeller!

Obviously some reference material should be sought regarding how the original aircraft looked, and a ready supply of detailed photographs from the Internet is invaluable in this respect, along with the many superb books available on the market today. Individual aircraft have been superbly described and illustrated in the Aviation Series of books, published by The Crowood Press: these include many classic British aircraft such as the Trident, Viscount and Vanguard as well as more modern types such as the Boeing B757 and B767. There is also a host of aviation and model magazines available, and there has been a recent trend in the modelling titles to include more articles on the building of civil aircraft. These often provide, not only educational tips, but also that all-important inspiration to open a kit box and start modelling yourself!

But if you truly need some inspiration, why not do as I once did and venture down to your nearest airport with your own camera and some sandwiches? But in this ever increasingly restricted world, where security at airports is heightened and even a 'plane-spotter' can be deemed a threat, do make sure that where you are taking photos from is not a prohibited area, and that your subject is allowed to be photographed. I'd rather not be responsible for any of you being asked: 'Would you mind accompanying us to the local station please, Sir…?!'

As a final reference to acquiring inspiration, the wonderful Britmodeller website (www.britmodeller.com), should be mentioned as this hosts not only pages of skillfully built models, but is coupled with a very active forum where modellers can share information and ask questions of other modellers. There are other forums and modelling related websites of course, and in this day and age we are certainly not short of online references for every subject that we can imagine! But as far as scale modelling goes, Britmodeller.com is certainly one of the friendliest places to visit and is about as close as you can get to a virtual modelling club. The Britmodeller website frequently gives me the necessary motivation to start my next project, as well as enabling modellers to join group builds where a given subject is the theme for the group to model. And yes, there has been an Airliner Group Build! So don't think that there are just a few commercial aircraft modellers around, there's more of us than you realize!

Commercial aviation is an area that, although not entirely neglected by the model manufactur-

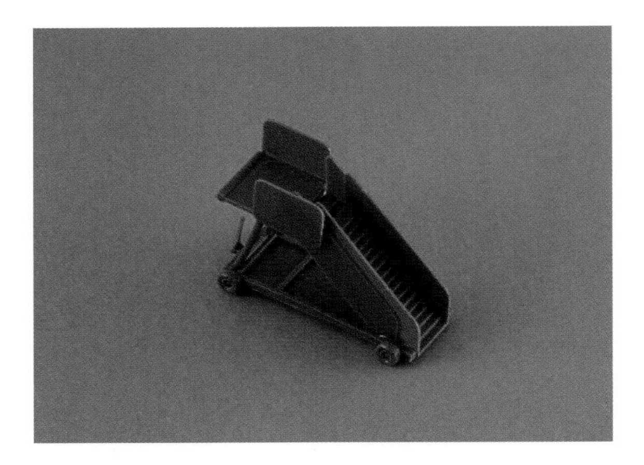

Airport dioramas are made easier with the addition of small kits like these steps from Bra.Z. Other items in their range even include baggage containers!

ers, has seen less support than the military aircraft modellers have always enjoyed. But with newer and more detailed models becoming available, this is certainly starting to change and at the annual ScaleModelWorld exhibition, hosted by the UK division of the International Plastic Modeller's Society, the IPMS (UK) (www.ipms-uk.co.uk), there is ample evidence of the growth in interest in commercial airliner models, as well as a host of other civilian aircraft types. After all, the myriad of liveries and colour schemes are extremely varied and attractive, and the range of aircraft available in kit form now allows a complete history of commercial aviation to be produced.

My own opinion is that modelling should not always be about creating an exact replica of your chosen subject. Yes, an exquisitely reproduced kit, especially in a diorama setting, is an absolute joy to see but, for me, the enjoyment gained from my modelling far exceeds my desire to get everything exactly right, and the learning of new techniques always keeps me interested in doing another kit. The research into the various types of kits also fuels my interest in learning more about aviation in general.

Some skills are specific to a particular field of modelling, but there are other skills that cross the modelling genres; such as in the case of building commercial aircraft, where the painting of the airframe requires particular skills more commonly associated with model car and motorbike builders. These are techniques which the average military aircraft modeller may not have learned or practiced and, if that is you, then this book might hopefully lure you away from your weathered matt greys, greens and browns and get you started on creating beautifully finished, gloss white fuselages! (Although I have mentioned 'beautifully finished, gloss white fuselages', the fact remains that airliners get very dirty too! So weathering can be incorporated and this is discussed in a later chapter.)

The layout of this book is chronological, by which I mean that the earlier aircraft designs appear towards the beginning and allows this book to (almost) tell the story of how commercial aviation has developed over the years. It's a fantastic history filled with triumphs and disasters but, above all, it is one of technological leaps of enormous proportions and, thanks to the engineers, designers and visionaries throughout the last century, we now take 'hopping on a plane' almost for granted.

I cannot take sole credit for this book as I received some wonderful help from two modelling friends: Brian Canell and Simon Lind. Simon has written a superb section on building a large scale Bristol Britannia, using a Vac-form kit as the basis of his build; it was this model that I admired during a visit to the annual ScaleModelWorld show back in 2008. It is a beautifully built model and I'm very happy to have been able to have Simon's permission to include it here. Brian writes about modelling to a theme and, very fittingly in his case, has chosen the aircraft of Pan American Airways, with an incredible build of a seemingly impossible kit. So to Simon and Brian, thank you both!

I do hope that this book will not only help to temp some of the die-hard military fans to stray away from their Spitfires and Messerschmitts, F-16s and Tornadoes for a while, but also act as an inspiration to the current airliner modellers to further enhance their skills.

As always, Happy Modelling!

Mark Stanton

This will probably be as close as I ever get to having an aircraft named after me!

CHAPTER ONE

A BRIEF HISTORY OF COMMERCIAL AVIATION

Aviation is proof that, given the will, we have the capacity to achieve the impossible. Eddie Rickenbacker

The history of aviation is well documented and, despite some tenuous claims to the contrary, mostly coming from New Zealand, it is widely accepted that Orville and Wilbur Wright were the original pioneers of heavier-than-air powered and controlled flight. That first flight in the Wright Flyer 1, on 17 December 1903, at Kitty Hawk, North Carolina, prompted a race amongst similarly minded and enthusiastic individuals to create better performing machines. However, that was just the start of what was to become an incredible history of development and it seems implausible to think that just sixty-six years later, Neil Armstrong was walking on the moon talking about small steps and giant leaps!

Alberto Santos-Dumont made a public flight in Paris on 13 September 1906, and across the channel in England, Henry Farman was not far from getting airborne as well. In fact, in 1908 Farman won the Grand Prix d'Aviation with a flight of just over half a mile (1km), although by this time the Wright Brothers were covering distances of up to 24 miles (39km). Around the same time, John Dunne, a lessor known pioneer, was instrumental in bringing aerodynamic stability to the earlier designs as a result of secret testing in Scotland, sponsored by the Ministry of Defence, but he never gets a mention anywhere.

It is widely accepted that it all began here, at Kitty Hawk, North Carolina on 1 December 1903. The Wright Brothers' first flight started a global race to achieve greater distances and with more passengers; a race that, it can be said, is still running.

In May 1908, Wilbur Wright performed what is believed to be the first, two-person, aircraft flight, with Charlie Furnas as a passenger; while on 8 July 1908, the first woman, Thérèse Peltier, flew as a passenger in an aeroplane in Milan, with Léon Delagrange at the controls. Sadly that year, Thomas Selfridge became the first person killed in an air crash during a military test in Virginia. The pilot was, rather ironically, Orville Wright who, despite surviving the accident, was then hospitalized for seven weeks.

In 1909, Louis Blériot saw that the English Channel was no barrier between England and France when he flew solo across the stretch of water in just thirty-seven minutes, thus securing his place in history. And in 2008, just ninety-nine years later, Swiss airline pilot Yves Rossy repeated the feat with nothing other than a jet-powered carbon fibre wing strapped to his body!

A lesser known American aviator, John Moisant, was the first pilot to fly from Paris to London, as well as the first to cross the channel with a passenger. He designed and built the first metal aeroplane in 1909. It is documented that in 1910 Moisant unfortunately crashed in Kemsing in Kent: he did survive this accident, although perhaps this was not such a great distinction, as Moisant crashed with great regularity across all of North Kent!

Later, in December 1910, he raced his Blériot monoplane against a Packard automobile over a

The early aviator John Moisant from the United States together with his cat: a sad loss to aviation at just forty-two years of age.

The First National Bank
of St. Petersburg
Pay to the order of The Benoist Air Boat Line.............. $400.00
Four-hundred &.......................00/100 Dollars
63-74

The original cheque and receipt for the first airline ticket: in today's money that is over $7000!

5-mile (8km) course; he lost. Sadly he died later that month in Kenner, Louisiana, whilst preparing for the annual Michelin Cup: this is significant only in as much as no one has ever heard of him! Sadly, the history of aviation is peppered with great feats of long forgotten heroes, and I have mentioned John Moisant here in order that he is, at last, immortalized somewhere in print! There have been many milestones in the development of heavier-than-air craft, but I would like to refer now to another, hardly mentioned but incredibly significant, landmark.

On 1 January 1914, the St. Petersburg – Tampa Air Line in the United States, operating a Benoist Mark XIV flying boat, became the first scheduled airline. In the cockpit was Tony Jannus, the first passenger being Abram C. Pheil, the ex-mayor of St. Petersburg and owner of a wholesale company. This first ticket was sold by public auction and Mr Pheil paid an astonishing $400 for the 23-mile (37km) journey: this equates to over $7000 in today's money and, if converted to dollars per mile, means Pheil paid over $300 for every mile travelled. It's incredible that today a passenger can pay as little as that to cover the 3,240 mile (5,200km) flight from London to New York; not including airport taxes of course!

As is sadly so often the case, a major conflict accelerated the development of technology and the First World War saw aircraft develop from simple, and rather fragile pieces of equipment, into faster and stronger designs capable of longer flights with heavier, and in most cases, highly explosive payloads. John Alcock and Arthur Brown used one such aircraft, the Vickers Vimy, for their successful attempt at the first non-stop crossing of the Atlantic. A perilous journey that saw Brown climb out onto the wings to chip away ice that had formed no less than six times! It may come as no surprise to learn that, despite living until after the Second World War, Arthur Whitten Brown never flew in an aircraft again! Today over 400 aircraft cross the Atlantic daily with, thankfully, rather more sophisticated anti-ice systems.

During the 1920s and 1930s, many pioneering flights were accomplished: one such flight was the incredible, transatlantic crossing in 1927 by Charles Lindbergh in a Ryan NYP aircraft, called The Spirit of St. Louis. Although Lindbergh was actually the 104th person to fly across the Atlantic Ocean, he was the first to achieve this feat solo, during a flight that lasted over thirty-three hours. If we consider that his aircraft had just one engine, and with most of the flight conducted just a few feet above the Atlantic waves, then the significance of his achievement might be better understood. Today's aircraft fly the same route with more crew, in fewer hours and at

The very first airline pilot: Tony Jannus, at the controls of the Benoist Mk.XIV flying boat. Pilots' uniforms have certainly come a long way since then!

The Benoist Mk.XIV flying boat: certainly no flat beds, large television screens or cocktails and canapés for those early passengers.

Captain John Alcock and Lieutenant Arthur Whitten Brown: who, for those of you who are interested in obscure facts, are wearing Burberry jackets.

John Alcock and Arthur Whitten Brown crash-land their aircraft in a bog near Clifden, Ireland, on 15 June 1919; completing the first ever non-stop trans-Atlantic crossing and winning them a £10,000 prize.

The Ryan NYP Monoplane, Spirit of St Louis in an early publicity photograph, prior to the famous solo trans-Atlantic crossing in May 1927.

significantly higher altitudes, not to mention that the in-fight catering and entertainment is considerably more sophisticated!

It was during this post-war period that engine and airframe development gathered pace and, with many skilled pilots left available after the Great War had ended, barnstorming, air races and commercial flights were soon a regular feature of life in the western world. It was really at this point, the end of the First World War, that commercial aviation (pardon the pun!) really took off.

During the 1930s, one of the most successful designs was the Douglas DC-3 Dakota and this aircraft really started the modern age of passenger airline travel. No longer the domain of the rich and famous, travelling by air became more affordable to the general public. Yet it was not much later that, once again, the political climate turned hostile and the Second World War broke out. By this time there were many airports situated in various countries around the world, and the impending conflict fuelled research and development into the technology behind aviation. This development would see aircraft becoming constantly improved, from piston engined biplanes, to jet–powered aeroplanes, with top speeds approaching mach one, the speed of sound. The output of the aircraft factories was relentless, with Britain adopting a 'ghost factory' method of production, whereby the production of military aircraft was farmed out to civilian assembly lines. One such factory in Wales set a world record when it constructed a fully airworthy and operational Vickers Wellington in under twenty-four hours!

The development of the aircraft from 1939 to the late 1950s saw incredible leaps and, within just twenty years, the distance and time between countries, and continents, shrank as the modern airliner as we know it, with ever- increasing passenger loads, became a common feature of the ever more populous skies.

Although designed some time before the Second World War, both sides used the jet turbine engine operationally on two of the most easily recognizable aircraft, the Gloster Meteor and the Messerschmitt Me-262. After the war, although development of the turbojet continued, it was the Vickers Company of Weybridge, Surrey that first installed the combina-

Possibly the greatest single leap in civil aviation history: with the DC-3 Dakota, air travel really did come to the masses.

Aaah, the Viscount! Four Rolls Royce Darts in close proximity to the ears meant that most ex-Viscount pilots now have some degree of hearing loss!

The Sud Aviation Caravelle was France's answer to the growing market for short to medium sized jet transport aircraft. It was the first of the 'clean wing' configuration airliners, with the engines mounted at the rear of the fuselage on pylons.

tion of a jet turbine with a reduction gear, driving a propeller onto an airframe: the result would become the World's first turboprop airliner, the four-engined Vickers Viscount.

The arrival of a commercially viable jet engine enabled companies such as de Havilland, Aerospatiale, Boeing, Douglas, BAC and Hawker Siddeley to begin developing jet-powered aircraft: again it was a British company, de Havilland, which would eventually launch the first turbojet-powered airliner, the DH.106 Comet. This was closely followed by the French Caravelle and the American Boeing B707 and Douglas DC-8: as the design of the aircraft and engines progressed, more efficient aircraft were developed and greater passenger capacities were sought.

Perhaps the ultimate development of that period was the original Jumbo Jet, the Boeing B747. So confident were Boeing of their huge B747 design that no prototype was actually produced, with the first production aircraft being used for initial flight-testing. In keeping with the leaps and bounds attained by the aerospace industry, barriers and hurdles were cast aside as each subsequent aircraft type brought with it advantages over earlier designs, yet there was still one major obstacle left to overcome.

Capacity and range were more often the primary considerations in the design of new aircraft, but speed was always one of the primary advantages of jet-powered aircraft. In 1962, BAC and Aerospatiale joined forces and began to design the iconic Concorde. From January 1976 until the final commercial flight in October 2003, passengers enjoyed this unique aircraft and the quality of service provided on board, in the world's only supersonic all first-class cabin.

If you go back and read that last paragraph again, but this time take note of the years mentioned, you may become more aware of the magnitude of the pace of development throughout the twentieth century. Incredibly, Concorde began commercial services in 1976, just seventy-three years after the Wright Brother's first flight!

In an extremely short time aircraft themselves have changed dramatically in appearance and,

Concorde – I don't think that adequate words have ever been written to describe the sheer beauty of this iconic aircraft.

Forty years after the original Jumbo Jet, the Boeing B747, entered service: more people than ever are sharing the same cabin air and eating meals at 39,000 feet in the Airbus A380!

although one modern airliner may look, to some, the same as any other, development of current aircraft is centred on efficiency and environmental impact; ideas that were far from the minds of the early designers! Instrumentation is now electronic and ergonomically laid out, computer-controlled systems are backed-up in duplicate or triplicate to avoid failures, carbon fibre and Kevlar have replaced aluminium alloys and new composite materials have been developed such as GLARE, a composite of glass fibre and aluminium used extensively in the construction of the largest commercial airliner flying today, the Airbus A380. (Although the term GLARE had seemingly been lost in the manufacturing of modern aircraft, it is the Dutch company Fokker that manufacturers the GLARE panels used in the Airbus.) Today's modern airliners have Fly-by-wire systems controlling the flying surfaces, landings in fog are a daily occurrence and the level of comfort on board one of today's modern airliners is far removed from that experienced by the early passengers.

Aviation has a fascinating history: always at the forefront of technological development and advancement and I wonder where the next 100 years will lead us, but then a certain Mr Branson has already approached that next step and bookings for space flight are now being taken!

CHAPTER TWO

SO WHAT'S DIFFERENT ABOUT MODELLING COMMERCIAL AIRCRAFT?

Basic skills, with which you are no doubt familiar, will be touched upon throughout the following chapters. However, the main emphasis with modelling commercial aircraft, and modern airliners in particular, is in the final finish and this book covers this area extensively.

Airliner model kits tend to have fewer parts and are less detailed than their military model cousins; this is primarily down to the scale of the subject, which leans towards a 'standard' of 1/144th (1in = 12ft) (2.5cm = 3.65m), rather than the larger 'military' scales of 1/72nd, 1/48th, 1/32nd or even 1/24th. There have been airliner models in odd scales, such as 1/96th, 1/100th, 1/125th and 1/200th, which have all reached the shelves of the local hobby store, but the generally agreed common scale with airliners is still 1/144th.

Airliner kits have been predominantly issued in 1/144th scale and this has been accepted as the 'standard' scale for the subject. However, Hasegana of Japan also produces a large range of civil aircraft in 1/200th scale and Airfix, Revell and Matchbox have all produced kits in the much smaller scales of 1/300th and 1/390th. On the larger side, Heller has released airliner kits in 1/125th and 1/72nd, whilst Doyusha has also chosen a larger scale too and has released some airliner models in 1/100th.

Despite this relatively small scale, the after-market industry has produced parts, mostly utilizing etched metal or cast resin, and more are now becoming made available as the hobby continues to grow. These additional parts enhance and add extra detail to the original kit. Areas that are often neglected by the model manufacturers, can easily be enhanced with a few scratch-building techniques: this book will certainly help you to target those areas that, due to the smaller scale, have been less well simulated by the manufacturers but are easily detailed by the modeller.

As mentioned earlier, the use of etched metal and resin parts allows greater detail to be added and, combined with resin and scratch-building techniques, this book will show how these techniques can be used in order to 'go to town' on your own favourite subject. Thankfully though, the original aircraft subjects are usually quite substantially sized so that, even in 1/144th scale, the model is still large enough to allow the keen or advanced modeller the scope to improve upon the original model kit. Although the detailing of any model is up to the individual, it is normally the case to leave the exposed engines, the highly detailed cockpits and the incredibly accurate weathering to the military modellers; but why? The only thing stopping you doing whatever you want to your model is your own imagination and skill. So go ahead! Start experimenting and adding extra detail as and when you want!

The liveries that airliners carry are a very good reason for many modellers to investigate the civil side of aviation. The standard liveries of most airlines are usually colourful subjects in their original format, but there are also special liveries representing, perhaps an airline's anniversary, a corporate sponsorship or occasionally, as in the case of the famous British Airways / Singapore Airlines Concorde, a dual livery representing a visual expression of a route shared by both companies. (On 9 December 1977, British Airways and Singapore Airlines started a service between London and Singapore, via Bahrain.)

My current favourites are the 'Retro' schemes, where the modern aircraft serving an airline are painted in special retro schemes, just as they would have looked in the past. Again, many of these schemes are becoming available as after-market decal sets, from the specialist decal manufacturers such as Two-Six decals.

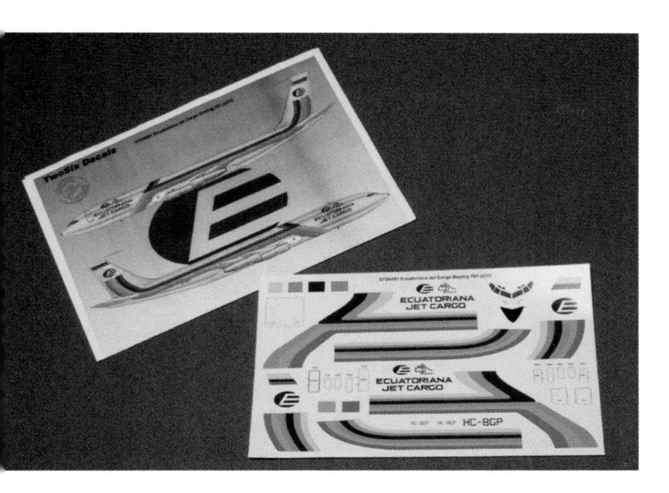

There are now many specialist decal sheet manufacturers that add an incredible array of liveries to those already supplied with the model kits. These decals, representing the Gold Boeing B707 freighter operated by Equatoriana Jet Cargo, will certainly get your model noticed!

Modern airline schemes certainly have come a long way in recent years, with ever more colourful liveries being introduced: Hungary's WizzAir is one example.

Very early liveries were painted by hand, normally just in black, onto a silver doped or painted airframe and quite often included just the aircraft registration, the name of the company and, possibly, a name applied to that aircraft. They were hardly ever creative but, as the airline industry grew, design studios created airline liveries that were painted onto the aircraft in large spraying facilities. Nowadays the liveries are designed on computer and large vinyl decals are printed. These decals are nothing more than large stickers, and have the advantage that liveries can be varied quickly with the addition of other graphics. These newer liveries are easily produced as decals for the modeller and the range available is now stunning in terms of subject matter, variety and quality.

Another colourful scheme: the North African low-cost carrier Jet4You.

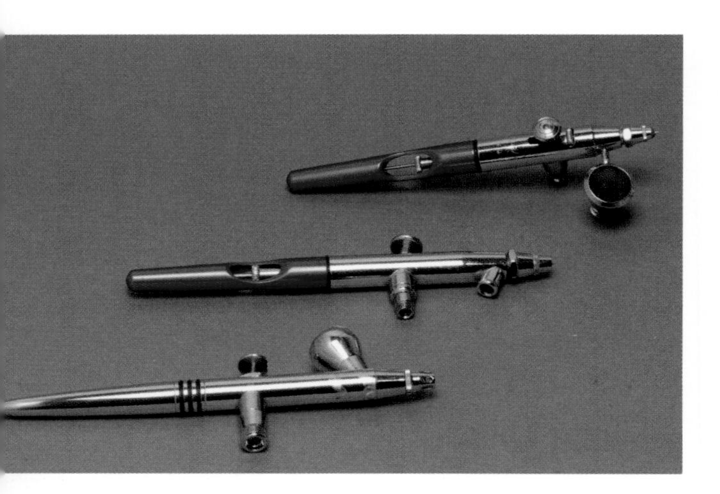

There are many different manufacturers of airbrushes, with varying levels of build quality. I have always used Iwata and Paasche and can highly recommend these brands. The three main types of airbrush are, from top to bottom: side feed, bottom feed and top feed.

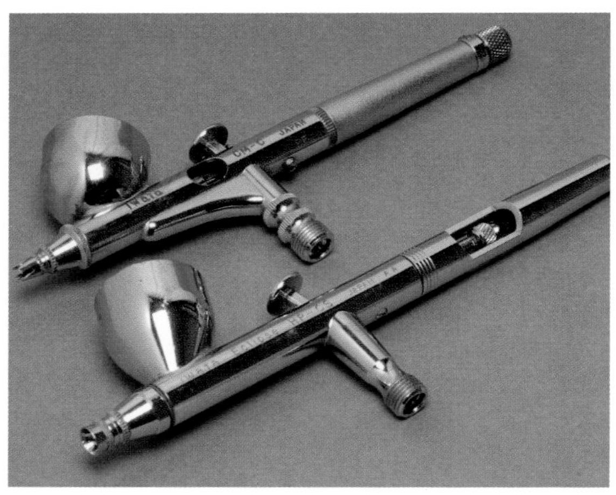

Iwata is a high quality brand of airbrushes, which give great results.

In order to fully exploit these schemes and their respective decal sheets, an element of care and patience needs to be used when preparing the model. It is always best to apply decals to a glossy surface to avoid 'silvering', the shimmering effect caused when air bubbles are trapped beneath the decal film; however, that's easier for the airliner modeller as the finish will invariably be a glossy one too. Nevertheless, a good clean finish is essential: it not only looks good but also allows the decals to adhere snugly to the model.

In order to achieve such a finish, we must enter the domain of the car and motorbike modeller, who will be familiar with a high gloss finish and the necessary skills required in order to achieve it. In this respect an airbrush is an important tool, in order to achieve a uniform and smooth painted finish on your models. There are alternatives to the airbrush and these will be shown as well, but if you are taking the hobby further, a good quality airbrush is indispensable and, along with a compressor, is a fantastic investment.

There are now many manufacturers of good quality airbrushes and there are also two distinct types: the internal and external mix airbrush.

The internal mix is the one for the serious modeller and this type comes in three different varieties, depending upon how the paint is supplied; either gravity fed from a top mounted paint cup, side fed, or siphon fed from a jar mounted beneath the airbrush. My personal favourite is the Iwata range and if kept clean and regularly serviced, these can also provide a lifetime of use. Beware of cheap imported imitations though, and always buy direct from a reputable dealer. Both Little-Cars and The Airbrush and Spray Centre provide good advice and are highly recommended to help in the selection of the right equipment.

With regards to the maintenance of your airbrush, thorough cleaning is always worth the time spent after every modelling session, and there are a number of products on the market that enable you to keep the brush looking like new. I use a strong solvent that will clean the most stubborn of paints, some cotton buds, pipe cleaners and a set of little brushes.

Thankfully the paint manufacturers have all kept up with the rest of the hobby and there are many ranges of acrylic and enamel paints available. Xtracolor has been producing matched colours of aircraft factory paints, as well as the correct colours for various airlines, for a few years now. So there's

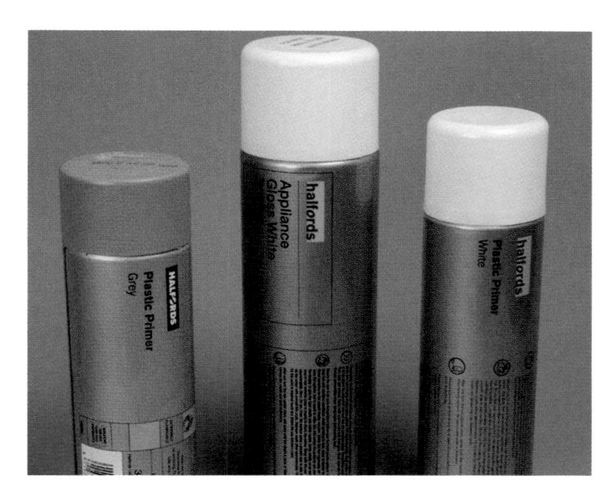

Halfords has become a mecca for airliner modellers and their range of spray cans, especially Appliance White, is an important part of the paint inventory.

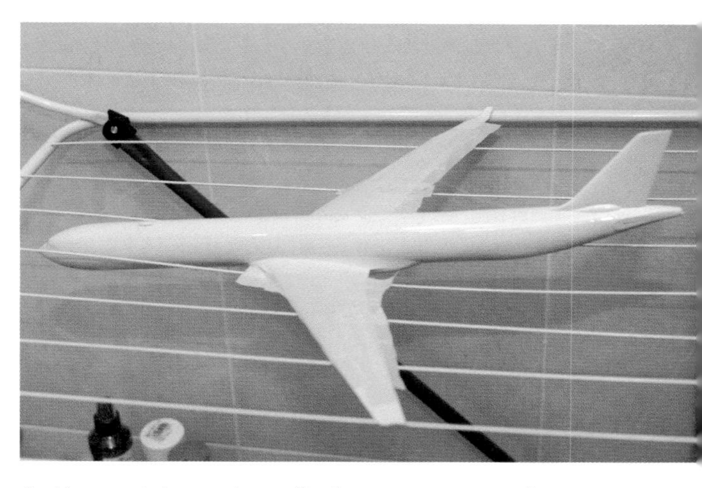

As the models can be quite large, space can be a problem when finding somewhere to allow the paint to dry. I've seen some novel approaches but I tend to use a clothes-drying rack, shown here in the bathroom!

no more guessing which grey to use on an Airbus's wings and, as for that elusive shade of purple for that FedEx freighter you are building? No problem, it's in the Xtracolour range too! There's even the correct shade of orange if you're building an easyJet aircraft!

But there are alternatives to specific modelling paints and one, well known, car parts shop has become something of a Mecca for modellers. There is probably a Halfords in every main town in the United Kingdom and amongst the spare bulbs, car hi-fis, maps and car cleaning products, lies a rack of spray paints that are simple to use and great value too! Amongst the range of colours are a few that are absolutely essential for me when I am building model airliners. The plastic primers, both grey and white, are important and some of the grey shades can come in useful, but none are more important than the Appliance White. This is a bright white that gives a glossy and hard finish to any model airliner fuselage and I would highly recommend it. Why it is called Appliance White though is a mystery, as I have yet to find anyone who has used the paint to spray a freezer or dishwasher, but it is a great basic white paint for us modellers, so who cares what it is called?

When using the Halfords' spray paints, the model surface is best primed and, although the range includes a plastic primer, I would also recommend either Tamiya's spray primer or the Mr Surfacer primer from Gunze Sangyo. Both of these products are only available from specialist model shops. However, regardless of the product used, the technique is the same: the fuselage, or other area of the aircraft that you are spraying, needs to be complete, with all seams sanded and polished before a very gradual build up of the primer is applied. First, just very lightly dust the surface with a quick sweep of the spray can. The nozzle should ideally remain at the same distance throughout the application and a few practice passes along the model will give you an idea of how far you should move your arm. For the first pass, start spraying just before the nozzle reaches the model and do not let go of the nozzle until after you've reached the end of the model. A quick pass at first ensures a light dusting and, as all the primers mentioned dry quite quickly, after a few minutes the process can be repeated with slower passes, ensuring that an even coat has been applied.

The process is identical for the topcoat: it is always better to build up the finish gradually with light coats, rather than trying to get a good wet coat on straight away – that way you'll avoid the paint running or pooling. As with any painted model, leave plenty of time before handling the model again to avoid fingerprints, and let the model dry in as close to a dust-free area as possible. There are various ways to support the model whilst the paint dries, but I find that with the large fuselages of a 1/144th airliner a cheap clothes drying rack comes in handy.

If you have brought this book, then I assume that you are in some way familiar with the basic construction of a model injected-plastic kit. As stated earlier, I don't consider this book to be a modeller's initial guide, as the emphasis here is on the subject matter, rather than teaching basic modelling skills; so it is assumed that you'll have at least a few kits on your modelling CV! In any case, the two earlier Crowood titles in this series, *Scale Aircraft Modelling* and *Advanced Scale Aviation Modelling*, more than adequately cover the basics of achieving some success out of a few injected plastic parts. Nevertheless, a little bit of revision is always useful, so let us have a quick look at some of the tools that are necessary in order to make the most out of the myriad tiny parts on those plastic sprues.

TOOLS

With respect to the tools required, there are some basic principles to follow: the main one I have adopted is that it is always a good idea to buy the best that you can afford. Buying cheaply is almost always a false economy, and this is especially true with tools. In this guide I have therefore recommended tools towards the higher end of the cost scale, purely because they will offer a lifetime of service. Over the years the average modeller will collect many tools and will always have his or her favourites: by following the principle that you should buy once and use forever, good quality tools will only help to enhance your skills and further improve the quality of your model building.

CUTTERS

The parts are removed from the sprue trees by using small side cutters. The Xuron range is particularly good in this respect and includes both side cutters, for plastic parts, and shears, specifically for cutting etched metal parts. I recently acquired a lovely set of cutters made in Japan by Tristar and these are also recommended.

TWEEZERS

To handle small parts, a set of tweezers is essential and there are two main types: those that spring open and those that spring closed. Over the years I've collected a few tools and I've been quite amazed at how many types of tweezers there actually are!

MODELLING KNIVES

Modelling knives have come a long way since the ubiquitous X-Acto sets that every young modeller had in the 1970s and 1980s! Today the sharpest knives available to us are basically surgeon's scalpels and these, made by the Sheffield based company Swann-Morton, are readily available in the best model shops and art shops. A range of blades is also available in various shapes and sizes but, to begin with, the standard straight edged no.11 and no.10A are possibly the best, although the curved no.10 and no.12 are also very handy to have in the toolbox.

HOBBY KNIVES

X-Acto, are still making hobby knives and there are a number of handles and blades available from this company to supplement the scalpels, as they can cope well with heavier work.

ADHESIVES

Technology advances have not only improved the quality of the kits, but also the types and varieties of the adhesives which we use. There are now specific adhesives, in varying thicknesses for the kit parts, as well as superglues, or cyano-acrylate adhesives (to give them their proper title), for attaching different materials together, such as etched metal detail parts to the polystyrene plastic of the kit. The main type of adhesive that I use is a very thin, toluene-based product which, when a small drop is applied to the join, will flow along it, via capillary action, and weld the two parts together by slightly melting the surfaces of each part. Thicker polystyrene adhesives are also used and they basically work in the same way,

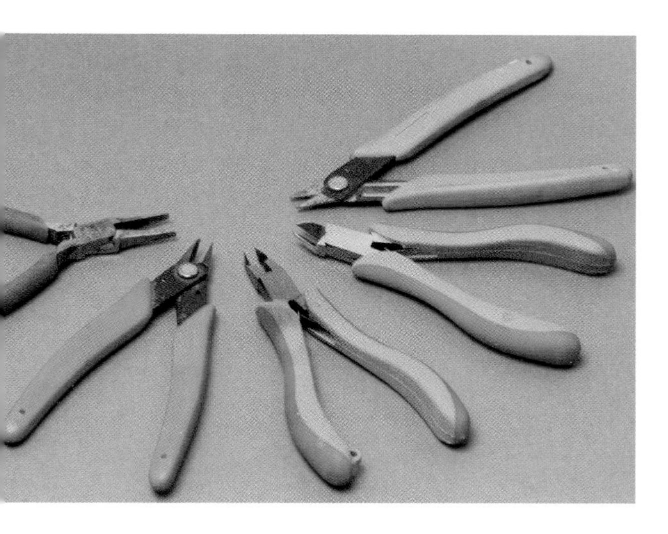

A modeller can never have enough tools! But always try and get the best quality that you can afford.

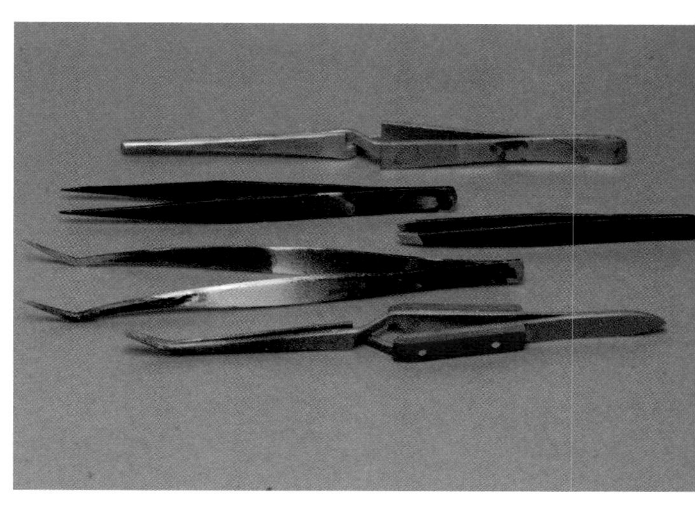

You will be quite surprised at the number of different types of tweezer available. But a good quality 'squeeze to close' and a 'squeeze to open' pair will easily suffice for most applications.

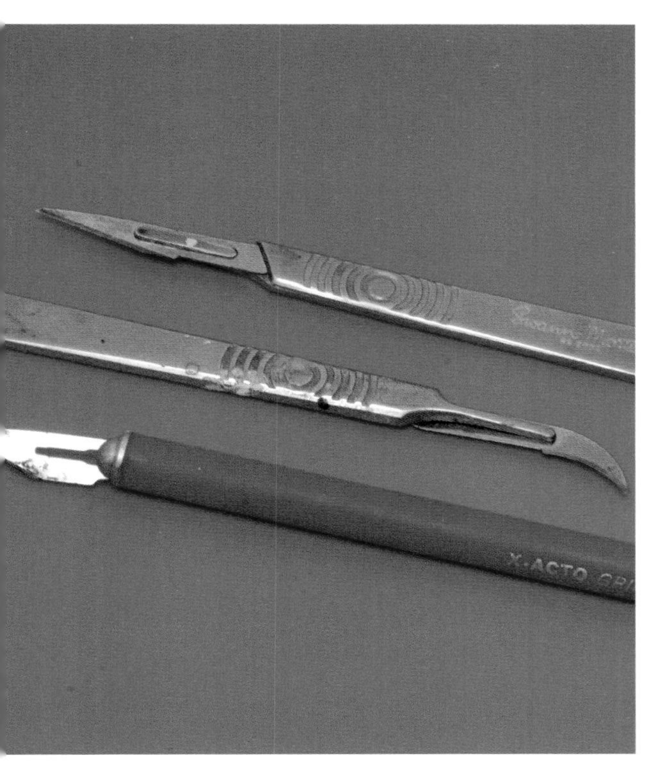

Over the years I have veered away from the standard hobby knife, preferring to use scalpels from Swann Morten.

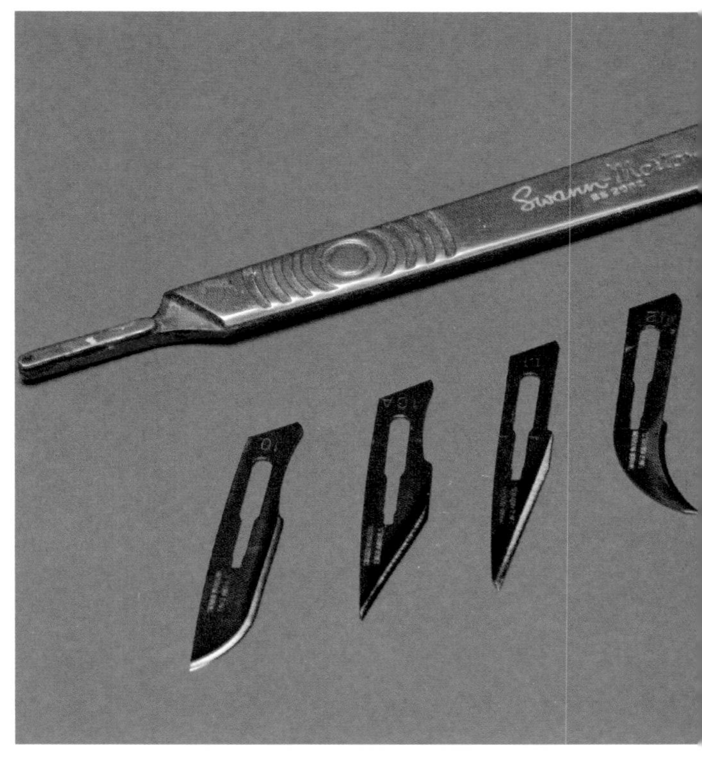

A good selection of blade types is available from Swann Morten.

although they will not flow along the join and set much less quickly.

Cyano-acrylate adhesives (the previously mentioned superglues, sometimes simply referred to as CA) are used for many purposes and the range of products is also extremely large, with different viscosities being the main property utilized by the modeller, as the thicker types are excellent for filling small gaps. Water-based PVA glues are used when attaching clear plastic parts, as these dry without the release of caustic or solvent fumes which would otherwise fog the clear plastic.

Finally, the two-part epoxy adhesives are also very useful: these not only attach different material types together but also dry, or more correctly cure, with an incredibly strong bond and are therefore useful when attaching metal undercarriage legs for example.

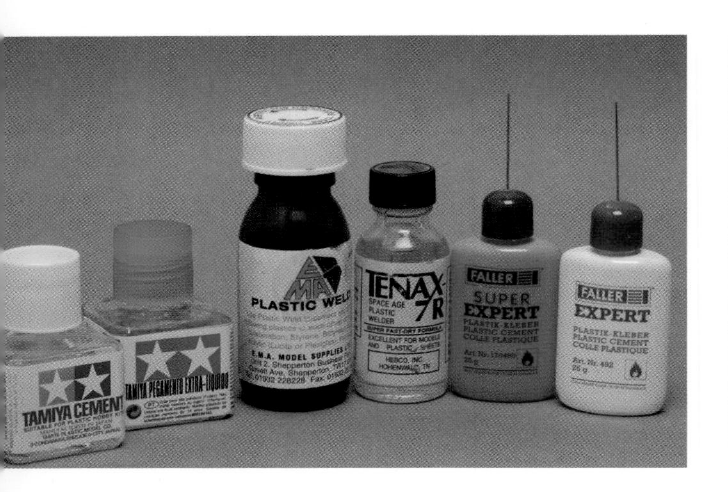

It used to be tube cement, but the serious modeller will have a selection of glues that are more effective than the old polystyrene cement!

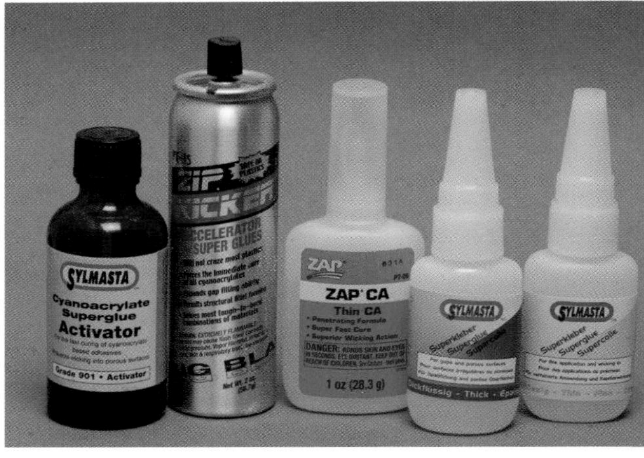

Specialist manufacturers of cyano-acrylate (CA) or superglue, have released various adhesives with varying viscosities. A bottle or spray can of activator is also very useful to set the CA immediately.

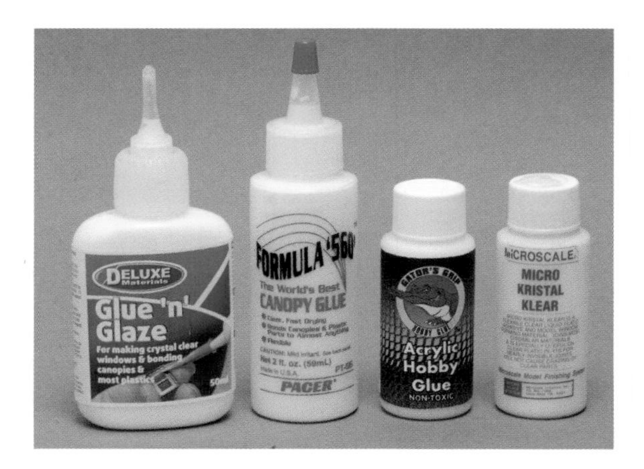

There are also many brands of adhesives that are used to stick transparent plastic parts in place: these are mostly PVA-type adhesives.

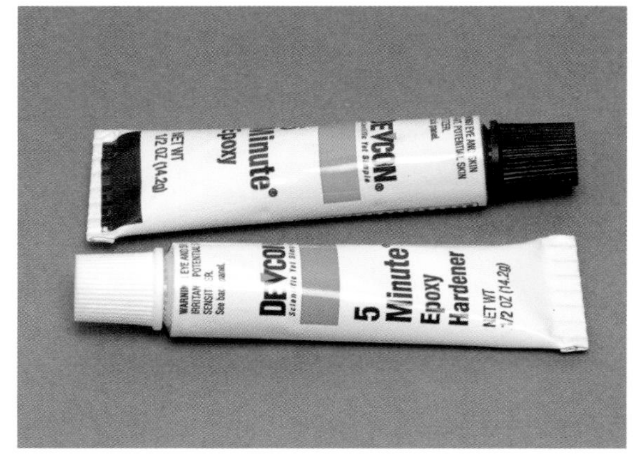

An epoxy-type adhesive is also a useful addition to the workbench.

SANDING STICKS AND PAPERS

After removing the parts from the sprue and carefully constructing the various sub-assemblies, there will usually be a need to smooth join lines, or to remove seam lines from the plastic parts, so the modeller's tool box should have a range of sanding sticks and papers in varying grades.

There are a few manufacturers of sanding sticks, specifically made with the modeller in mind, however a trip to a chemist or beauty salon will also be worthwhile, as there are now numerous styles and designs of nail files that also meet the modeller's needs. My own favourite is a four-sided sanding block with differing grades of abrasive paper on each side, and this was found in a beauty salon (I can't remember why I actually went in there initially though!)

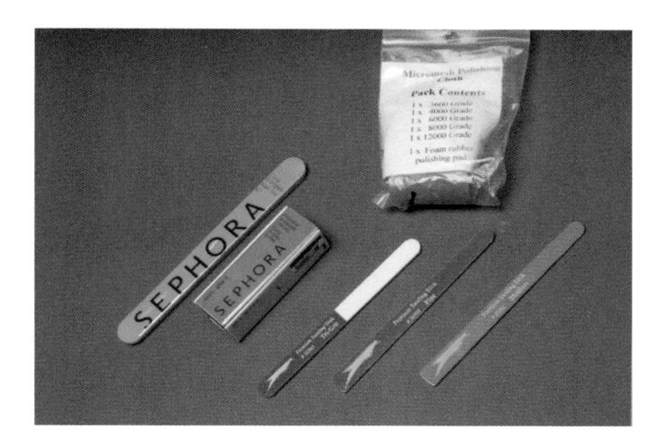

Sanding sticks and nail files, along with some fine grade polishing cloths are all essential when constructing and preparing the model for painting.

SCRIBING TOOLS

After the model has been constructed, and the seams and any filled areas have been sanded smooth, the recessed detail that has been moulded into the plastic is inevitably lost; this can be recovered by scribing the lines back into the plastic and, again, a whole range of tools are available for this purpose. You might even think of befriending your dentist and asking for some of his used tools, as these are also handy implements, not only for de-scaling teeth, but also as scribing tools!

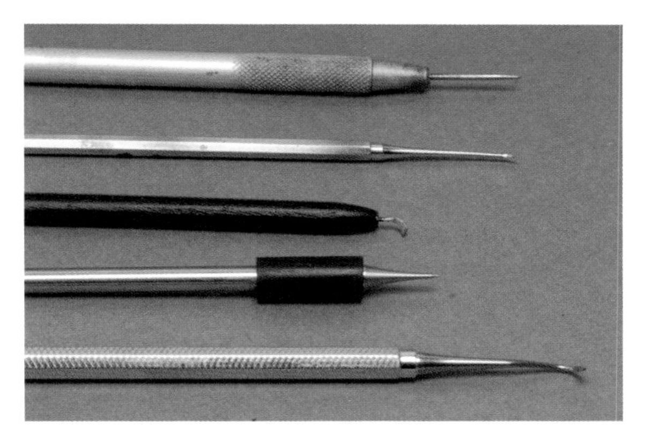

A selection of scribing tools, used to recover lost panel lines, after the model has been sanded.

PAINTBRUSHES

And finally, despite the main tool for painting being the airbrush, it is still important to have a good selection of paintbrushes. If cared for properly, a good quality set of different sized brushes is also a great asset to have and will give years of service. Again, don't get the cheap ones, treat yourself to some good quality sable brushes with a good point: if treated with care these brushes will always be an asset in your modelling toolbox.

So that's enough of a preamble. I hope that for the beginner the above has provided you with a good basic knowledge of everything that you will need, and for the skilled modeler, I hope that there has been some useful information for you too. So, what are we waiting for? Let's open the first box and begin…

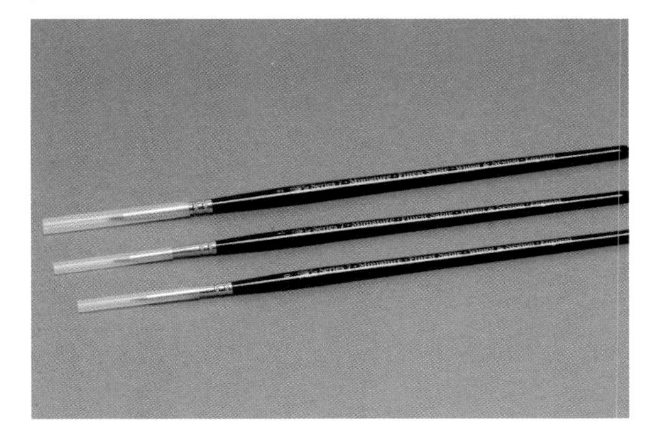

Despite my primary painting tool being the airbrush, good quality paintbrushes also have a place on the workbench, for painting small parts and details neatly.

CHAPTER THREE

IN THE BEGINNING...

RODEN 1/48TH DE HAVILLAND DH.4

As already mentioned in the first chapter, the first airline passenger was flown on 1 January 1914, in the United States. However, it was not until after the end of the First World War that the first British passenger was flown.

At the end of the Great War, surplus aircraft were converted to passenger use; one particularly successful aircraft in this respect was the Geoffrey de Havilland designed DH.4. This was operated by some long forgotten airlines such as: Aircraft Transport and Travel, Handley Page Transport and the Belgian airline SNETA. It was on an AT&T aircraft, G-EAJC, that: 'a reporter from the Evening Standard newspaper and a load of newspapers and other freight' was flown from Hounslow to Le Bourget on 25 August 1919, the reporter thus became the first British airline passenger. No doubt treated to the VIP status he deserved, it is rumoured that he did not even have to pay for his own coffee and a bag of peanuts!

Up until now, you will have read all about Airfix and Revell and how 1/144th is the 'standard' airline scale, it may surprise you then that the very first model in this book is from neither stable, nor is it in that scale! But in keeping with the intention to compile a general history of commercial aviation, here we start the modelling with a look at Roden's 1/48th de Havilland DH.4A (Passenger).

Roden are a relatively new manufacturer from the Ukraine and utilize the most up-to-date CAD/CAM techniques to create virtual models, from which they make their own mould patterns. During their brief history they have managed to accrue some high accolades, including a number of 'Kit of the Year' awards. Roden does not hesitate to release some very esoteric subjects, mostly concentrating on the first half of the twentieth century, and both the quality of the kits and the accuracy of the subjects are produced to a very high standard.

The de Havilland DH4A (Passenger) is one of Roden's latest issues; the box art shows the aircraft

The Roden De Havilland DH4 is available in many guises: here we take a look at the passenger variant.

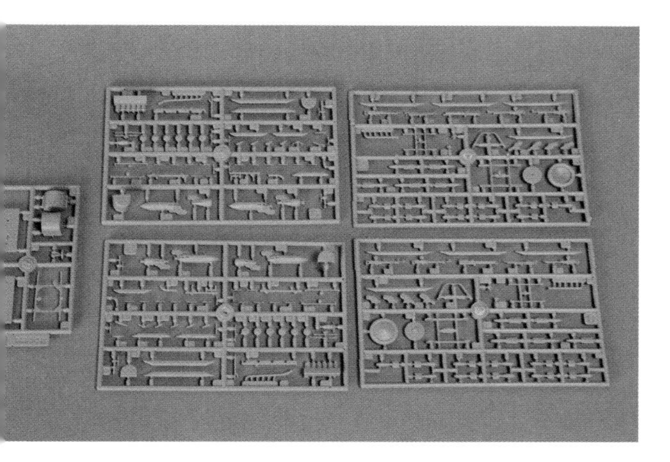

Eight sprues contain the 170 parts, although many are redundant when building this version.

The decal sheet includes two variants, one military DH4a, F5764 of No. 1 Communication Squadron based at Kenley in 1919. The subject of this chapter, though, is the civil DH4a, G-EAJC, operated by A T & T, at the time of the world's first commercial flight, from London to Paris in 1919.

looking as if it is ready for service on a warm and balmy day in the summer of 1919. On opening the box the first thing that struck me was the number of parts. There are no less than 170 individual parts on the eight sprues but, on further investigation, it appears that only sixty-four of those parts are used to create the passenger version. As the kit shares the same basis as the military DH4, the kit contains so many options that this results in over 100 parts going to waste, or at least into the spares box!

The Roden kit is included here simply because it is a model of an aircraft at the very genesis of commercial air travel, a kit of one of the very earliest airliners and, as such, an important inclusion in the book. It obviously has a strong tie to the military variant and the kit requires many of the skills associated with military modelling, but it is a great starting point as it introduces a few interesting techniques which are peculiar to a limited run kit. So, at the risk of upsetting some of you advanced modellers, I'd just like to go back to basics and briefly describe the methods used to detach the kit parts from their plastic sprues.

The hot injected plastic that forms the kit flows through the moulds and along the sprues, which form the 'framework' that holds the parts. Depending upon the quality of the kit, the parts are attached to the sprue by varying sizes of sprue gates. The limited run, low quantity releases, such as this kit, tend to have larger gates, but the principle is the same with respect to getting the parts free from the sprue. By using a good quality side cutter, the parts are cut from the sprue and this will inevitably leave a small tag of plastic on the part that can easily be tidied up with the use of a sanding stick. Once detached the various parts needed for the sub-assembly are kept safely together and then assembly of the first stage can begin. Should the gate be too large for the side cutters to cut through cleanly, then the part can first be detached by sawing through the gate with a razor saw and then tidied up with a sanding stick.

Not surprisingly, construction starts with the cockpit area and the fuselage interior. The basic components for the cockpit and passenger areas need to be painted in a natural wood finish which I'll come onto shortly, but before that the smaller components: seats, control column etc., should all be painted according to the instructions. The fuselage interior is not really visible so is just given a coat of aluminium with the airbrush. The fuel tank is painted gloss black, before being sprayed with Alclad

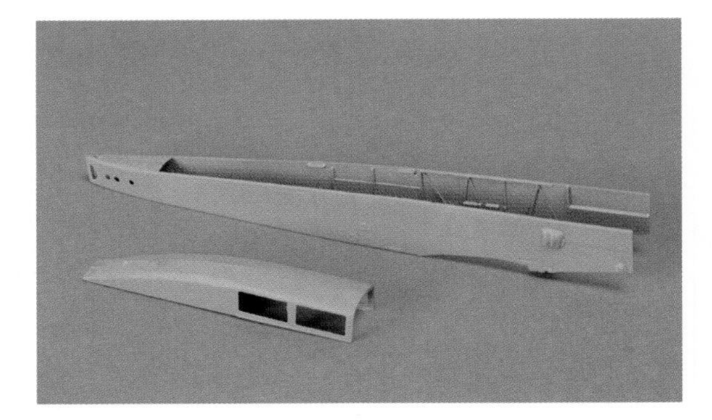

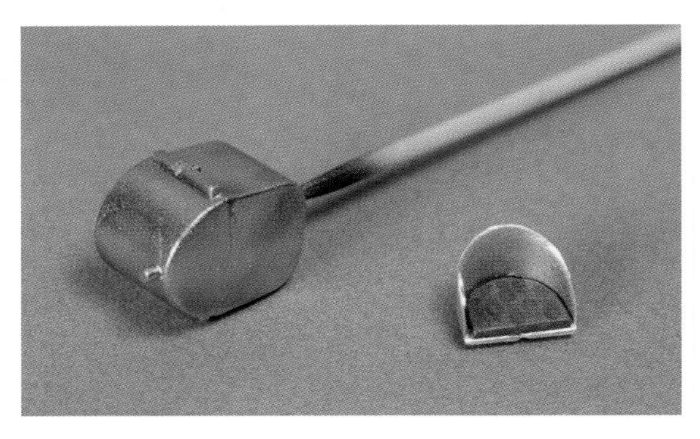

CLOCKWISE FROM TOP LEFT:

The fuselage sides and cabin area after preparation.

The fuel tank is first painted gloss black, prior to the Alclad II metallic paint being sprayed.

The fuel tank and seat after painting: the Alclad II paints really are excellent at representing metallic finishes.

II Polished Aluminium and given a really nice highly polished finish, almost indistinguishable from a piece of metal!

On an open cockpit aircraft, the interior is on view and can be as detailed as the modeller wishes, but as you'll see, most of the following builds have nothing visible of the interior, so any detailing will be in vain. But, where relevant, the various areas that are on view can be as detailed as you wish.

The natural wood areas, and this includes the propeller, are all painted in Tamiya Desert Yellow as an undercoat for the oil paints that will be used to create a wood effect. The basic technique that I use with the oil paints is to start with a lighter brown, almost dry-brushing the component, which will leave streaks of the colour on top of the Tamiya base coat. By using progressively darker shades and following a pattern of wood grain, the oil paints blend well together to give a nice rendition of a natural wood finish.

The engine components are all painted and assembled as per the instructions and then added to the fuselage sides. A light dry brushing with a lighter aluminium colour reveals the detail moulded on the plastic parts and really brings the assembly to life. The finished cockpit area, passenger seating area (of which there are just two seats!) and the fuel tank are all added once the fuselage halves are joined. The lower wing completes the construction for now, and the model kit really does come together very quickly. In fact I was rather surprised at how quickly, given the number of parts in the box, but as mentioned earlier, over 100 parts are redundant.

The passenger cabin itself is formed from two halves that sit on top of the fuselage, above the passenger seating area. This assembly has four windows, two each side, which are supplied on a small piece of plastic sheet and need to be cut out but before they are adhered to the inside of the cabin; the cabin section is set aside to be painted, along with the main fuselage and wheel struts. All these parts need to be painted blue, to match the shade of the registration letters on the decal sheet.

The specific shade used for the fuselage comes from the Tamiya range of acrylics and is their Flat Blue, XF-8, lightened slightly with white. All flying sur-

The four-bladed wooden propeller after painting using acrylics and oil paints.

The wooden floors of the cabin area really do contrast very nicely with the metal seats. Not exactly first class travel though, compared to the expectations of today's airline passengers!

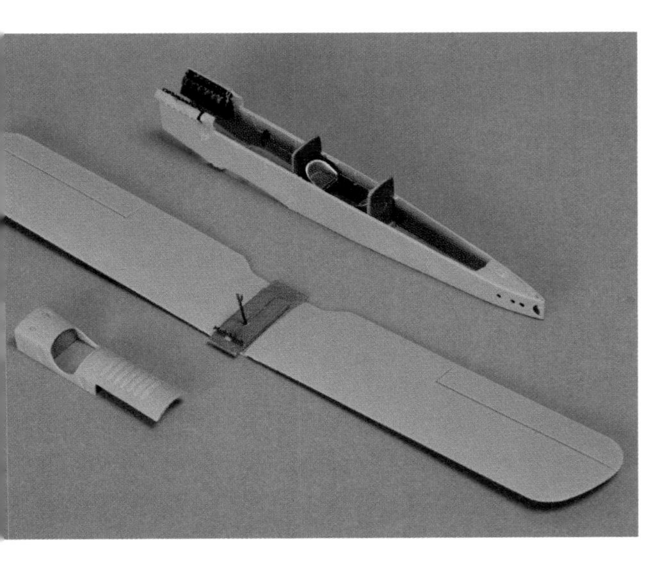

The cabin areas: shown here for the final time before concealing it all behind the fuselage parts.

It is not too long before she starts to look like an aeroplane!

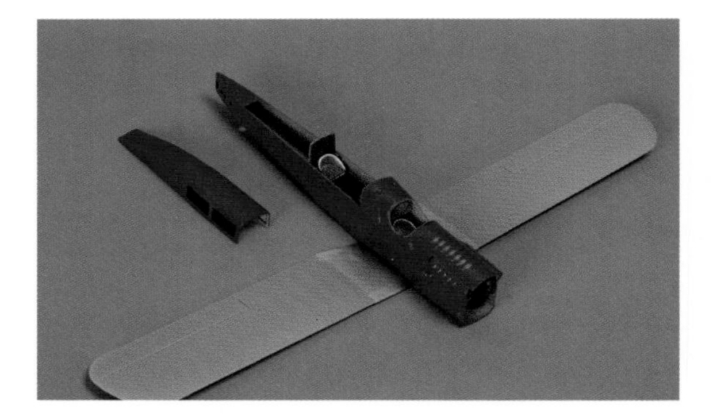

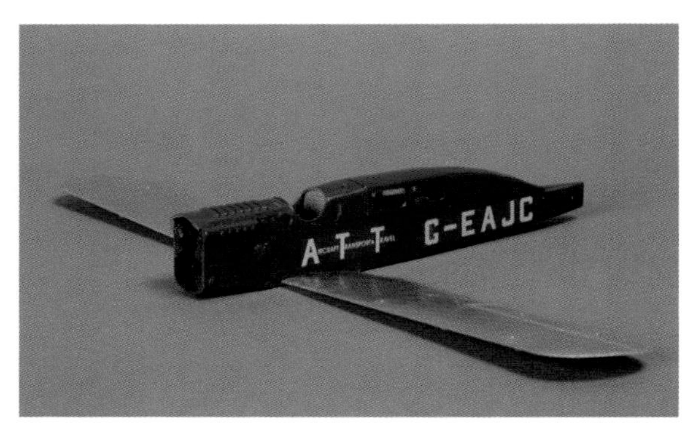

CLOCKWISE FROM TOP LEFT:

Tamiya's acrylic XF-8 Flat Blue is lightened with a small amount of white to obtain the correct shade.

The white decals are very opaque and contrast well with the blue fuselage.

The main components: prior to the fiddly final assembly.

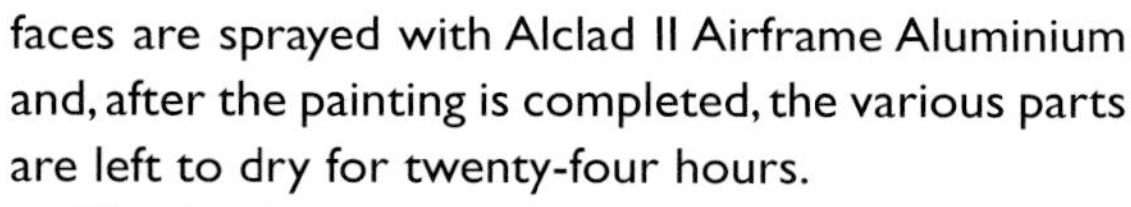

faces are sprayed with Alclad II Airframe Aluminium and, after the painting is completed, the various parts are left to dry for twenty-four hours.

The decals are applied now prior to final assembly, as the kit is quite fragile and the model should be handled as little as possible once the upper wing is in place. There are few decals to apply and this is easily completed in around half an hour. It is now time for the daunting task of getting the upper wing in place!

The tail surfaces are added and, a quick tip on enhancing these is simply to drop the elevators: on early aircraft (and indeed on most light aircraft) the control surfaces were not hydraulically powered and would naturally drop with gravity. So, a simple score along the elevator hinge line with a scriber thins the plastic enough to be able to just bend the elevators down. If you do this, don't forget to also displace the control column in the cockpit in the appropriate direction! In this case the stick should be forward of the neutral position. I don't think anyone will argue with you about the exact position, but any displacement will show that you've made a little bit of effort with respect to your attention to detail! The final finish is achieved by spraying a coat of satin varnish over the whole airframe to seal in the decals and create a uniform appearance.

Before the intimidating job of attaching the upper wing, some of the final details are painted including: the propeller hub and brass protection plates on the propeller blades, as well as the radiator detail.

And now it's on to the next task, attaching the upper wing to the lower, by way of eight thin struts! Prior to doing this though, I prepare all the struts and undercarriage supports and place them on a sheet of card, all numbered, so that with reference to the instruction sheet I will know which is which and where each one goes. The whole upper wing has to balance on these struts as the glue sets and it would be easy to imagine the whole assembly wobbling away with no intention of setting in the correct position!

One of my memories from my much younger days is of playing with Lego; it's amazing what you can use this for when modelling, but here it can be used to create a jig for supporting assemblies whilst they dry, which is exactly what I have done here. By

The propeller's hub and blades and the radiator are all painted using Alclad II.

In order not to get them mixed up, the wing struts are all placed on a sheet of card and, after painting, each one is numbered.

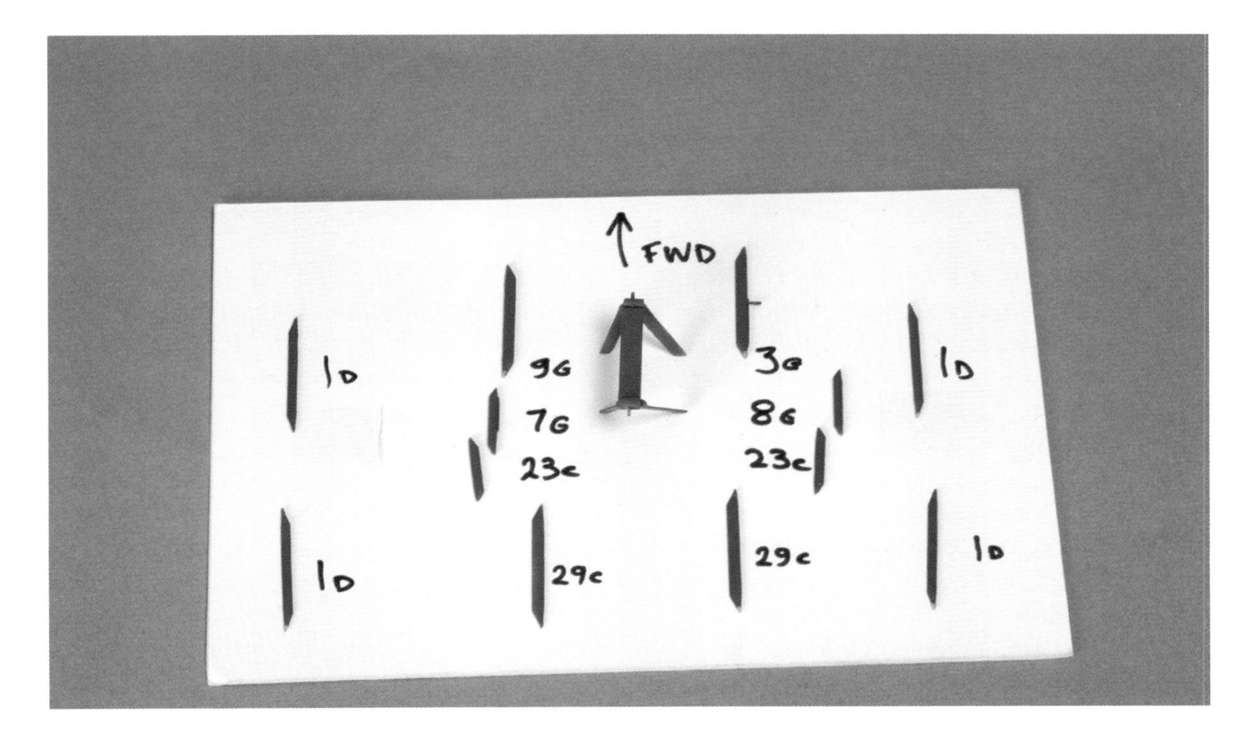

ABOVE AND ABOVE LEFT: ***Lego is still very much in demand in my home; although the applications are less obvious than they used to be!***

creating a jig, the upper wing is supported in place as each inter-plane strut is glued in place: for this I use a cyano-acrylate, or superglue adhesive, as it gives me the required strength of bond, as well as a fast setting time.

Once the struts are all in place I do not touch the model again for another twenty-four hours, to make sure that the adhesive has dried fully. The next phase of assembly is to add the small struts supporting the upper wing surface to the upper fuselage. These small struts are also adhered with cyano-acrylate and with these in place the whole assembly feels a lot stronger.

After the whole aircraft is complete final details are painted, such as the pitot tubes, beautifully moulded on one of the front inner struts. The exhausts are painted in a dark rust colour, again from the Alclad II range. This time, appropriately enough, the colour is called Engine Manifold. These are glued in place and the wheels, painted with a dark grey with the hubs in Aluminium, are placed on the axles and she sits, unsupported, for the first time! But now it is time for another daunting task: that of rigging the attractive little biplane.

As most early airframes were of biplane configuration, the rigging lines between the upper and lower wing surface, as well as the control wires, were all visible and, if replicated on a model such as this, really do make a huge difference to the final appearance. This is an area that is an art in itself and there are almost as many techniques in recreating the cables and wires as there are biplane kits! In the build of the Handley Page H.P.42, in the next chapter, the rigging was completed with fine steel wire, however there are many materials that can be used and, over the years, I've used fishing line, fine nylon sewing thread, fine lycra elastic, as well as actual human hair (the latter was obtained humanely from my daughter's hairbrush!). However, on this model I've used stretched sprue, created by heating a length of waste plastic sprue over a candle and when the plastic starts to melt, quickly drawing the ends apart, away from the heat source so that you end up with metres upon metres of very fine plastic thread, perfect for rigging biplanes!

Each length is roughly guessed at and, when the stretched plastic is presented to the area that it is destined for, the length can be more accurately measured and cut to size with a scalpel blade. Each end is dipped in cyano-acrylate glue and placed carefully using a pair of tweezers. Finally, each length is attached very carefully and, slowly but surely, the rigging is completed.

Fine strands of stretched sprue are used to rig the biplane and, just like the real thing, the rigging provides quite a bit of strength to the finished model.

The finished model is placed on a wooden base, complete with a patch of grass and, I must say, looks splendid in the display cabinet! But seriously, the DH.4 provided the early passenger with a method of transport unimaginable even ten years earlier and is captured by Roden extremely well in scale form.

The next few years saw aircraft develop quite rapidly and, after the success of the early biplanes, the embryonic airlines started to demand more capacity; after all, just two passengers were hardly ever likely please the accountants! The next airliners were not only able to carry many more passengers, but were also able to carry them further. Although the next kit manufacturer needs no introduction, the aircraft might be unfamiliar to some readers. However, this was an important machine during the beginning of airline travel.

CHAPTER FOUR

THE DAWN OF AIRLINE TRAVEL

AIRFIX 1/144TH HANDLEY PAGE H.P.42W

Just sixteen years after the honourable Mr Pheil became the first holder of an airline ticket, the fledgling airlines of the world were beginning to develop their route networks far beyond home shores. In the early 1930s, Great Britain's Imperial Airways operated the H.P. 42 'Heracles' and 'Hannibal' class of airliners, which were the world's first practical, four-engined airliners. There were two versions of the H.P. 42: these were known as the 42E or Eastern Class, usually known by the name of the flagship 'Hannibal', and the 42W or Western Class known as 'Heracles'; another aircraft, 'Helena', the subject of this build, was also a 42W variant.

Externally the aircraft were practically identical, however it was the slightly different engines and internal fittings that differentiated between the two. The 42W, powered by the larger 555hp Bristol Jupiter XFBM engine, operated mainly throughout Europe and on part of the India service, carrying thirty-eight passengers. The 42E Class operated primarily from Egypt, Pakistan and Africa and was powered by four Jupiter XIF engines of 490hp each. Just twenty-four passengers were carried but the 42E had a greater airmail capacity.

In service the H.P. 42's proved completely successful and were probably more popular with their passengers than any other airliner in the world at that time. Although never a fast aircraft (the H.P. 42 was said to have a built-in headwind!) it was exceptionally comfortable and was the only airliner capable of offering a full catering service, with between four and seven-course meals and drinks served from a trolley. The cabin was quiet, and as it was slung beneath the wings all the occupants enjoyed good visibility; the low fuselage also meant that high steps were not required for boarding. Outstanding amongst the H.P. 42's virtues was her safety record: the aircraft was absolutely reliable and in their years of service with Imperial Airways each airliner flew over 12,000 hours and reached an aggregate of over ten million miles.

G-AAGX, a HP42E: getting airborne from Croydon Airport during her proving trials.

First issued by Airfix in 1965, the seventy-four parts faithfully capture the biplane configuration of the early airliner.

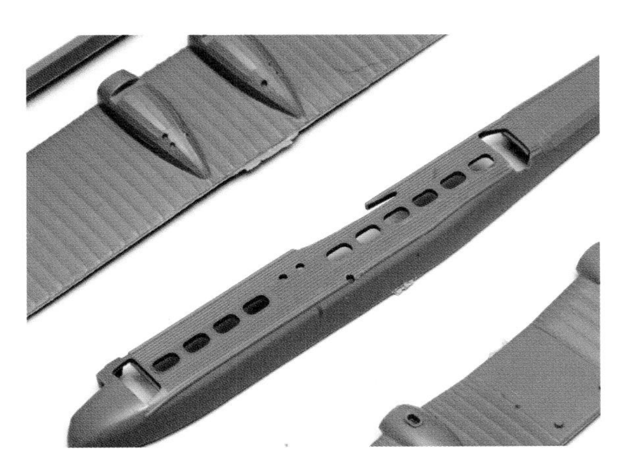

The parts do indicate the age of the moulds, with some flash present – seen here on the trailing edge of the wing.

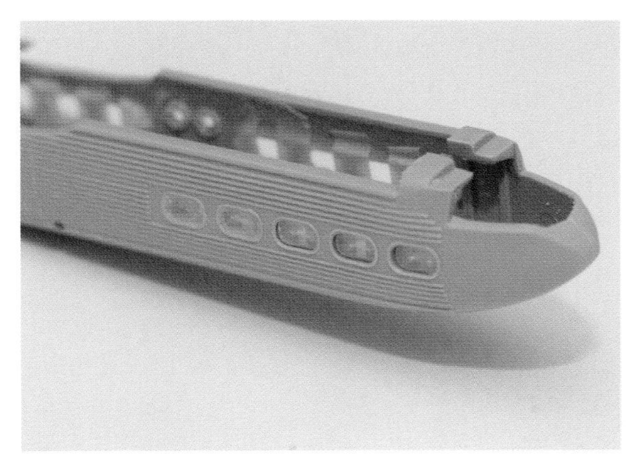

Cabin window curtains are represented by simply adhering some strips of masking tape to the inside face of the windows.

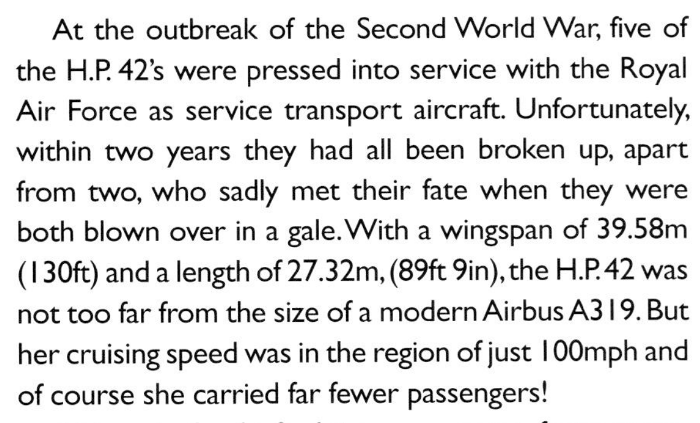

At the outbreak of the Second World War, five of the H.P. 42's were pressed into service with the Royal Air Force as service transport aircraft. Unfortunately, within two years they had all been broken up, apart from two, who sadly met their fate when they were both blown over in a gale. With a wingspan of 39.58m (130ft) and a length of 27.32m, (89ft 9in), the H.P. 42 was not too far from the size of a modern Airbus A319. But her cruising speed was in the region of just 100mph and of course she carried far fewer passengers!

Although the Airfix kit is now some forty-years-old, it is still very easy to find. The seventy-two parts are nicely moulded for a kit of this vintage and certainly allow for some subtle detailing. The kit was released as part of the SkyKing series and, as such, is in 1/144th scale. The SkyKing range was chosen as Airfix' airliner range and the smaller 1/144th scale was chosen to allow the larger aircraft, such as the Boeing B747, to be more manageable. However, the downside meant that the smaller aircraft, like the H.P. 42, were relatively small kits and there has been much discussion about the fact that this kit should have been in 1/72nd. But we are lucky to have a representation of this important early airliner in plastic at all, so let's have a look at what Airfix have given us.

As is normal in an airliner model, there is no interior detail at all, although there is certainly some scope here for those who want to scratch-build a cabin and seating. Following the instructions, construction begins with preparing the window parts, carefully gluing these into place on the interior of each fuselage part. Polystyrene, or any solvent-based adhesives, and transparent plastic parts, are sworn enemies, as any glue getting onto the transparent parts will render them opaque; therefore, when cementing these parts to the fuselage sides, special care must be taken. An alternative would be to use a PVA-based glue: these water-based glues tend to dry clear and are easy to wipe off with a damp cloth should any errant glue get onto the model's surface. There are now many PVA adhesives available from the larger, specialist model shops.

If you look at period photographs of the H.P. 42, and there are plenty to be found on the Internet, curtains can clearly be seen in the passenger windows and these are replicated here on my model with the use of small pieces of masking tape. After the window parts have thoroughly dried, use a scalpel, a cutting mat and a very steady hand, to cut out small pieces of tape and then adhere them to the inside of the windows.

The technique is very simple but the effect is worth the few minutes that it takes. Once all the windows had been given their 'curtains', the fuselage halves are attached together. As soon as this sub-assembly is dry it is time to have a look at a rather large and

After securing the two fuselage halves together, Berna clamps are used to keep the two halves firmly together. A large gap will be worked on after the assembly has completely set.

The lower fuselage gap is filled with Tamiya plastic putty.

unsightly gap, visible along the lower fuselage join. This gap needs a bit of attention before continuing with any further construction.

A gap such as this is not uncommon on an older kit, although most modern kits are moulded to much finer tolerances, using up-to-date, computer-designed masters. But it is a very simple process to put right and can be repaired using, in this case, Squadron's White Putty, although any number of other fillers could also be used. Smearing a line of putty along the gap and working it in, using a scrap piece of plastic, fills the space nicely. Squadron's putty is solvent-based and will stick very effectively to the plastic: once dry the area is easily workable by simply sanding and polishing using progressively smoother sanding sticks. Once completed, the filled gap will simply disappear under a coat of paint.

The tail surfaces are all carefully removed from the sprue and cleaned up, prior to constructing into a surprisingly sturdy sub-assembly. At this point the elderly kit really begins to look rather smart!

The wing assembly, which looks incredibly fragile even on the full size aircraft, is the next, very daunting task. However, the wing struts that support the upper wing are sturdy and supplied as one single piece for the front and rear struts. There is also a small template, supplied as a moulded part on one of the sprues, which helps with aligning the upper and lower wing halves correctly. As the area to which this is attached will be hidden from view once assembly is complete, the template can actually be adhered to the lower wing surface and this helps both correctly place and support the upper wing, whilst the whole assembly dries. The whole wing assembly only takes around thirty minutes to fully construct: once complete and with the template piece carefully removed, it is bonded onto the fuselage using a thin polystyrene cement. With the wing and tail surfaces nicely square and in place, the model is left to allow the glue to dry completely: now is not the time to let accidents happen!

When the upper fuselage panels are set in place, it is apparent that there will be a small gap either at the front or rear of the panels, as these are just a little too short to fill the top of the fuselage completely. Therefore, everything: front panel, wing and rear panel, are pushed back as far back as possible, resulting in one single gap at the front, just above the cockpit. This is then easily accessible and is filled using two small strips of plastic, cut to shape and sanded. The front windshield can now be glued in place and the model is now ready for masking, prior to painting.

The embryonic Imperial Airways had a simple scheme of silver doped fabric surfaces, metal areas were left bare and the livery itself was nothing

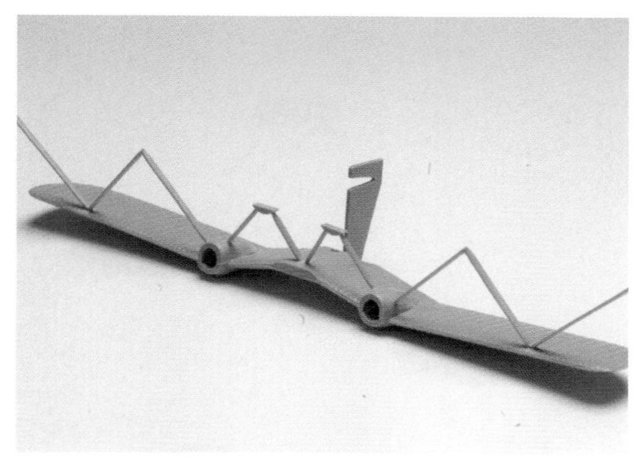

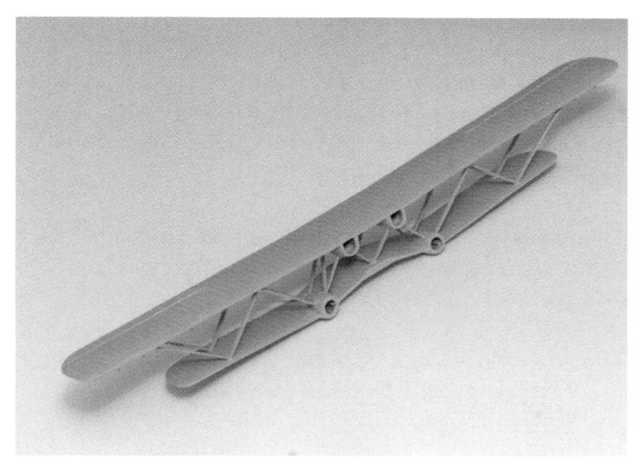

CLOCKWISE FROM TOP LEFT:

The rear tail surfaces are carefully assembled, as any out of alignment will be very noticeable.

The upper wing is assembled prior to adding the struts. This assembly needs to be fully dry before assembly of the lower wing can begin.

The completed wing sub-assembly is surprisingly strong.

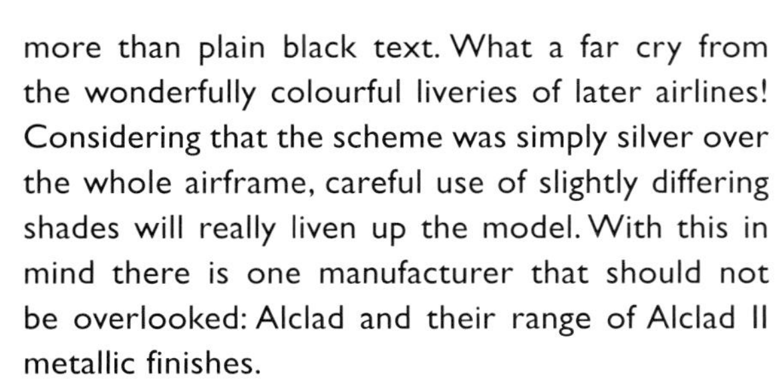

more than plain black text. What a far cry from the wonderfully colourful liveries of later airlines! Considering that the scheme was simply silver over the whole airframe, careful use of slightly differing shades will really liven up the model. With this in mind there is one manufacturer that should not be overlooked: Alclad and their range of Alclad II metallic finishes.

Prior to spraying, all the windows are masked off and for this I use Tamiya tape on the main windshield areas, but for the oval passenger windows I use Windsor and Newton's liquid paint mask. This flows extremely nicely into the recesses and areas that would be hard to mask with tape and being similar to a PVA-type adhesive, dries to a rubbery layer that is easily peeled off after the paint has dried. Preparation for spraying the model with Alclad II involves applying a smooth, gloss black finish: for this I used my last can of Tamiya TS-14 Black. The TS range of paints is fabulous and they give an incredibly smooth and hardwearing finish. Unfortunately, they were removed from sale in the UK, apparently due to labelling issues, although I do understand that they will be on sale again soon. (As of August 2009, the TS range of Tamiya spray paints was due to be released again in the UK).

After the black finish has dried, load the paint cup of an Iwata airbrush with Alclad's 102 Duraluminium shade. These metallic paints cover the base coat beautifully and, after a few careful sweeps with the airbrush, a final coat is applied and the little H.P. 42 airliner really starts to come to life.

Finish off the painting by masking off a few panels, the nose area and control surfaces, in order to give them a coat of the brighter 106 White Aluminium shade. Use a wash of darker metallic colours to add detail and liven up the small 1/144th scale radial engines. Paint the exhausts matt black and fix them

CLOCKWISE FROM TOP LEFT:

After the model has reached this stage, it is left aside for a couple of days in order to allow the glue to fully set; you certainly don't want any accidents at this stage!

The small gaps behind the cockpit area are filled with strips of plasticard, which are cut and sanded back flush to the fuselage.

The lower fuselage gap can be seen here, after the Tamiya filler has been sanded.

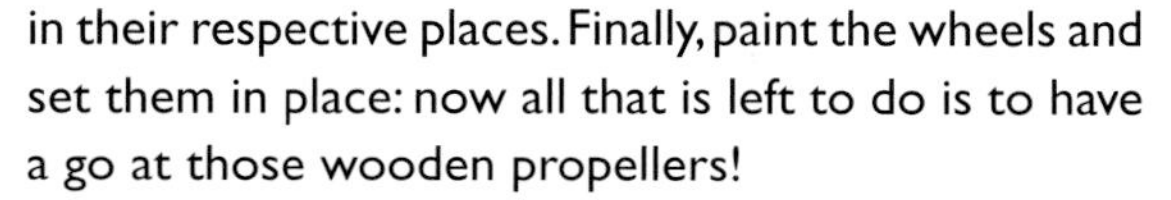

in their respective places. Finally, paint the wheels and set them in place: now all that is left to do is to have a go at those wooden propellers!

The early propellers were manufactured by laminating together layers of different woods, mostly mahogany, oak and walnut in order to provide strength, but that just makes it difficult for us modellers to reproduce that effect! My preferred technique is to use artist's oil paints. By painting the propeller in a light shade, such as Light Raw Umber, the light base colour can be gradually dry brushed with strokes along the length of the propeller blade using progressively darker shades, such as Raw Umber and Burnt Sienna. A little investment in these shades is definitely worthwhile if you are planning to paint early wooden propellers effectively and a tube of each colour will last a modelling lifetime!

Once dry, the four little propellers are placed onto their engines and the final details are added. Surprisingly for an aircraft of this vintage there is no rigging on the main struts of the wings, other than a simple cross-brace on the outer two struts. By using short lengths of steel wire, these are nicely reproduced, but the rear tail surfaces have a more complicated pattern of rigging, which is reproduced using very fine, surgical stainless steel thread. While this material is obviously very strong, it is difficult to handle in long lengths, and is therefore best used where shorter lengths of rigging need recreating. A small drop of cyano-acrylate glue, or superglue, is all that is needed to secure each end of the steel threads in place.

In some original photos of the H.P. 42, a prominent nose skid is evident and this is reproduced by using fine steel wire: this time an old top E string from my guitar provides the raw material! Another length of guitar string is formed into a loop to replicate the ADF aerial above the forward fuselage. In some

A liquid masking fluid is used to mask the windows prior to painting.

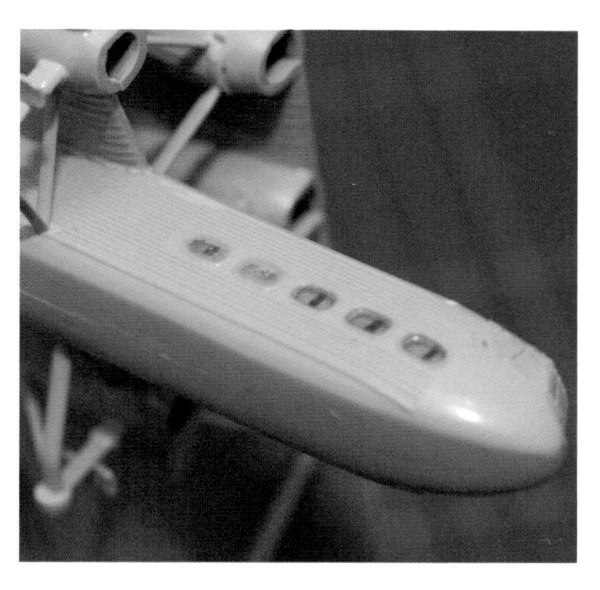

The masking fluid dries to an almost clear finish.

Alclad II metallic paint is used as the final finish and is best applied to a gloss black undercoat, applied here using Tamiya TS-14 spray paint.

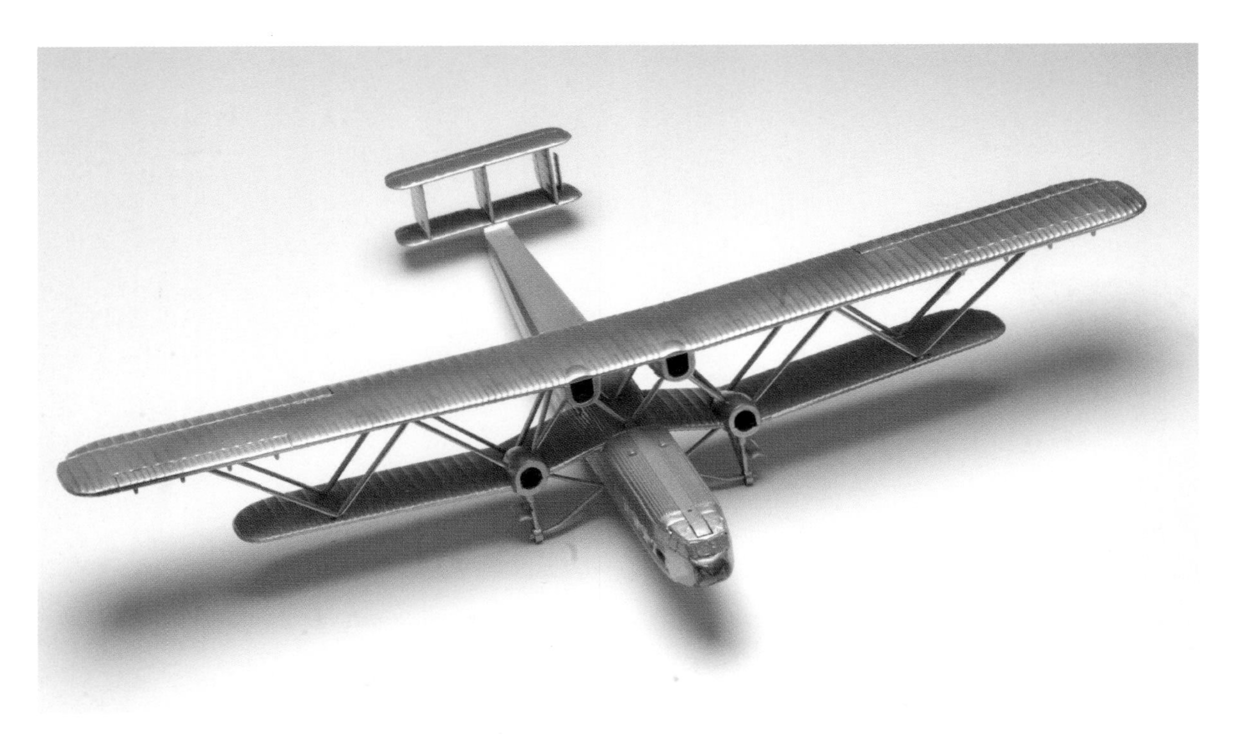

The final coat is applied by airbrush, using Alclad II 102 Duraluminium.

As a contrast, the bare metal panels around the nose are sprayed with Alclad II 106 White Aluminium.

With the final details attached, the H.P.42 sits in my display cabinet.

photographs a nose mounted light is also clearly seen and, although it may be taking a little 'artistic licence' to incorporate this detail into this model, I did so with the help of one of the lovely little model railway lenses I have in the spares box. (Little-Cars stock a full range of model lenses in various sizes and colours.)

Although Airfix provide a flagstaff, no flag is supplied and many period photos of the H.P. 42 clearly show the Civil Aviation Ensign flying from the mast. After doing some research on the Internet, I found a design that could be reduced and then printed onto a white decal sheet to reproduce this feature.

To allow for trial and error, I printed out three copies of the flag in both left and right-handed patterns, in order that both sides of the flag could be correctly represented. The white decal sheet is available from model stores and can be printed on using a standard ink-jet printer, but the image has to be sprayed over with a sealing coat of clear varnish to waterproof the image. As you can see from the photo the idea worked and the image can now be treated like any other water slide decal.

The flag is cut from the decal sheet and, after wetting it and sliding it from the backing sheet, it is placed onto a small piece of tin foil, before wrapping it around the flagstaff. Using tin foil as a backing to the decal, allows the flag to be realistically moulded and draped naturally.

Finally all the masking is removed and there she is finished, awaiting the first group of passengers to embark upon what, in the early 1930s, would have been quite an adventure!

CHAPTER FIVE

INTO THE THIRTIES...

AZ MODEL 1/144TH AVRO TYPE 618 'TEN'

During its most successful period in the 1920s and 1930s, the Dutch aircraft manufacturer, Fokker, dominated the civil aviation market. In fact, it could also be argued that they have dominated this book, as this is the first of three aircraft designed by the Fokker Company represented within these pages!

The original Walter Rethel design of 1924 was a single-engined, high-winged monoplane. Anthony Fokker modified the design with two additional engines to enter the inaugural Ford Reliability Tour in 1925, which it won. Consequently, the production versions F.VIIa/3m, F.VIIb/3m and F.10 all had three engines, and the aircraft became popularly known as the Fokker Trimotor. The Avro type 618 'Ten' was a copy of the F.VIIB/3m built by the British manufacturer under licence to Fokker. Ingenuously enough, the Avro designation 618 'Ten' was adopted as the aircraft was capable of carrying two crew and eight passengers. Later variants were known as the Type 619 'Five', a five seat aircraft, the Type 624 'Six', six seats and the Type 642 'Eighteen' with, unsurprisingly, eighteen seats. Very clever, those early aircraft designations!

A small, etched metal sprue contains some of the finer elements, such as the engine support struts. Finally, there are three resin engines, although 'engines' is really an optimistic description for what are, essentially, just little lumps of resin. These are not the best representations of a radial engine but help is at hand in the form of Aeroclub Models. Aeroclub have been casting generic and replica metal parts for model aircraft for some time and in their range they have a generic, nine-cylinder radial engine that is a perfect replacement for the resin parts.

Construction begins with the cockpit and, although I have previously stated that many airliner models, particularly in 1/144th scale, do not have interior detail, this diminutive kit does come with a basic cockpit area, complete with two seats, an etched metal instrument panel and control columns!

The resulting completed assembly is quite a joy to behold, given the scale, and although impossible to

AZ Models' Avro 618 'Ten'.

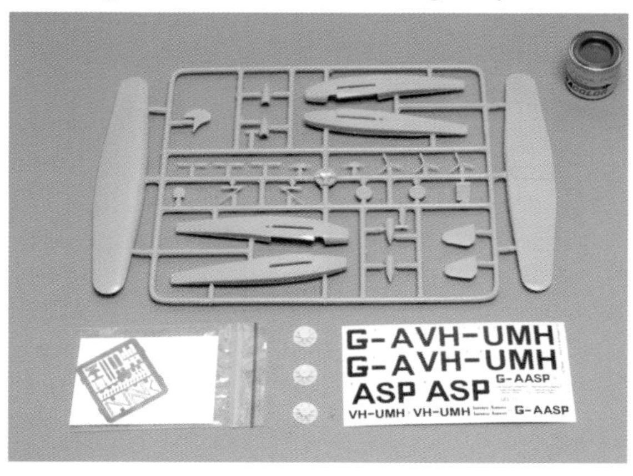

With just one sprue holding the complete kit, the size can be seen here compared to a standard paint tinlet.

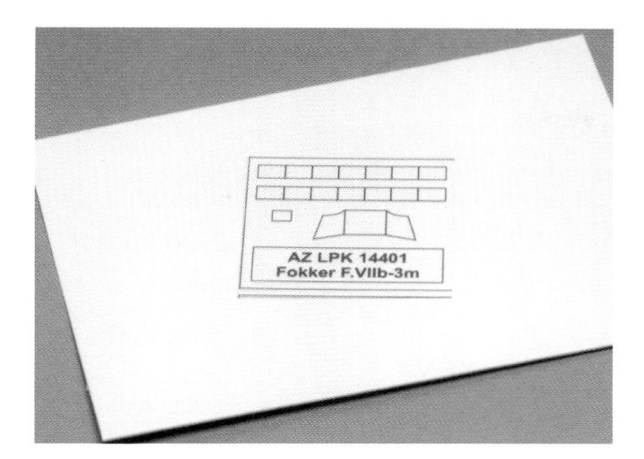

The transparent parts are included on a small acetate sheet.

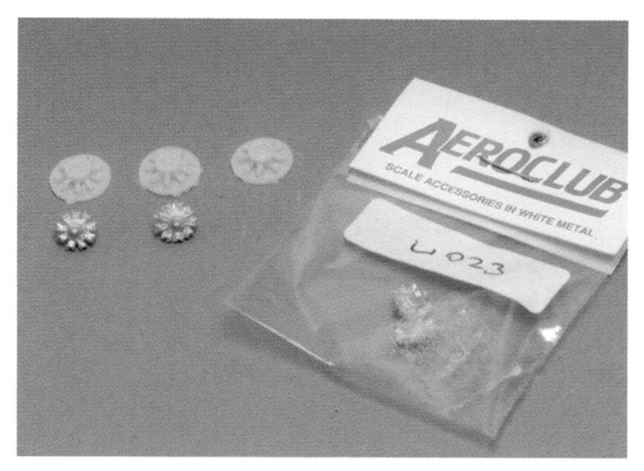

Replacement white metal engines are used instead of the kit's resin parts.

see once the fuselage halves are adhered together, it is always nice to know that the detail is there! The side window glazing is supplied on the clear printed sheet and each side window needs to be cut from the sheet using a small, sharp pair of scissors. Although this sounds rather daunting, the window parts do not need to be cut accurately as there needs to be an overlap, which will provide a good surface to apply the adhesive to. In this case I have used a thin cyano-acrylate, carefully applied in small stages with a pin, followed by a quick application of accelerator to speed up the setting time.

Once each half of the fuselage has had the glazing applied, the cockpit assembly is installed in one side and the two halves glued together, this time using very thin viscosity plastic cement, applied by brush. There are various brands available and care should be taken, as the fumes that they give off are rather noxious! These types of adhesive are very thin and flow quickly along the seam: with a little pressure applied on each side, the join will set rapidly.

The resulting join is perhaps not as clean as could be achieved using a modern kit, but it is certainly easily cleaned up with varying grades of sanding stick.

The single wing is supplied as two halves, upper and lower and, in comparison with the fuselage, looks huge! Comparison with contemporary photographs shows that the wing was incredibly thick and the kit parts represent this very well. The wing halves are stuck together, again using the thin plastic cement and, once this has set, are sanded down to hide the join lines. After the wing has adhered to the top of the fuselage the tiny model really begins to ooze character, but the following part of the construction is certainly more daunting!

The engine nacelles are effectively hung on struts under the wing and also form part of the undercarriage structure, by holding the main undercarriage legs. These are supplied as extremely fine plastic mouldings, while the wing to engine struts are supplied on the etched metal fret and these parts are almost microscopic! Using a steady hand, thin superglue, a scalpel, a needle, a magnifying glass and a lot of patience the engine nacelles are secured in place. Once the nose-mounted centre engine is attached you can afford to let out an audible sigh of relief!

Now that the basic airframe is complete, thankfully the whole assembly is painted silver; I don't think that I could cope if there was a detailed and intricate scheme to be applied! Using Alclad II Light Aluminium, the entire airframe is sprayed and left to dry. The next step is to consider how best to represent the exhaust rings.

In some kits, especially limited run editions such as this, it is often left to the modeller to provide additional detail by scratch-building components. The exhaust collector rings around the rear of the cylinder heads of this model are an example and, after a search through my 'detailing bits' drawer in my

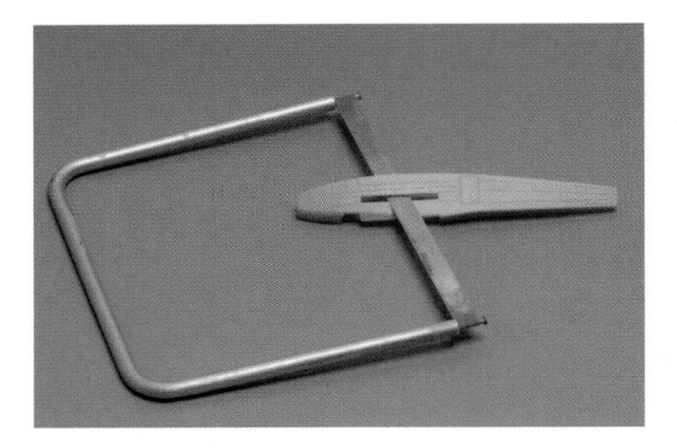

Cleaning up the inside of the window openings is made easier with the use of a flex-i-file sanding tool.

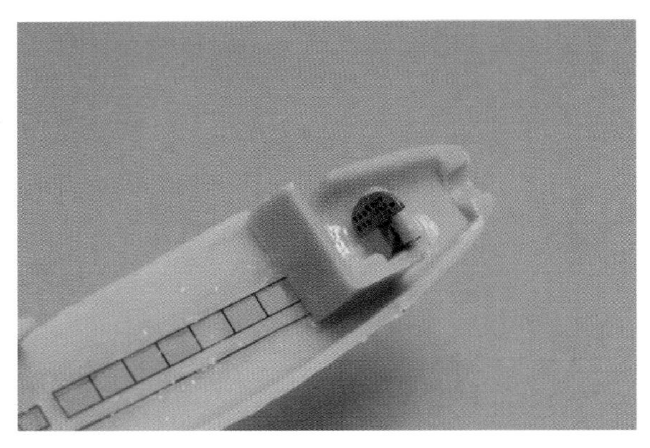

The acetate sheet windows are adhered in place with a very careful application of thin superglue.

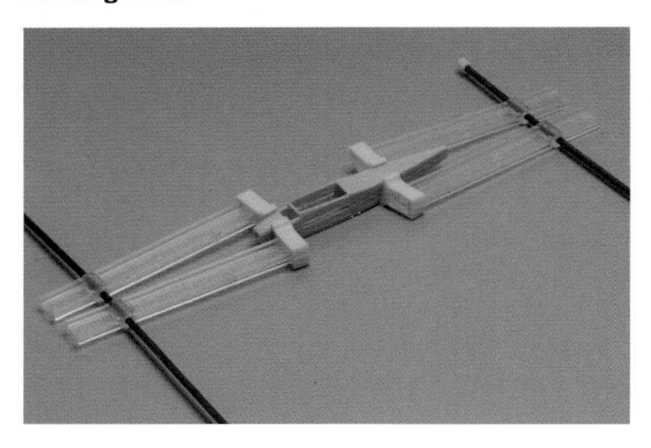

The two fuselage halves are again held with the aid of the Berna clamps.

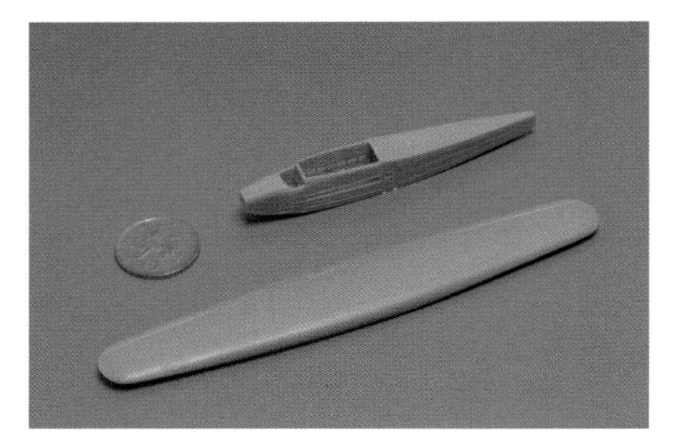

After just a few hours' work, the main components are seen here with a British ten pence piece for scale. Yes, the model really is that small!

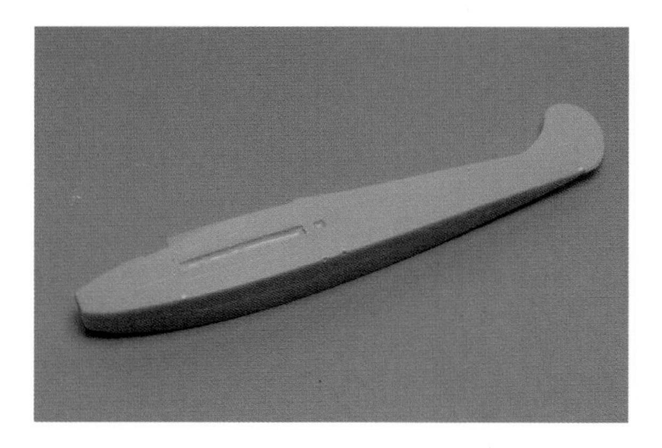

The windows are masked using Humbrol's Maskol, another PVA-based masking fluid.

The tail surfaces and wing are all attached and the centre, nose-mounted engine attached with CA. Once more, the size of the model is easily apparent when seen next to the ten pence coin.

The painstaking task of attaching the wing mounted engines and undercarriage is completed with care, patience and a large magnifying glass!

The wing-mounted engines are attached with very fine, etched metal struts.

modelling cabinet, I decided to use some fuse wire of an appropriate diameter. Fuse wire is an inexpensive and extremely useful addition to the inventory, as it is available in many diameters and, although usually silver in colour, can be sanded and the nickel plating removed to show the copper core. After sanding three short lengths, revealing the copper, these are wrapped carefully behind each engine and bent to represent the exhaust pipes.

Against the completely silver finish of the aircraft, these really show up, especially after each engine is given a wash with a dark steel colour to reveal the amazing detail cast into these tiny little Aeroclub engines.

Once more I decided to use the Imperial Airways scheme provided on the decal sheet, the alternative scheme being an Australian registered aircraft. Once the decals are applied the final assembly begins with the addition of the wheels, tail-skid and control horns; these are also reproduced as tiny parts on the etched metal fret. The propellers are attached to the engines and painted in the same way as those of the H.P. 42 in the previous chapter.

The diminutive Avro 618 'Ten' sports her final livery: as it was the 1930s, this means overall silver!

Copper fuse wire is used to represent the exhausts.

The windscreen is made up by using stretched sprue to represent the frames. The Wooden propellors are painted using various colours of oil paints, over an acrylic undercoat.

Certainly an exercise in patience, AZ Models' tiny Avro 618 'Ten' is an absolute joy to build.

The final result is worth the patience and the kit itself is an absolute joy. Sometimes it is really worth seeking out an alternative to the major manufacturers in order to stretch your modelling skills a little although, after this build, I decided that I had to have something slightly easier to construct!

CHAPTER SIX

THE GOLDEN AGE

HELLER 1/72ND DE HAVILLAND DRAGON RAPIDE

The de Havilland DH.89 Dragon Rapide was a British, short-haul passenger airliner of the 1930s. Designed by the de Havilland Company in late 1933, it was really nothing more than a twin-engined, scaled-down version of the four-engined De Havilland Express DH.86 and shared many common features with the larger aircraft: including its tapered wings, streamlined fairings and the De Havilland Gipsy Six engine. The DH.89 ultimately became the most successful British-built, commercial passenger aircraft of the 1930s.

The prototype first flew on 17 April 1934 and 205 were built prior to the outbreak of World War Two. One famous incident involving the use of a DH.89 occurred in July 1936, when a British MI6 intelligence agent, Hugh Pollard, flew with General Francisco Franco in a leased Dragon Rapide from the Canary Islands to Spanish Morocco at the start of the military rebellion in Spain, thus marking the beginning of the Spanish Civil War. That aircraft is now wonderfully preserved in the Spanish Air Force Museum at Cuattro Vientos airfield near Madrid.

At the start of World War Two many Dragon Rapides were impressed by the British armed forces and served under the name of the de Havilland Dominie. They were used for passenger duties and radio navigation training, although over 500 more were built specifically for military purposes, powered by improved Gipsy Queen engines, to bring total production to 731. Many survivors entered commercial service after the war, and eighty-one were still flying on the British register as late as 1958. Both De Havilland and Brush Coachworks Ltd, the

The Heller release of the DH.89 Dragon Rapide; the same model has also been released by Airfix.

latter making the greater proportion, completed the Dominie production.

The DH.89 proved a very durable aircraft despite its relatively primitive plywood construction and many were still flying in the early 2000s. In fact several Rapides are still operational in the UK and a few owners offer pleasure flights in them. (These are quite often available from Shoreham Airfield in Sussex, where the combined 1930s vintage aircraft, along with the 1930s era control tower and terminal building, provide an unforgettable experience.)

As Trevor Snowden has already mentioned in his foreword, the French company Heller were, at one point, 'in bed' with Airfix. The two companies shared their releases and many kits appeared as different variations on the same theme in each of the company's boxes: the Dh.89 is one example and the Airfix version includes decals for the RAF military variant, whilst Heller's is a civilian example.

Despite the age of this kit, the parts are crisply moulded with good surface detail. However the kit was produced before moulding technology allowed the integration of recessed panel lines on kit parts; thus the panel lines are raised, but a swift wipe over with a fine grade sheet of wet 'n' dry sandpaper will remove these if desired. There is something so very 'familiar' with kits of this vintage and many modellers of my own age will be instantly reminded of their youth when looking at the sprues of silver grey plastic, raised panel lines and only a slight representation of an interior. With modern injection-moulding methods, after market etched metal and resin detail sets, how we are spoiled today!

By now you should be getting used to the order of assembly and this kit is no different: the interior is completed prior to the fuselage halves being assembled, followed by the wings and tail surfaces, before the smaller details are added. So no surprises there and, in no time at all, this lovely model is almost at the painting stage.

The interior is sparse and can be neatly detailed far beyond the level of detail supplied. The cabin seats are provided, as are the pilots' seats, but there is so much scope here that it would be a shame not to have a go at reproducing something a little more detailed than that provided. For reference, you need

The Heller DH.89 Dragon Rapide, modelled by Rico Christmann.

look no further than the Internet and a search for images of the Dh.89's interior quickly reveals that the passenger seats are slightly different in shape to those provided in the kit, with the seat backs being much taller and with a more pointed profile.

Over the years I have seen many of the Heller kits built into lovely replicas of the original. But this particular model, built by Rico Christmann, really caught my eye: although the livery really highlights the lines of the Rapide, I think that the setting and the miniature people, sourced form a model railway supplier, really shows the aircraft as she would have been seen on the apron in the 1930s.

The DH.89 is such a classic design and instantly recognizable as being from the de Havilland stable: from the rudder profile, to the tapered wings, there are many clues as to its heritage.

CLASSIC DESIGNS LONG FORGOTTEN

During the research for this book, I looked at the complete history of civil aviation and always thought that the most development took place during the 1950s and 1960s, when the jet engine became the preferred power plant. However, the designs that most appealed to me were certainly from the 1930s: it is from this decade that I can look at the civilian aircraft and see a huge difference in the design of

RIGHT AND BELOW: ***The Welsh Models' vac-form kit of the Armstrong Whitworth AW.27 Ensign.***

RIGHT: ***The exceptionally skilled Alex Bigey built this particular model. More of Alex's models can be seen at his website, www.freewebs.com/aeroscale.***

the aircraft, from the beginning to the end of that ten-year period. I suppose that I should not be too surprised, as you only need to look at the development of the motorcar during the same period to see the huge technological leaps that were made.

However, when such leaps are made, the brand new design becomes redundant all too quickly and the lifespan of many aircraft during this period was incredibly short. After all, the Boeing B737 has been in constant production for over forty years and even more modern designs such as the Airbus A320 have been in service for over twenty years. But during the 1930s many airliners were produced with service lives of as little as two years.

To many enthusiasts and model makers, some names are familiar, such as: the de Havilland DH.91 Albatross and the German Focke-Wulfe FW200 Condor, which later, in its military guise, became known as the Scourge of the Atlantic, due to the heavy losses it inflicted on allied shipping during the Battle of the Atlantic. But how many of you have heard of the Armstrong Whitworth AW.27 Ensign? A beautiful, four-engined airliner operated by Imperial Airways at the end of the decade, this aircraft has been produced as a vac-form kit by Welsh Models and a superb example of one is shown here, built by the extremely talented French modeller, Alex Bigey.

The list of 1930s Airliners is enormous and every industrialized country seemed to have at least one major manufacturer designing and producing civilian passenger aircraft. Many of these designs were destined to be short- lived but some, such as the Lockheed L.10 Electra, were to see much greater service operating as military aircraft during the Second World War.

The L10 Electra was immortalized as it was in one of these aircraft that Amelia Earhart disappeared over the Pacific Ocean during her attempted round the world flight in 1937. The L10 was further developed into the L12 and, later, the L14 Super Electra. Again, the aircraft achieved some notoriety, as it was in a Lockheed L14 Super Electra, operated by British Airways, that British Prime Minister Neville Chamberlain flew to Germany in order to try to achieve a peaceful accord with Hitler. It was a short-lived 'Peace in our Time' as Germany invaded Poland the following year and the rest is history.

The Special Hobby 1/72nd model of the L10 Electra with Tally Ho decals: once again the work of Alex Bigey.

The Junkers F24, a conversion completed by Michel Leornardi from the old VEB Plastikart model of the three-engined G24.

This large, four-engined flying boat is the Sikorsky S.42, completed by Michel Leornardi from the RCM vac-form kit in 1/72nd scale.

More exceptional vac-form building by Michel Leornardi: this is the Short Mayo Composite in 1/72nd scale from the AIM kit.

Germany was still operating under restrictions with respect to the production of military aircraft, but the aircraft manufacturers, such as Focke Wulf and Junkers, were all working hard to design civilian aircraft that could be easily converted to military use: both the Heinkel 111 and the FW200 began life as airliners. Another exceptional modeller of aircraft from this 'Golden Age' is Michel Leornardi: shown here is one of his models of a Junkers F24, the single-engine variant of the three-engined G24. This is a superb conversion from the old 1/72nd kit produced by the East German company VEB Plastikart.

During the 1930s, there was strong competition between Pan American Airways and Imperial Airways on the longer, trans-oceanic services using large flying boat airliners. Shorts and Boeing both produced aircraft that would also see wartime service, but during their pre-war lives they were responsible for the first trans-Atlantic services joining Europe with the United States. The Shorts C-Class Empire flying boats competed head on with Boeing's 314 Clipper series. The experience gained during these flights became important for the wartime operations over the Atlantic, as well as for the post-war development of one of the busiest routes in current airline operations.

More of Michel Leornardi's work is shown here with the Sikorsky S.42 being the 1/72nd vac-form kit by RCM. The Short Mayo Composite is a long-range seaplane combination of the Short S.21 Maia, similar to the C-Class Empire flying boats, and the Short S.20 Mercury. The kit is the AIM vac-form kit that Michel enhanced with Aeroclub Bristol Pegasus engines and Hamilton props for the S.21 Maia; the Napier Rapier engines were sourced from four Matchbox Fairey Seafox kits for the S.20 Mercury. The final finish was achieved with Tamiya's TS-17 Gloss Aluminium spray.

The 1930s was indeed the Golden Age of Aviation and, had it not been for the Second World War, the most produced and flown post-war airliner may well have been a British, French or German design. So, now to an aircraft that, despite being designed and first flown in the early 1930s, I am sure will be immediately recognizable to everyone.

CHAPTER SEVEN

AIR TRAVEL COMES TO THE MASSES

MINICRAFT 1/144TH DOUGLAS DC-3 DAKOTA

Does the Douglas DC-3 need any introduction at all? So many books exist and so many words have been written on what is, truly, one of the greatest aircraft designs of all time. Of course, the aircraft is known in military circles as the C-47, but the Douglas DC-3 was never a converted military aircraft, in fact it was the other way around, with the design being a commercial airliner first that later gained a reputation as a good military aircraft. Just to emphasize how successful the aircraft was as an airliner, it is an astonishing fact that, prior to World War Two, nine out of every ten, airline passengers in the United States were flying on board the DC-3.

With over 16,000 made, the DC-3 is still the most produced airliner; however it was only put into production after a telephone call from American Airlines' CEO, C. R. Smith, to Donald Douglas, who finally agreed to go ahead with development after Smith informed him of American's intention to purchase twenty aircraft. The initial derivative of this new aircraft first flew on 17 December 1935; just thirty-two years to the day after the Wright Brothers flew the Wright Flyer at Kitty Hawk. More than 2,000 DC-3s are still flying today, with over 300 still in commercial service.

So with such an illustrious history, why then was this aircraft neglected by the model manufacturers in the 'standard' airliner scale? There have been many kits of the aircraft in 1/72nd and even in 1/48th but there was a gap in the market for a traditionally scaled Dakota and Minicraft eventually came up with this, a very nicely moulded 1/144th DC-3 Dakota.

I discovered when opening the box just how tiny the aircraft is! That has to be the answer to my earlier question as to why the manufacturers neglected moulding the kit in 1/144th scale. Compared to the earlier H.P.42, also in 1/144th scale, the DC-3 really comes across as very small indeed. The kit itself has just thirty-seven parts; all very nicely moulded with engraved panel lines, with the main landing gear

The Minicraft Douglas DC-3 is available in a number of different releases: shown here is the United Airlines release.

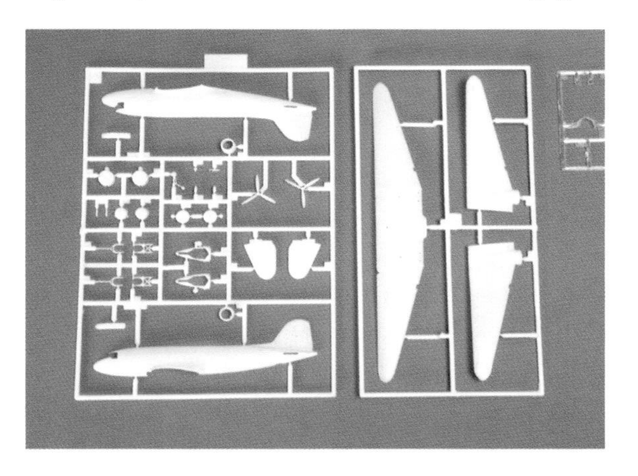

The three sprues are all that is needed to hold the small number of parts.

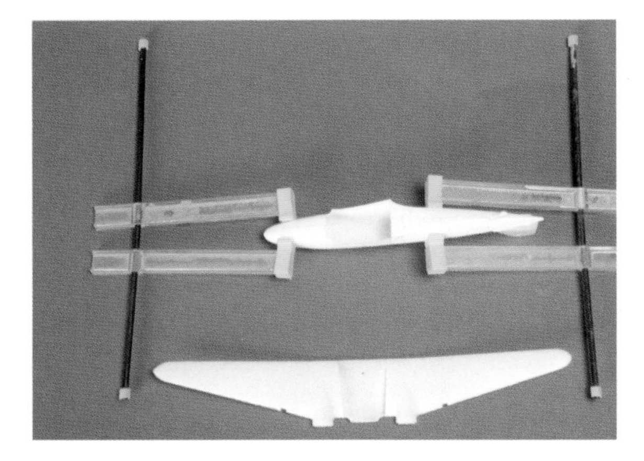

The Berna clamps in action again!

Tamiya masking tape is used here to hold the dihedral angle of the wings whilst the adhesive sets.

Plasticine comes in very handy here, to hold the tweezers that the model is supported by.

especially well represented. There have been a few reviews of this kit mentioning that the fuselage shape is slightly wrong, with a heavy nose and too long a tail cone. These are not a problem: the basic nose shape can be reformed with a sanding stick and the tail cone can easily be shortened.

There is a small clear sprue, which includes the windshield and landing lights, but the cabin windows themselves need to be represented by decals. I also found that the model kit includes the twin row Pratt & Whitney radial engines, used by only a few airlines pre-World War Two but, accuracy issues aside, this is one aircraft that had to be included in this book and, in my own humble opinion, there is only one livery that she should be modelled in.

Most of the parts come together very easily indeed: the wing and vertical tail trailing edges are nicely made with sharp edges, even though they are moulded in upper and lower halves; the lower wing is moulded in one piece, tip to tip, and the upper wing halves fit well to the lower half. The wing to fuselage fit is not very good however, a view supported by other reviews of this kit, but there are essentially three ways to rectify this problem: the first is to glue the wings to the fuselage, before gluing the lower front fuselage halves together. This leaves a much easier gap to fill along the lower fuselage seam, instead of having to deal with the hard-to-access wing roots.

Another solution is to spread the wing roots out with a length of sprue after the fuselage halves have been cemented together. This does then leave the wings at a rather shallow dihedral, and the lower fuselage at the wing roots takes on a fatter appearance.

The third option, which I have adopted for this model, is to cement the fuselage halves together and, once they have set, adhere the wings in place. Then, using a length of masking tape, force the upper wing roots to set in place. Once dried the wings spring back slightly, but leave a more defined dihedral than before and with no gap at the wing roots.

The engines have already been painted and as stated earlier, are the Pratt & Whitney R1830 radials that, although not appropriate for a pre-World War Two aircraft, are the correct ones fitted to this par-

CLOCKWISE FROM TOP LEFT:

The model is primed using Gunze Sangyo Mr Surfacer.

After the primer has fully dried, the DC-3 is sprayed Light Aircraft Grey and after drying, masked ready for the white upper surface coat.

Removing the Tamiya masking tape reveals a nice sharp edge, dividing the upper and lower surface colours.

More masking is required in order to spray the engine nacelles.

These metallic paints can be mixed to give an infinite number of shades and I really feel are an essential range of paints to have in your modelling inventory.

The Minicraft DC-3 is now ready for the livery to be applied.

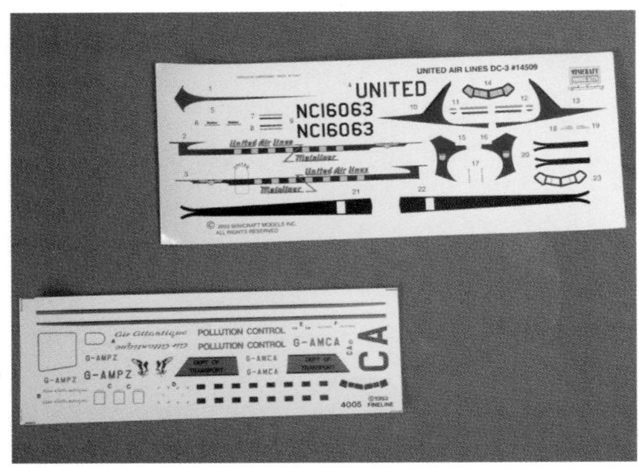

The kit's decals (above): with the decals of the chosen livery, Air Atlantique, supplied by Fineline Decals.

ticular aircraft. These are placed in the cowls and attached to the wings. With the horizontal stabilizers in place the model is now ready for the initial coat of paint and is best primed beforehand with a coat of Gunze Sangyo´s Mr Surfacer.

This grey primer provides a great base, as well as being a micro-filler that shallows the rather deep panel lines. After the primer coat has dried, the little DC-3 is sprayed Light Aircraft Grey from Xtracolor´s range on the lower fuselage and wings, with the upper fuselage surface being sprayed white.

After the wings have been masked, leaving the engine cowlings exposed, these are then sprayed Aluminium and the undercarriage is fitted, having previously been sprayed with a mix of Aluminium and Steel, both from the Alclad II range. These metallic paints can be mixed to give an infinite number of shades and are an essential range of paints to have in your modelling inventory. Leave the model for a few hours to allow the metallic paints to harden: they do not take as long as enamels or even acrylics. The masking is then removed and the diminutive DC-3 is now ready for the initial decals.

Coventry Airport might not be too familiar to many airline passengers, but it is home to an astonishing, small independent airline that operates a number of historical types. General Aviation Services started operations in 1969 from Jersey in the Channel Islands, but in 1977 the company adopted the new name Air Atlantique and started freight operations using the Douglas DC-3. The scheme that I have chosen for my model is G-AMPZ whilst she was in service with Air Atlantique. The decals were available from Fineline Decals, but are quite hard to find now. Occasionally they do pop-up on the Internet auction sites but, when trying to source decal sheets, the best way is to head off to the major model shows. You will be surprised what you can find at these events!

The kit's own decal sheet provides the de-icer boots but after looking at these, the sheet does show a few cracks. Initially I did try and use these, by first spraying the de-icer decals with a coat of flat varnish and cutting the boots out close to the edges. Once on the model, the flat-coated decals respond well to decal solvent, and the result is not bad, but not as good as a painted-on look. In order to achieve that look there is only one option left: to remove the decals by covering them with sellotape and quickly ripping the tape off, removing the decals with it. The leading edges of all flying surfaces are then masked and sprayed matt black, resulting in a much better finish.

Once the matt black de-icing boots have dried the main decaling can begin. This really is my favourite part of any model kit build: the model just springs into life and quickly begins to adopt the familiar green and white scheme of Air Atlantique. All the windows are decals and in this scale I find it quite acceptable, especially on a model as tiny as this.

ABOVE: ***The application of the livery really starts to bring the model aircraft to life.***

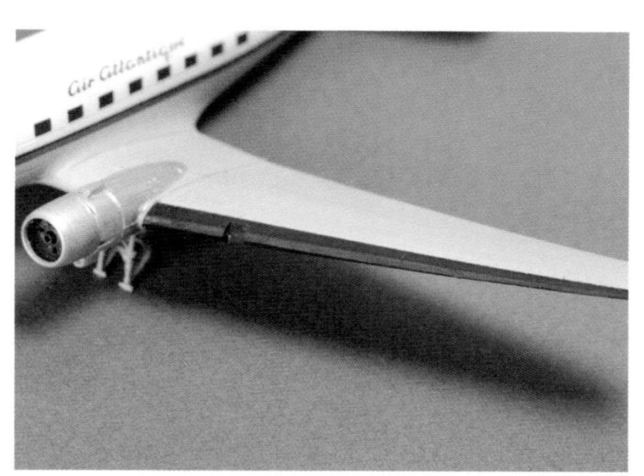

ABOVE RIGHT AND RIGHT:
The leading edge de-icing boots are sprayed matt black.

The propellers are sprayed matt black, the wheels and tyres are sprayed with steel, and matt dark grey respectively, and then attached to the model. Final detail painting includes the rear tail wheel and attaching the fine aerial on the upper fuselage, which is represented with a small length of stretched sprue.

Finally, using a suitably sized model lens from the MV Products range, the prominent wing root light is created. The light cover is represented by nothing other than sellotape which being flexible, thin and clear is a fantastic product to have to hand.

After finishing the model I really feel that it deserves to be displayed on a base. There are many suppliers of ready-made bases, as well as the hundreds of suppliers of model scenery products with which the model railway and military vehicle modellers will be familiar. And so, armed with a selection of static grass, some modelling earth and a suitably sized base, work can begin on creating somewhere for the DC-3 to sit.

I chose to place the DC-3 on a taxiway, adjacent to a grassy area. The wooden base is marked out with tape indicating where the grass is to go. Vallejo produce a range of scenery products and these are spread across a portion of the base, after it has been severely scored and scratched in order to give the terrain paste something to grab on to.

The small radio aerial is represented by a small piece of stretched sprue.

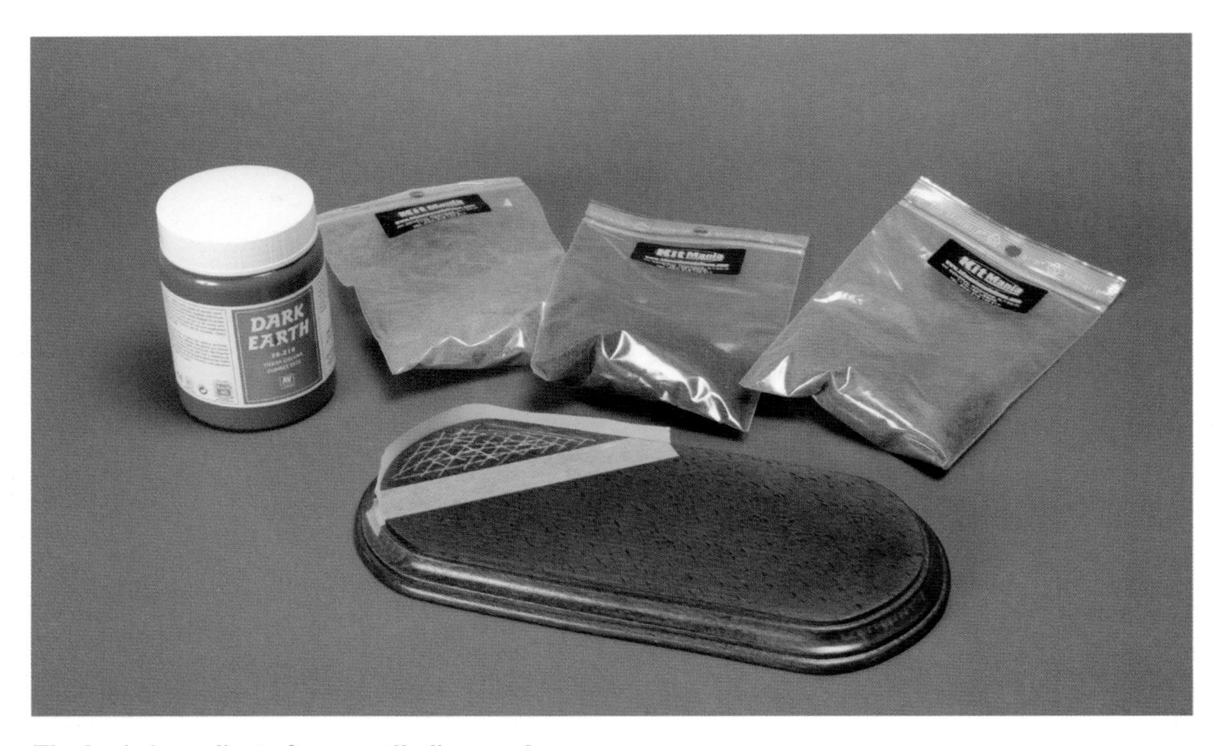

The basic ingredients for a small, diorama base.

The area that is going to receive the terrain paste is masked off and the paste applied with a wooden stick.

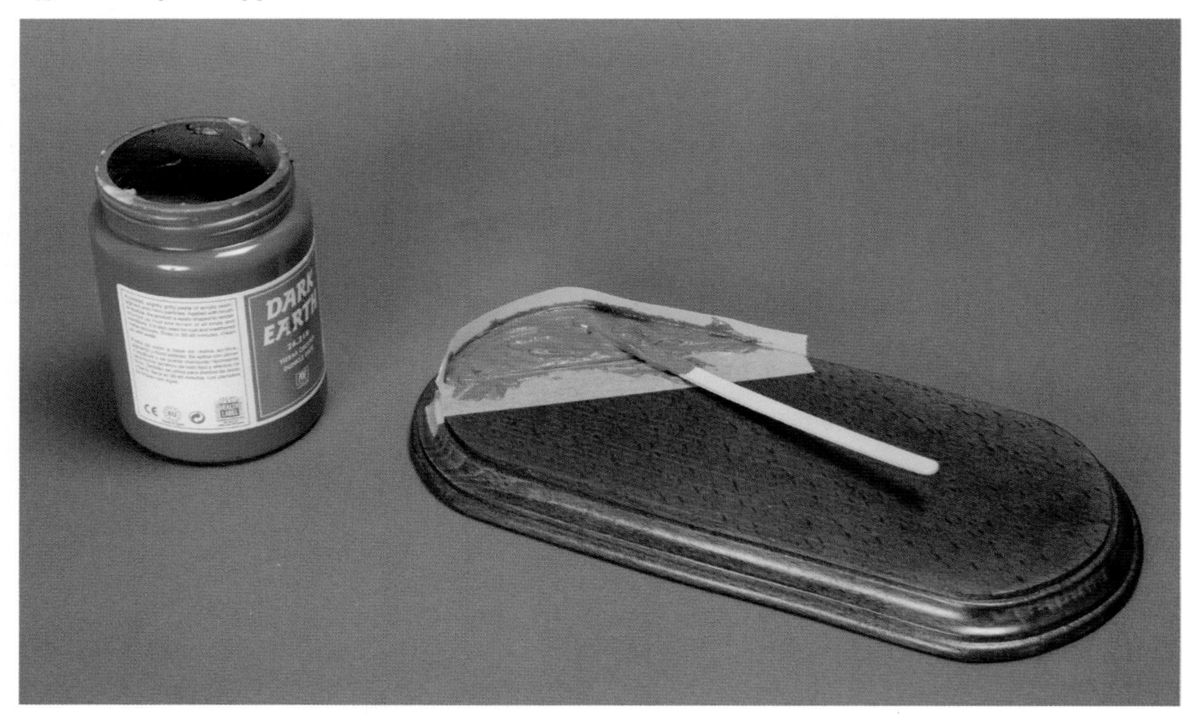

The static grass is sprinkled over the wet terrain paste and allowed to dry. The tarmac area is painted and a small taxiway light is made using sprue and clear blue resin.

After the modelling terrain paste had been spread on, various shades of static grass are used in order to create a less uniformly coloured area. The grass is just sprinkled over the paste and left to dry. The taxiway is sprayed with dark grey and scuffed a bit to give some tonal variation. Finally, a small taxiway edge light is made from a small blue resin light from CMK's resin lights set and some scrap pieces of plastic.

The Air Atlantique DC-3 is placed on the base ready for the photographs and, as I normally display my models on glass shelved cabinets; the addition of a simple base really brings the model to life.

The Minicraft kit is good. It needs some help to bring it up to its full potential, but it nonetheless fills an important gap in any 1/144th transport collection.

CHAPTER EIGHT

THE BEAUTY OF FOUR RADIAL ENGINES

MINICRAFT 1/144TH BOEING 377 STRATOCRUISER

During the Second World War, the development of aircraft engines was at a pace subsequently never matched. Just as an example, the Rolls-Royce Merlin, the famous power plant of not only Great Britain's front line fighters, the Spitfire and Hurricane, but also of the Lancaster and Mosquito, as well as many other types, started at the beginning of the war with an output of just over 1,000 horsepower. Towards the end of the engine's development, and fitted to the de Havilland Sea Hornet, it was producing over 2,000 horsepower. The Merlin was, of course, a V-12 configuration piston engine with the advantage of a smaller frontal area than a radial engine, thus reducing drag. Although Great Britain did have many aircraft powered by the radial piston engine, with one of the most notable producers being Bristol, it really was the American forces that saw the radial engine type more widely used in both fighter and bomber aircraft.

As with the DC-3, Minicraft has released the Boeing 377 Stratocruiser in a number of boxes with different liveries.

The DC-3 Dakota had used the Wright 1820 series in the earlier production aircraft before changing to the hugely successful Pratt & Whitney R1830 range. The Pratt & Whitney Wasp range began with a fourteen-cylinder radial engine, producing just 800 horsepower and throughout the war was subject to intensive development, resulting in the R-4360 Wasp Major. This magnificent engine had a displacement of 71.5l from its twenty-eight cylinders and produced up to 4,300 horsepower. Many museums have examples of these: some are shown in a cutaway configuration and really show what a true feat of engineering this engine was.

The list of aircraft powered by the Pratt & Whitney Wasp series is an absolute encyclopaedia of 1930s to 1960s aviation: ask anyone for the name of any airliner from that period and the chances are that it was P&W powered. As far as we modellers are concerned, we have a good choice of some fantastic model kits of these large, radial-powered airliners.

Minicraft, once again, have come to the rescue of the airliner fan with the release of the DC-4 and DC-6 aircraft from the Douglas stable. Both versions have been released in various guises, with the military variants of each type being covered as well; there are also versions of the DC-6 released as US Presidential transport aircraft. Revell produce a kit of, what many believe to be, the most beautiful airliner of all, the Lockheed L.1049 Constellation. When released, this model took many airliner fans by surprise as Minicraft already had a 1/144th Constellation in their range, but the Revell release is far and away the best, featuring extremely fine details and fantastic decals from the box. Of course, there were many users of Lockheed's elegant aircraft and there are many other decals available to produce a 'Connie' in your favourite livery.

The Constellation shared the airways with the Douglas aircraft to destinations all around the globe and gave the adventurous traveller the chance to sample long-haul flying properly for the first time. With respect to Douglas, the ultimate development of their piston-engined aircraft was the DC-7 and a recent release by Roden in 1/144th almost completes the Douglas range of piston airliners. I say 'almost' as, to the best of my knowledge we are still waiting for the lesser-known DC-5 to appear in injected plastic kit form. Planet Models, of the Czech Republic, do produce a resin kit of the DC-5 in 1/72nd though, should you really feel that you need one in your collection!

At the time of the introduction of the Constellation and DC-7, Great Britain was also developing its own, indigenous large piston-engined airliner. This was not a four-engined aircraft, but an eight-engined behemoth with a wingspan greater than the Boeing 747. This ultimately ill-fated aircraft flew just one prototype from 1949 to 1953, when it was eventually scrapped. The aircraft is the Bristol Brabazon and was another aeroplane that, it was hoped, would turn the favour of the airlines towards the British market. The engines that powered the Bristol Brabazon were the same as that of the Hawker Sea Fury, the sleeve-valved Bristol Centaurus, and this engine too, was an absolute feat of technical engineering. In model form we are certainly fortunate with the Brabazon, as the French company, F-RSIN, has produced a very nice, although quite costly resin kit of the Brabazon in 1/144th scale.

One important aircraft missing from the above list is an airliner developed from the Boeing B-29 Superfortress: the Boeing 377, but known as the Boeing Stratocruiser, was Boeing's answer to the growing demand for a large, long-range airliner. It was built shortly after the end of World War Two and was a development of the C-97 Stratofreighter, itself a military derivative of the B-29 Superfortress. Powered by the Pratt & Whitney R4360 Wasp Major, the Stratocruiser first flew on 8 July 1947.

The Boeing Stratocruiser had surprisingly low fuel consumption for the time and, due to a pressurized cabin, was able to cruise at 32,000 feet. Airlines were now able to meet the demand for trans-continental flights with an aircraft that must have provided

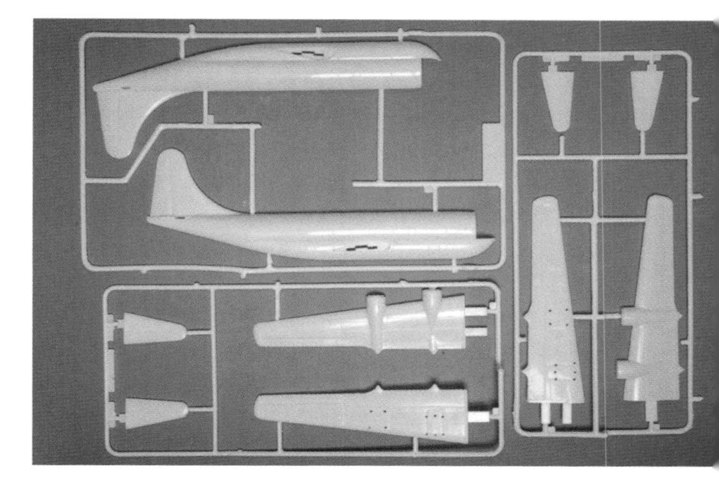

The model is nicely moulded with some very finely detailed parts.

exceptional comfort and relative luxury. The Boeing 377 featured two passenger decks, not seen again until another famous Boeing product, the B747. The upper deck was for economy class customers, while the lower was a VIP lounge and bar. The lifespan of the large, piston-engined airlines was limited though, as the introduction of the jet airliner was imminent. Piston-engined aircraft, such as the Stratocruiser simply became uncompetitive for the major airlines. Many aircraft were scrapped, but the lifespan of the Stratocruiser was given a boost with some airframes being converted by Aero Spacelines to 'Guppies'. These aircraft were versions of the Stratocruiser with an enlarged fuselage and turboprops. One version, the Super Guppy, was used by Airbus to transport aircraft parts between factories, a role now carried out by the converted Airbus A300, the Airbus Beluga.

The Boeing Stratocruiser has been quite well treated in the modelling world: Academy has a 1/72nd scale aircraft model in their catalogue, whilst the 1/144th scale kit is released by Minicraft and it is this kit that is the subject of this chapter. Minicraft is certainly to be congratulated, not just for this lovely model kit, but also for their commitment to bringing us a great series of classic airliners. Not only do Minicraft produce the civilian Boeing 377, but also the military KC-97G and C-97G.

Inside the box there are five runners holding the injected moulded parts, all in white plastic. These have engraved panel lines, which are not the most finely produced, but they will soften in appearance once a coat of primer and paint have been applied. White plastic is not my favourite colour of plastic to work with as it tends to hide any imperfections, but once the parts are assembled the model will be primed and then any areas that require more work will be revealed. Other reviews of this kit have made mention of some moulding flaws, however I found this example to be very cleanly moulded.

Once again, Minicraft has produced some very finely moulded landing gear legs and wheels, but the landing gear doors are on the thick side. Although I have used them in this build, they would benefit from being replaced with some thin plasticard cut to size. But the main omissions in the kit are the engines! Yes, the nacelles are nicely represented but, on close inspection, the engine fronts are just plain, blank plastic. All is not lost as these are available, along with some nicely manufactured metal propellers, as after-market resin sets from Cobra. (Cobra products are available direct from the company at www.cobracompany.com.) As is common in this scale, the wheel wells are also blank canvases that the serious 'super-detailer' can work on.

Along with the white plastic parts, there is a single clear moulding that forms the complete upper nose area of the aircraft. The cockpit windows are moulded into this part and can either be masked prior to painting, or represented, as in this case, with a decal. The advantage of supplying such a large clear part is that the areas that require cleaning up after the part has been attached are clear of the window areas themselves.

The fuselage parts are a 'one-size-fits-all' as they are, presumably, made to cover the civil and military variants of the aircraft. One main area that can easily be improved upon is where the forward doors have been scribed onto the lower deck area. To make the civilian version, simply fill in the scribed door on the left-hand side of the fuselage.

Starting work on the fuselage, the two halves are joined after a substantial amount of nose weight has been fixed in the nose area, she would definitely be sitting on her tail otherwise! The clear cockpit parts are then attached and the joint itself, as well as the main seam along the fuselage, have a few gaps and need filling. The whole assembly is sprayed with Tamiya's white primer, which is a relatively thick primer that softens the deep, coarse panel lines, but also dries very quickly, allowing work to continue at a fairly fast pace. The upper and lower fuselage joins are masked either side and a thin line of Tamiya filler applied and left to set prior to sanding and polishing smooth.

This only takes a short time as the Tamiya filler responds well to being sanded and polished with a four-sided nail polisher. After the joins have been finished, another coat of Tamiya primer is applied and the join line simply disappears.

Following the assembly of the fuselage, the model quickly takes shape with the wings being dry-fitted to the airframe. There are no problems with the join here and these are left in situ to give the modeller something to hold as the model is worked on. As the Stratocruiser is going to receive a gloss varnish coat later, leave the Tamiya primer as the main colour for the upper fuselage: this can then be masked off, ready for the gloss black undercoat, applied using a technique that I tried out on this particular model.

Prior to this, the red fin of the Northwest Airlines scheme needs to be masked and painted; although sourcing a matching red to the decals proved to be harder than I thought! I needed a relatively bright red and help came to hand from a most unlikely source. I had just completed a model car, a Ferrari, and for these I use the excellent range of colour-matched paints from Zero Paints. (The Zero range of paints is available from Hiroboy UK at: www.hiroboy.com/catalog/zero_paints.php.) It was here that I found that the Ferrari Rosso Corsa, number 322 in their range, was a perfect match for the decals. These spray superbly and dry to a matt finish; they dry quickly and are almost immediately ready for a coat of gloss varnish once the model is finished.

I mentioned previously that there was a particular technique that I wanted to try: the representation of the highly polished, bare metal areas on the lower fuselage of the Stratocruiser. To achieve the desired finish I used Alclad II's Chrome paint. As is normal with all the Alclad II range the undercoat needs to be a gloss and, with the Chrome paint, this really does need to be gloss black: Alclad provide their own undercoat exactly for this purpose.

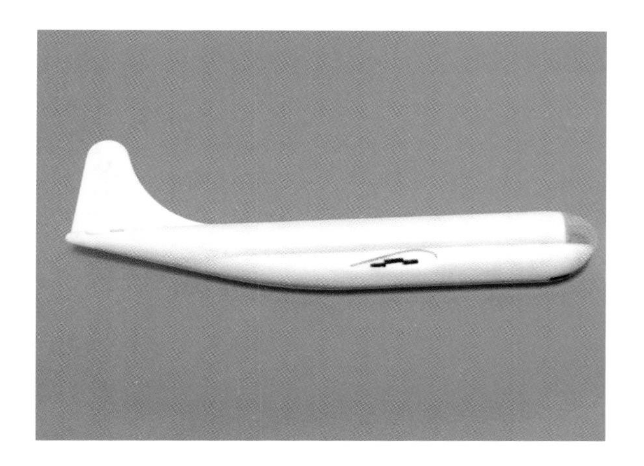

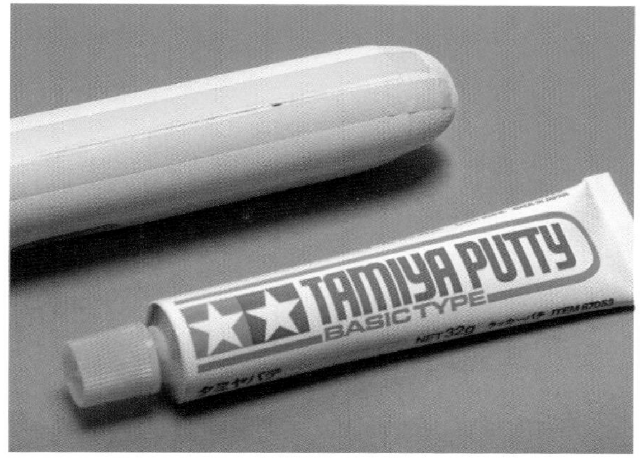

CLOCKWISE, FROM TOP LEFT:

The fuselage halves, together with the large single piece transparency in place.

The seams along the fuselage are masked and filled with Tamiya Putty.

Removing the masking tape reveals a neat thin line of filler.

The fuselage, once it has been sanded and primed using Tamiya's Surface Primer.

The wings are dry-fitted in place in order to assess the fit, which doesn't need any filler at all.

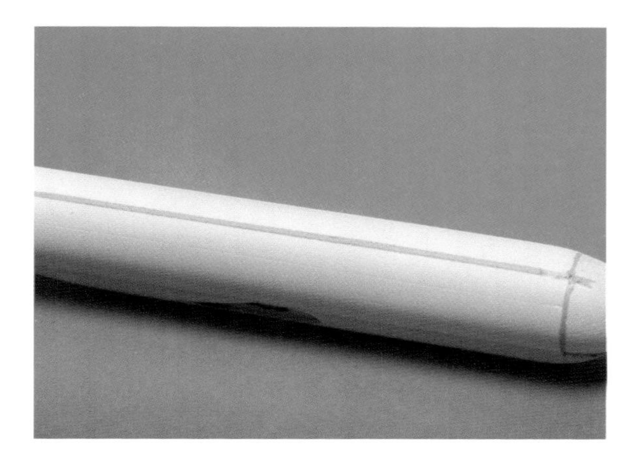

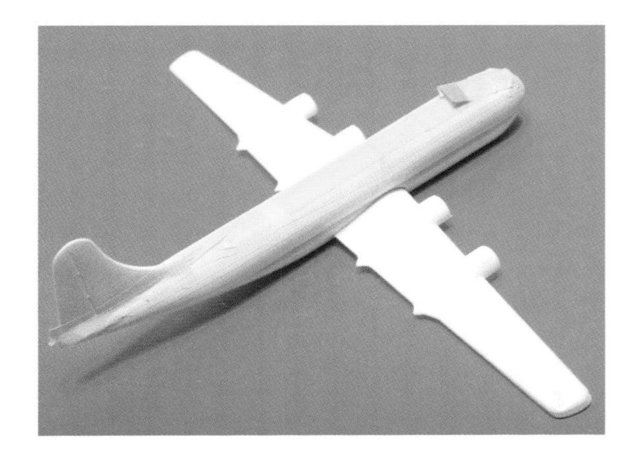

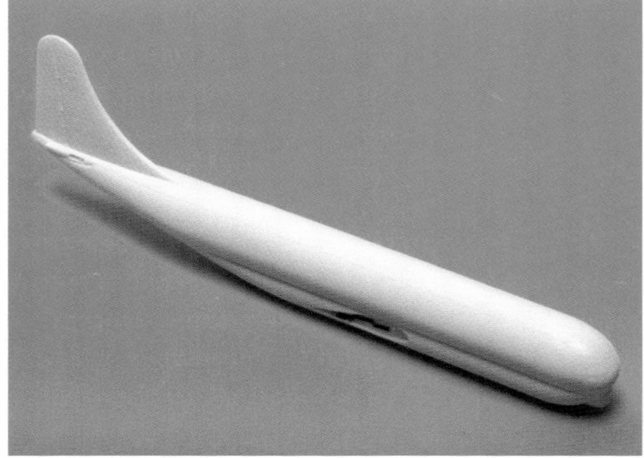

A shade of Ferrari Red from Zero Paints proves to be the best shade to apply for the NorthWest livery.

And here she is, in full gloss black finish ready for the metallic coat.

The final fuselage finish is achieved using the Alclad II metallic paints over a gloss black undercoat; first, however, the upper white section of the fuselage is masked.

Alclad's primer is thinner than others I have tried and dries exceptionally fast: no sooner has the initial dusting coat been applied, than it is dry enough to receive a second, wetter coat; finally the last coat is applied to give a glossy, smooth finish, ready to receive the Alclad II Chrome finish. The small bottles of Alclad II do tend to settle over time and require a good shake prior to being sprayed; the chrome paint is then sprayed in very fine coats. After the first coat has dried, after only about ten minutes, the process is repeated until a uniform finish had been achieved. Looking at this finish, it is impossible to distinguish it between actual metal foil, as seen on the McDonnell Douglas DC-9 prepared earlier. I certainly cannot recommend Alclad II enough; it has every property that is required of a modelling paint: thin enough to spray, quick drying and a realistic finish.

The wings are now removed from the completed fuselage and prepared with the Alclad II primer: this time various shades of Alclad II are used to create the different shades that are present on the original's wings. The engine cowlings receive a coat of chrome to highlight them and you can see in the above picture the lack of engines in the nacelles! As already mentioned, a replacement resin set is available from Cobra Company.

Prior to the final assembly of the smaller details, the decals are applied and yet again, as soon as the decals are in place, the whole airframe really comes to life! It does not take long before the propellers and horizontal stabilizers are attached and the undercarriage is fixed in place.

For the next chapter, we are going to stay with the radial engine, but this time we are coming back across the Atlantic to Great Britain, where the Bristol Centaurus, the eighteen-cylinder, sleeve-valved power plant of the Hawker Tempest and Sea Fury, was developed to produce over 3,000 horsepower. It was two Centaurus 663 engines, producing a combined 4,800 horsepower that equipped the next aircraft.

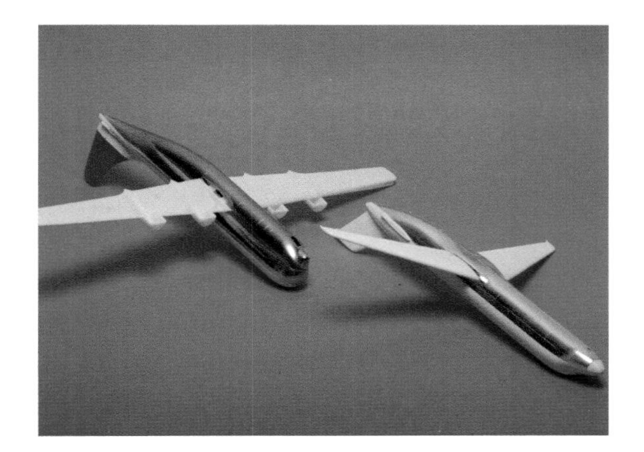

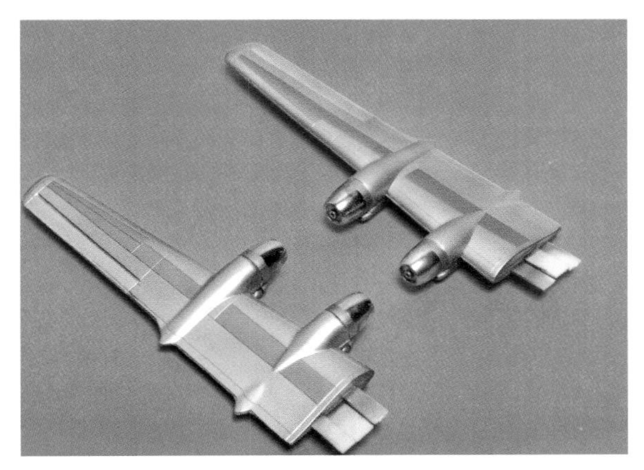

ABOVE LEFT: ***The Stratocruiser, finished in Alclad II Chrome, shown here with a DC-9 that has the lower fuselage covered in bare metal foil. I will let you decide which is the more realistic finish!***

ABOVE: ***The finish achieved using the Alclad II range is superb.***

LEFT: ***The wings are sprayed in different shades of Alclad II to break up the finish.***

BELOW: ***The purposeful looking Stratocruiser in her NorthWest Airlines livery: this model has certainly encouraged me to start the BOAC version, sooner rather than later!***

CHAPTER NINE

SMALL AND PERFECTLY (VAC) FORMED

WELSH MODELS 1/144TH AIRSPEED AMBASSADOR

Sometimes I see photographs of an aircraft type and just wish I had been old enough to watch them come and go from the airports that I used to visit: the Airspeed Ambassador is one such type. With its high wing, elegantly shaped fuselage and the very prominent tail surfaces with the three vertical fins, the Ambassador just looked full of character.

The original design was from as far back as 1943 and was one of the aircraft design requirements that was set out by the Brabazon Committee (set up in December 1942, under John Moore-Brabazon, 1st Baron Brabazon of Tara, to investigate the future needs of the British Empire's civilian airliner market). This was the Type IIA design that was being looked at to replace the venerable Douglas DC-3 in the twin-engined, short to medium-range category. Airspeed Ltd. was originally asked to study and design a non-pressurized model, which was in the lighter weight class of 14,500Kg. The engines chosen for this earlier design were the Bristol Hercules radial engines, which were used quite extensively on military aircraft during World War Two.

But as air travel was almost booming during the post war years, inevitably the design requirements changed and it was not long before the powers-that-be asked Airspeed to produce two prototype aircraft, with pressurized cabins and almost twice the gross weight. The aircraft would now need more power and this came from the Bristol Centaurus radial engine. How the onlookers must have stared as the Airspeed Ambassador began services from the UK to Europe. She was an incredible diversion away from the 'standard' design of aircraft at that time. Sleek and elegant, with long, tapered wings, the Ambassador shared a similar look to the Lockheed Constellation and was so very different from the tail-wheeled, ex-military aircraft that had been in airline service during the early 1950s: in fact she must have looked rather 'futuristic'!

The aircraft was used extensively by BEA on its European routes and achieved the highest number of flying hours per year of any of the airline's fleet; they were named the 'Elizabethan Class' in honour of the United Kingdom's new Queen. The very first scheduled flight was from London's Heathrow airport to Le Bourget airport in Paris and, as well as serving on the European routes, the Ambassador was also used extensively on the domestic network. But technological advances were rapid in those post-war years and it was not long before the advent of the turbo-prop airliner gave airline passengers greater comfort, faster flight times and longer routes. Thus in 1958, the Airspeed Ambassador was withdrawn from service with BEA in favour of the new Vickers Viscount.

But as is often, if not always the case, the dropping of a fleet by a major carrier is generally good news for the smaller, fledgling carriers and so it was with BEA's disposal of the Ambassador when a Mr Davis and a Mr Newman purchased them for their own carrier to support their holiday sales: thus the package holiday was born; and the name of that carrier? Well, just look at the initials of Davis and Newman and you will see that they are instantly recognizable to anyone with an interest in aviation: the airline was, of course, Dan-Air.

Along with establishing the new holiday routes with Dan-Air, as well as serving with BKS Air Transport and Autair, the Ambassador also had an important role as an engine test-bed aircraft and was used by both Rolls-Royce and Bristol in the development of new turbo-prop engines. Sadly, however, the aircraft type suffered two fatal accidents during its service and as a result of advances by the newer turbo-prop and jet powered aircraft, it was not long before the Ambassador was no longer to be seen gracing the aprons of Britain's airports.

(The Airspeed Ambassador was the aircraft involved in the famous Munich Air Disaster when, during a refuelling stop in Munich on the way back to England from Yugoslavia, the aircraft crashed on take-off, killing members of the Manchester United Football team, along with members of the British press travelling with them.)

WELSH MODELS

I started looking seriously at modelling airliners long after I began making military aircraft and the Airfix range was, at that time, my main source of kits, followed later on by Revell. But even combined, their ranges are limited and some of the more esoteric subjects are simply not economically viable for these larger manufacturers to produce as injected moulded kits. So it has been left to what has become known as the cottage industry, to fill the huge gaps in the line of airliners that have never seen the light of day as model kits. The biggest manufacturer is Welsh Models, who have for many years been the main producer of airliner kits in not only 1/144th, but also the larger scale of 1/72nd.

When I first ventured beyond the mainstream kits I found these kits very daunting but soon realized that, with care and patience, once the vac-form parts are separated from their backing sheets and sanded down, what you are left with are a selection of plastic parts that now look no different from any other injection kit. With their recent releases, Welsh Models now also supply their models with resin components and, therefore, some models have just the two fuselage halves as vac-form parts, the rest being in beautifully cast resin. With the smaller components, such as propellers and the undercarriage, being in cast white metal these kits are truly multi-media and are also supplied with decals. You'd therefore expect the prices of these kits to be very high, but the opposite is true and they represent great value for money. I'm now a huge fan of these kits and, after all, where else could you find a 1/144th Airspeed Ambassador?

DEALING WITH VAC-FORMS

Just like I myself, many of you may feel some trepidation towards attempting a vac-form kit, thinking that this particular type of model is the domain of the advanced modeller. However, if you just follow a few simple steps and accept that there is more work in getting the parts ready, you should have no problem at all in getting great results from this kind of kit.

'Sucking' a heated sheet of plastic over male moulds produces the main components; the result is that you will see a single sheet of plastic with the model parts formed into it. The technique used to remove these parts really depends upon the size of the part and proximity of other parts to the one you want to remove. Before removing any part though, a thin line should be drawn around it using a marker. I use a CD marker pen with a relatively fine tip. This not only defines the shape of the part more clearly, but is also important later on when you start to sand the parts down. Smaller parts can be cut free using a scalpel to slowly score deeper cuts around the part until it is free, whereas the larger parts can be scored around using an Olfa P-Cutter or similar. Once the parts are scored around, they can be carefully snapped out of the backing sheet. I use an old spare model kit box to put all the parts in and, once they are all free of the backing sheet, work can begin on preparing them.

As I mentioned earlier, the use of a marker to define the edges of the part also acts as a guide to the amount of sanding required, in order to get the mating surfaces of the part properly prepared. I use a sheet of wet and dry, adhered to a large flat floor tile: using some water, carefully and slowly start to sand the part down until the last remaining piece of the backing sheet becomes so thin that it detaches itself from the part. It is a process that is quite hard to describe in writing, but you'll know when this happens! But critical to the success of your first and subsequent vac-form kits is the test fitting: it is so tempting to just get on with the sanding and before you know it you will have gone too far. Test fit regularly and you'll see how much further you have to sand to get the perfect finished part.

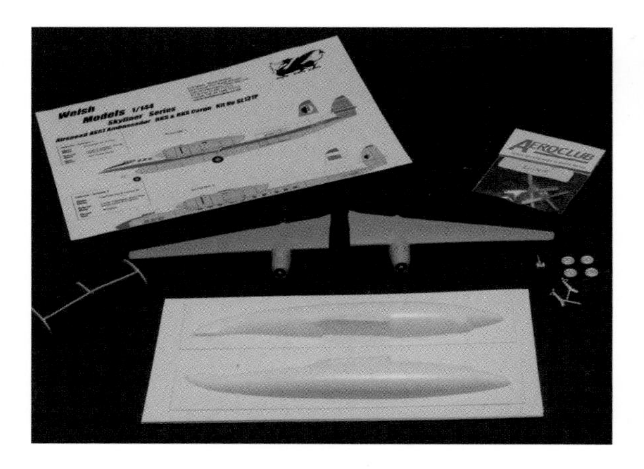

The components of the Welsh Models kit with the Aeroclub propellers: with plastic, resin and metal, this is a true multi-media kit!

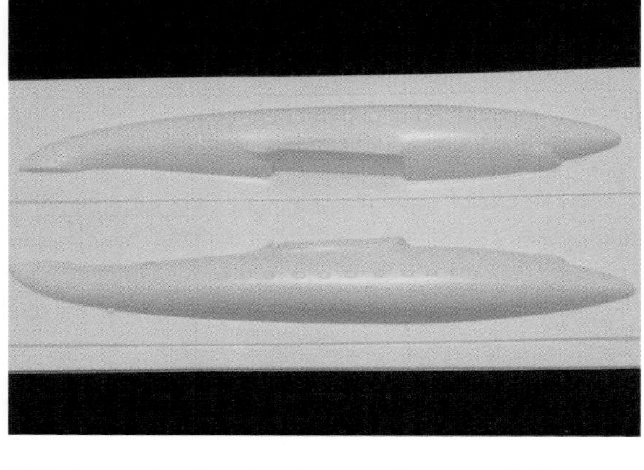

This is a superb entry to vac-form modelling, as the only parts that need separating from the backing sheet are the two fuselage halves.

Once the parts are prepared the model can be assembled just like any other kit, with the exception that there are no locating pins. On large parts, such as fuselage halves, I adhere small tabs on the inner face of the fuselage that act as locating tabs and provide greater strength to the sub assembly. I doubt that any vac-form kit has been assembled without the use of some filler, so be prepared for some further work with filling and sanding and after creating your first model of this type, you will see that the vac-form kit presents no real hurdle at all, it really is all in the mind! (For a useful account of how to construct vac-form models go to: www.worldmodelkits.com and follow the links.)

Now we've had a general look at vac-form models, let's go back to the Airspeed Ambassador: on first inspection the fuselage halves are beautifully moulded as vac-form parts, the wings and the rear surfaces are resin, and the propellers, undercarriage legs and wheels are in white metal. I did have a spare set of propellers for this kit from Aeroclub, the set is W010, which looked slightly better and so I used these instead of the kit's own set. The tail surfaces are moulded as a single piece, that's three vertical stabilizers and rudders as well as the horizontal stabilizer all in one, so that saves quite a lot of work straight away!

In preparation for cutting the fuselage halves off of the backing sheet, they are drawn around with a CD marker and then very carefully scored around using an Olfa P-Cutter. With a suitably deep score around the fuselage halves, they are then snapped away.

The mating surfaces of the two halves are then sanded down until that thin slither of backing sheet comes away.

As you can see, the backing sheet has become so thin that it peels away and that is the time to stop sanding! Check the fit of the two halves and correct any imperfections carefully with a sanding stick. The other parts are all cleaned up, although there is very little to do with the resin parts, they really are very nice indeed. However, with that large chunk of resin sitting at the rear of the fuselage, there is no way that this model is going to keep her nose on the ground without a substantial nose weight and for this I use a suitably sized ball bearing. This is held in place with some filler and the fuselage is given some thin tabs, made from plasticard, as location tabs. These provide a much stronger assembly once the two halves are glued together and held whilst setting with two Berna clamps.

The two halves are cleaned up after setting and the wing surface is placed on top to test fit. It is obvious that there is going to be some filling required and so, after adhering the wing in place with cyanoacrylate, as obviously plastic cement will not touch the resin parts, the resulting gaps forward and aft of the wing are filled with Tamiya's plastic filler.

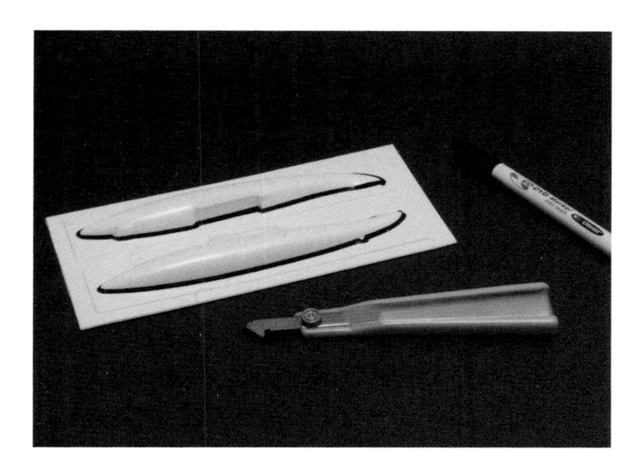

The tools required are simply a black marker and an Olfa P-Cutter.

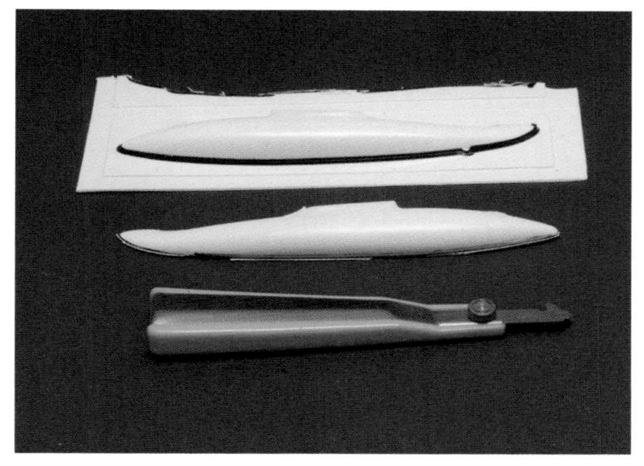

The plastic parts are drawn around with the marker and then scored around with the P-Cutter. The fuselage halves will then easily snap clear of the plastic sheet.

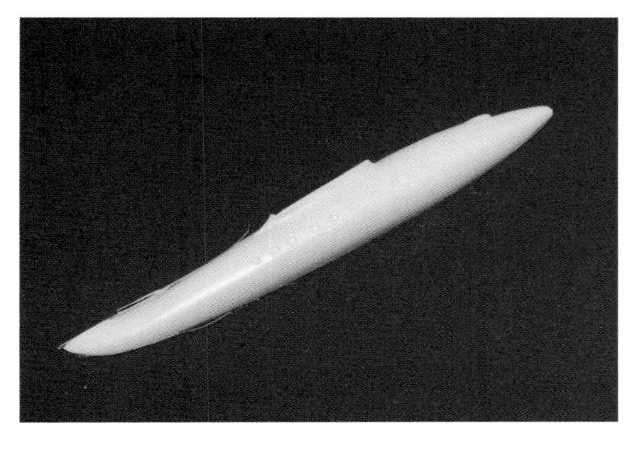

After preparation is complete, the vac-form part looks just like any other injected moulded component.

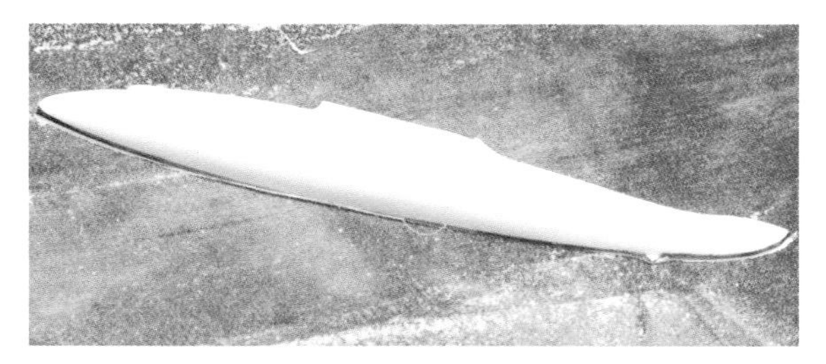

The wet 'n' dry paper that I use is stuck to a flat floor tile and the plastic parts can be sanded down to the black line that remains at the edges. You know you've done enough sanding when the last remnants of the backing sheet peel away from the kit part.

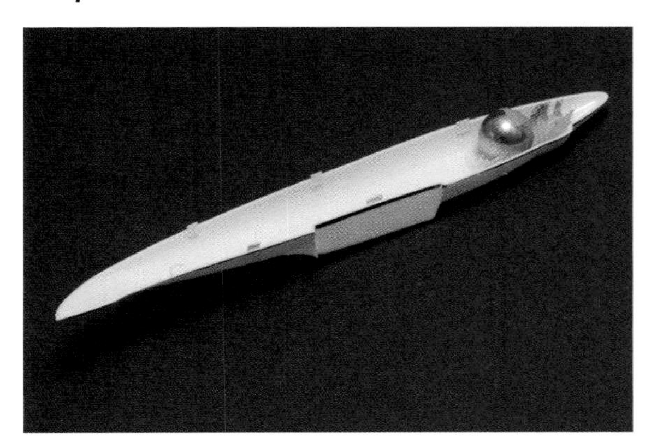

With those resin tail surfaces, this model would definitely be sitting on her tail unless a substantial nose weight was used.

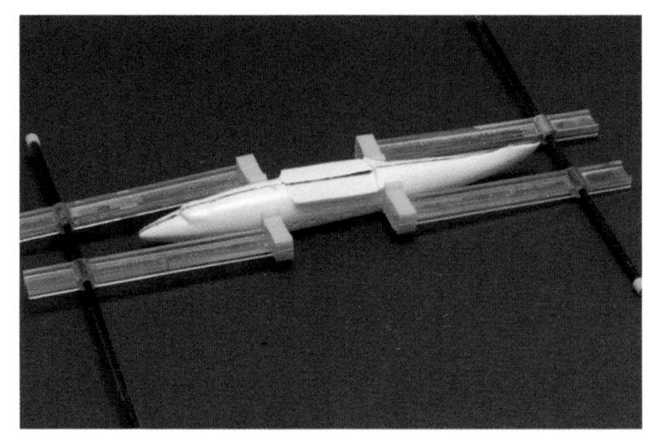

The fuselage halves are joined as normal, with just a touch of extra care due to the lack of locating pins.

CLOCKWISE, FROM TOP LEFT:

The wing to fuselage join needs smoothing using plastic filler.

The completed airframe: showing the graceful, beautiful lines of the Ambassador.

The window indentations on the fuselage are filled and sanded smooth. It is better to complete this before the wing is attached.

The completed model just prior to painting.

And here she is in her initial coat of white.

Once the tail surfaces are in place as well, the graceful lines of the Ambassador are obvious!

As the windows are represented on the decal sheet, the small indentations on the fuselage sides are masked and filled before sanding flush with the fuselage. After which the model is primed and then sprayed with Halfords' Appliance White paint, decanted from the large spray can into a pot that can then be used to pour the paint into the air-brush cup.

The fuselage is masked in order to spray the wing and tail surfaces, as well as the lower fuselage. These are all going to be in a bare metal finish and the lower fuselage is going to be something of a challenge as the decals show the cheat-line to curve around the nose area in quite a complex curve that is difficult to do just by eye. In order to get the curve corresponding to the decals, I used strips of Tamiya masking tape, laid onto a mirror and torn off repeatedly to lessen the adhesive's strength as these are going to be placed directly onto the decals. There is a heart-stopping moment as the strips of masking tape are laid and carefully traced around the curve line before very, very carefully the tape is removed from the decal sheet, hopefully without removing the decals with it! Although the plan did not quite work, I did now have two strips of tape with the correct curve that I used to mask the fuselage: I then had to source another set of decals, but more about that later!

All painting is then completed and, once again, I use the Alclad II Aluminium shade. But to add interest some panels on the wing surfaces are masked off and sprayed in a slightly darker shade.

The final painting job is to paint the tips of the three tail fins and rudders in a matching red shade to the decals and, once this is completed, the tiny Ambassador is ready to have the decals applied.

As I mentioned earlier, the decals did lift with the masking tape when I tried to create the masks to paint the fuselage and sourcing a replacement set proved difficult, especially in the BKS livery that I had already masked the fuselage for. Of course, the simplest way would have been to just buy another kit, but that seemed a waste so I tried to salvage the piece that had stuck to the tape. As it happened, the decal piece came away from the tape in one piece and so all was not lost after all!

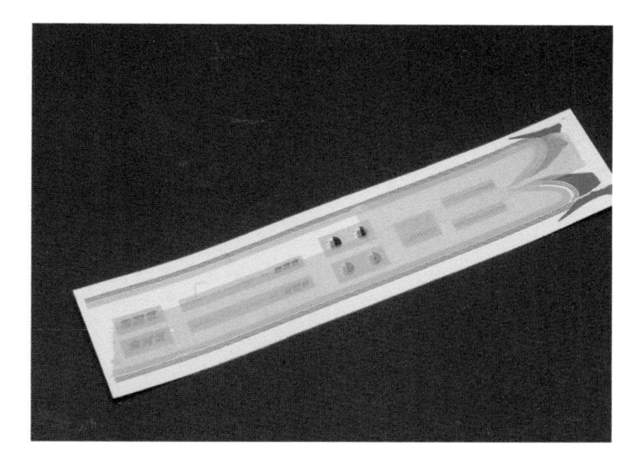

The curve of the cheat-line is copied onto masking tape.

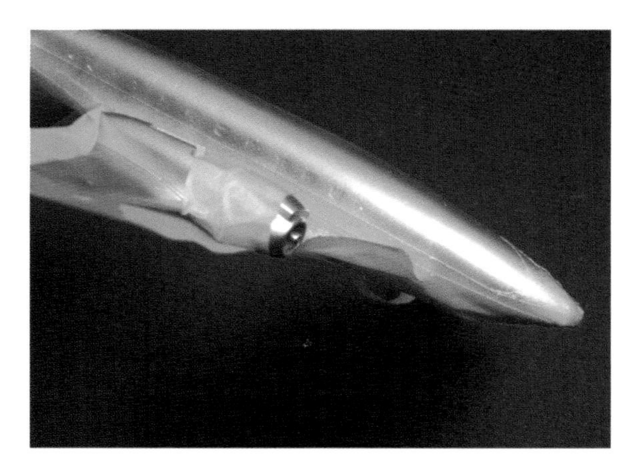

With the masking tape in place and silver paint applied: copying the decal pattern onto the tape ensures that the demarcation line between white and silver follows the same curve as the decals.

The decals are placed on the model with the use of the decaling solvents Microsol and Microset. Microsol is a decal softener that enables decals to 'mould' onto the surface and Microset is a product that provides additional adhesion for the decal. I have been using these products for years and even the most compound curves can be covered with a decal when using Microsol and with careful use of a

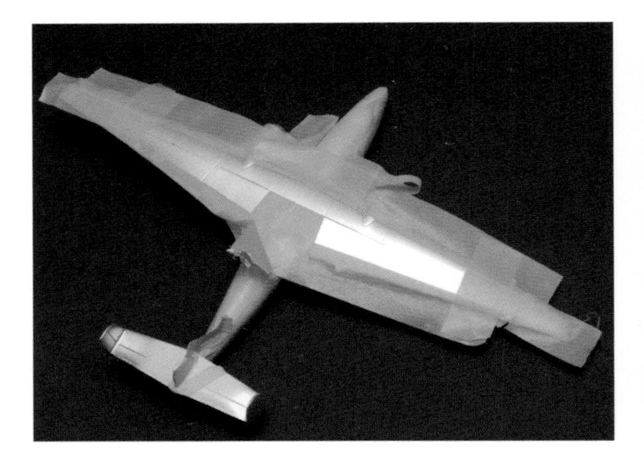

The centre panels of the upper wing surfaces are masked in order to receive a contrasting shade of silver.

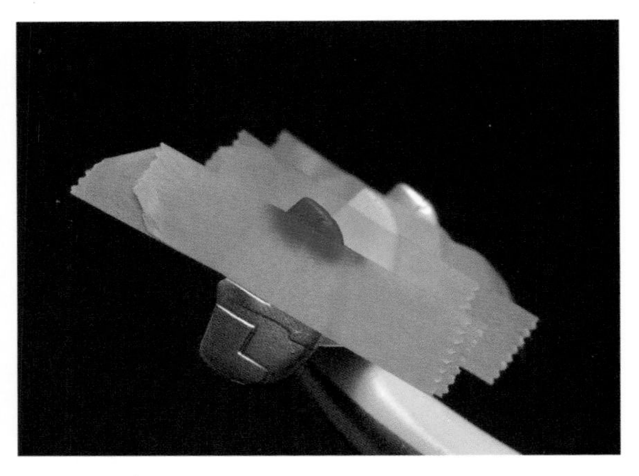

Final details include masking and painting the tips of the tail fins.

Finally, the undercarriage is attached, the propellers are painted silver and the de-icing areas are painted matt black, prior to attaching them to their respective engines.

hairdryer, a blast of hot air can really get the most stubborn decals to conform!

On the Airspeed Ambassador, the decals are fairly straightforward with just the nose area requiring some persuasion. But once the model is completed I do think that she looks very smart indeed in her red, white and silver finish. A final coat of Johnson's Future floor polish is enough to seal the decals and give the model a final glossy sheen.

I hope that the above is enough encouragement for you to go out and try a vac-form kit for yourself. They really are not to be feared and they nearly always result in a unique subject to add to your collection.

Over the years I have met many fellow modellers that share my passion for airliners and I'm now going hand over to a fellow modeller with a passion not just for airliners, but also for a particular airline and who has been modelling the aircraft of Pan Am for many years.

CHAPTER TEN

MODELLING TO A THEME

PAN AMERICAN AIRWAYS, BY BRIAN CANELL

Talk to most modellers who have taken up this hobby and many will tell you they collect and make models to a theme. Themes can be any subject: Royal Air Force Squadrons, trainers, Japanese World War Two fighter planes, aircraft manufacturers etc. Of course there are those that just build anything that takes their fancy, and why not!

I, too, have a few themes and one collection I have been putting together over the years is the aircraft of Pan American Airways. This has a special connection to me for the simple reason that my father flew and was killed flying for Pan Am. In 1968 I was just a few months old and my father had been working for Pan Am for a number of years. He was a First Officer and was very shortly due for promotion to Captain. One of the last flights as First Officer was a routine flight in a ten-month-old Boeing 707-320C (N494PA 'Clipper Malay') from New York City to Caracas Venezuela on 12 December 1968. As the flight was on approach to Maquita airport no problems were reported but suddenly the aircraft disappeared into the sea with the loss of all passengers and crew; there were fifty-one people on board.

To this day no one really knows what happened, as the accident happened before the advent of the digital flight data recorder. Some suggestions have been the flight deck undershot the airport: Maquita airport is almost at sea level and the town rises steeply into mountains; it has been suggested that the night lights create an optical illusion and you think you are higher than you actually are, however this has never been proved. Other theories include: aircraft failure, sabotage and rumours circulated at the time that there was an altercation between the purser and the flight deck. Sadly, we will never know.

When I was around seven years old I gained an interest in aviation and model building. I always wanted to build a Pan Am 707 but my local model shops (there were a lot of them back in the 1970s) never seemed to have any. I had to wait until I was in my mid-twenties and returned to modelling after a ten-year break to find one. It was in a model shop in Cambridge when I saw a Russian kit of a Boeing B707 in a rather plain box, with very poor box art that certainly did not show what airline livery was contained inside. When I opened it I was delighted to see Pan Am decals; the collection had started!

Not long after buying and building it I was told about a rather big model shop in North London 'Next to Colindale tube station' – it was Hannants. Wow! Modelling paradise! I never knew there were so many extra bits and pieces available to enhance and improve your models. They also had decals, hundreds and hundreds of them and I found a set of Pan Am ones for a 1/144th scale Boeing B747. I had built one many years earlier (badly) so I bought the new decals to restore it. Now my collection had doubled!

Over time more and more kits and decals became available for my new theme. Airfix did a B727 in their SkyKing series, as well as a B314 Clipper Flying Boat. In the late 1990s Minicraft released a series of classic airliners with Pan Am decals, mainly of Douglas and Boeing types, and over the past few years I have discovered how E-Bay can be so useful in finding old kits; including many high priced and sought after ones, such as some Aurora kits from the 1960s. Just last year I obtained two vac-form kits of the Sikorsky S38 and S42 flying boats, which now takes my collection back to the early days of the airline.

About twelve years ago I was in a model shop a few miles from home, where I would pay a monthly visit in order to top up on materials and take a general look around. High on a shelf there was a huge Heller box containing a massive 1/72nd scale Boeing 707-320, but with Lufthansa and Air France decals. That was it! I just had to buy this kit, as this would be the model I needed to make as 'Clipper Malay'. It stayed in the loft for around six years until I finally found a set of Pan Am decals for the kit, produced by Two-Six Decals. The decal set shown on the original release had a different tail number and Clipper name so I decided to contact them directly; imagine how I felt when they very kindly printed a set for me with the correct markings on! But the wait to build 'Clipper Malay' was not over as it took a further two years until I got around to making the kit, coinciding with the fortieth anniversary of the accident.

Over the years I have built around twenty Pan Am aircraft and have a further fifteen to make. The collection is not complete however, as there are a few aircraft that were operated by Pan Am that I can't seem to find model kits of anywhere, such as: the Fairchild FC-2, Consolidated Commodore and de Havilland Dash 7. There are also decals that I need to source for some of the kits that I have in the collection; however, that shouldn't be too difficult as the Internet has enabled modellers from all over the world to get together and help each other out with making and designing unique decals.

That illustrates the interest I have in Pan Am and I am sure that you will all realize why the airline has a special significance for me. But let's now have a look at, in many ways, a unique kit: the Maquette Boeing 307 Stratoliner. This is in the larger 1/72nd scale and I will show you how I built one of the most challenging kits of my modelling life!

This Russian made kit contains the old FROG tooling of the Boeing B-17E Flying Fortress, so that dates the kit's origins to the early 1960s! But to replicate the Stratoliner, the FROG kit is minus the original bomber's fuselage and replaced with a new injected one, along with various decals for the United States Army Air Force (USAAF), Trans World Airlines (TWA) and Pan Am.

Although the old FROG parts seem to be free of ejector pin and sink marks, there is quite a bit of flash, the thin slivers of excess plastic that leak out of the main mould. This is quite easy to clean up, with a sharp scalpel blade and a sanding stick, but there are also quite a few parts that won't be used on my airline version such as: the original B-17 bomb doors, the crew and other military parts.

The worst parts, though, are the fuselage halves and they have the dubious distinction of being, probably, the worst moulded fuselage parts of any aircraft I've ever built! I did wonder what was going on with the side windows, as each side doesn't match. Naturally I thought there must be a mistake but, looking at my references they do seem to be accurate, as the starboard side had drop down bunks with small windows and the larger port windows were the normal seating area. I'm not aware of another set up like this on an aircraft.

As if that is not bad enough, the decals are inaccurate and incomplete for the Pan Am version. The blue is too light and there are no wing registrations, no 'Clipper' name decals and no 'Pan American Airways' decal that goes around the entry door. Also the starboard 'Pan American Airways System' decal leans the wrong way; they are both supposed to lean back towards the tail. Oh dear, I think I've some work to do!

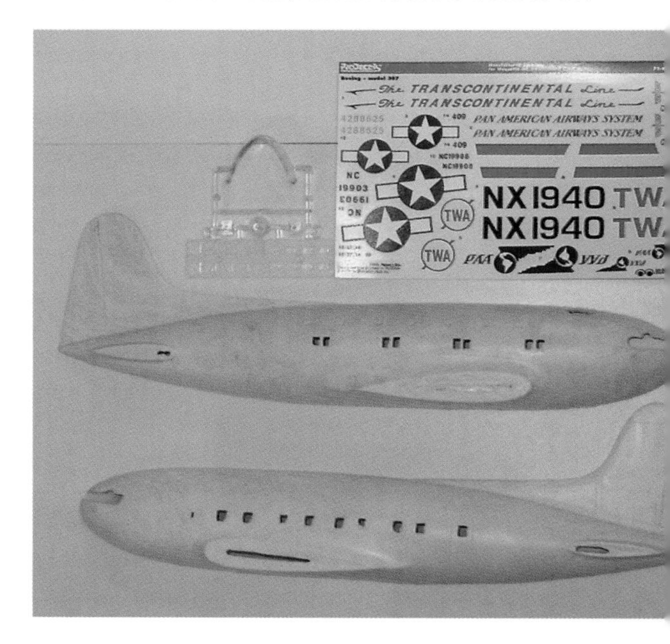

The Maquette kit combines a new injection moulded fuselage...

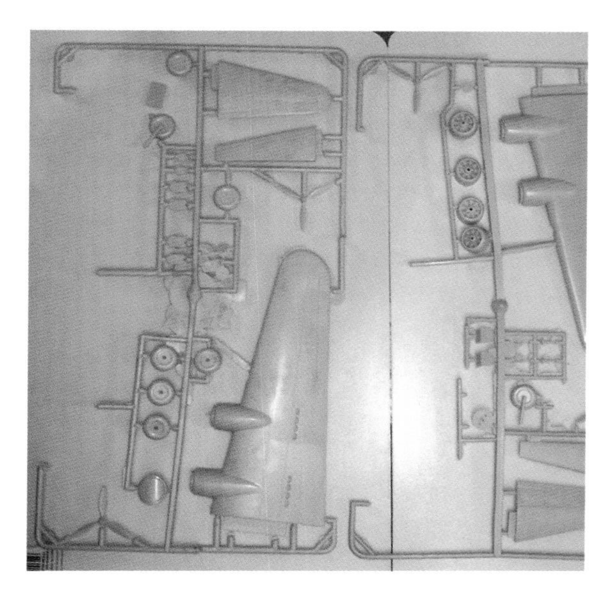

... with the old kit of the B-17E Flying Fortress, issued by FROG in the early 1960s.

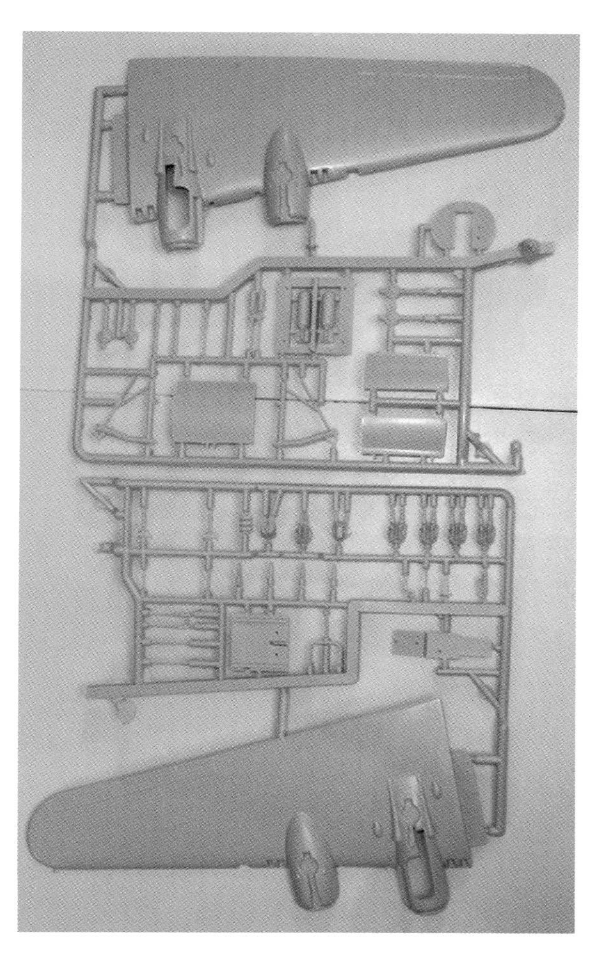

CONSTRUCTION

The original FROG tooled parts, despite their age, are actually quite good in terms of quality and fit, it's the Russian parts that cause problems. The instructions say to start by installing the tail wheel into the retainer in one side of the fuselage, before fitting the fuselage halves together. The first problem I encountered was the fact that there is no retainer! Therefore, I made one out of Milliput, a two-part epoxy putty, superb for this kind of work.

Make up retainers to join the fuselage halves and make a cockpit bulkhead out of the original FROG piece, plus some more Milliput to make it bigger. I haven't detailed the interior as it won't be seen, but I have done the bulkhead in order to catch the windscreen piece that I just know will drop inside when I fit it! The interior is then painted Matt Black.

Superglue and accelerator are used to fit the fuselage halves together. The fit is, well, rubbish! One side seems bigger than the other so I have lined up the top half as best I can and let the bottom half just stick where it touches: it needs an incredible amount of filler!

I have used an acrylic automotive spray primer for priming one wing, sprayed in three light coats. I have

The tail wheel is attached in place with Milliput epoxy putty, as there is no location moulded into the fuselage halves for the wheel.

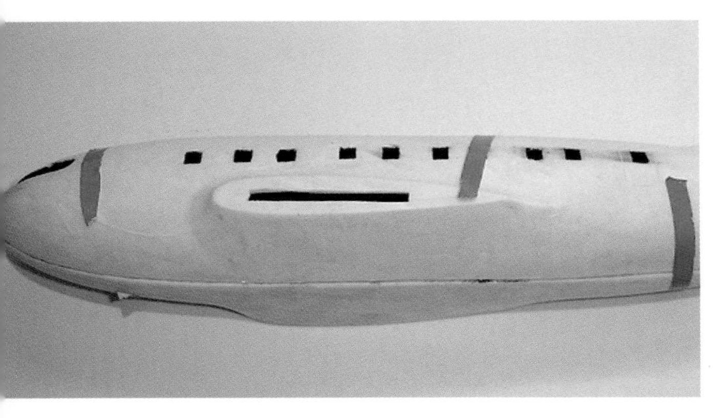

The fit of the fuselage halves means that an enormous amount of filler will be needed along the bottom seam.

Like most modellers, it's nice to go outside the assembly and painting sequence to 'just see what she'll look like!'

With the main components together and, after hours of filling and sanding, the model finally receives a coat of primer.

also started painting the engines, just to get an idea of what they will look like, after which both wings can be fitted and cemented into place.

Once the cement has fully set put a layer of filler along the front and rear wing joins and then give the model a good coat of primer. Once the primer dried I realized the joins were pretty poor, again I think because of the poor quality fuselage, rather than the inside faces of the wings. I therefore had to fill, sand, and prime a total of four times to get rid of all the gaps! I was quite pleased with the result though.

PAINTING

When I built this kit in early 2008 I did not own an airbrush but having owned and used one for nearly a year, I don't know how I managed to paint models without one! The finish of an airbrush is so much better and covers much more quickly than a brush. Also some paints dry faster when sprayed, as the final finish is usually a thinner layer of paint. There are plenty of books and Internet forums describing different airbrushes and what you can expect from them. All I would say is that I agree with Mark and recommend that you buy the best you can afford. Do be aware that cheap ones won't perform that well, and if you decide to upgrade later, then buying that cheap one was just a false economy. A good compressor is a must too.

As this model is brush painted I'll explain how to do it. Metallic paints can be very difficult to apply with a brush. Firstly it's very important to stir the paint for some minutes so all of the pigment and metallic flakes are thoroughly mixed together. It's also important to keep stirring the paint as you use it as it can start to settle very quickly. Metallic paint dries to the touch within minutes, but can actually take weeks to fully harden off. Brushed metallic paints also don't like to be recoated unless you put a barrier between coats, more on this later.

To paint this Stratoliner I chose a wide flat brush using Humbrol's Metalcote Polished Aluminium (product code H27002). I use this paint as I've found that the metal particles seem smaller, therefore the paint seems smoother and the finish seems less grainy than other metallic silvers, such as Humbrol's infamous H11 Silver.

Begin by painting the fuselage in long strokes without going over the same area twice if possible; try to cover the grey primer in one go. However, as it will have extra coats, don't worry too much if the paint looks a little patchy at this stage.

Just paint the fuselage and engines for now; the model needs to be handled quite a lot and it's best not to keep touching metallic paints too much until they've been sealed with a topcoat of varnish as the finish can rub off. After about half an hour apply two coats of 'Klear'.

Johnson's Klear is an acrylic-based varnish that is sold for use on floors to refresh the shine. Recently the formula has changed and it has a new name in the United Kingdom of 'Pledge with Future shine' however, I believe it's basically the same product that is sold as Johnson's 'Future' in other countries. It's great for modellers as you can obtain a glossy finish prior to adding decals; it can also be used as a model varnish to protect applied decals and paint. It's very thin and can be applied with a brush without streaks.

Once the Klear has dried add a second aluminium coat, in order to try to replicate individual panels on the aircraft. Looking at pictures of the Boeing 307 on the Internet the fuselage is made up of lots of rectangular panels. It's amazing what tips you can pick up along the way and I used those little yellow sticky Post-it notes as a paint mask. These are great as they are not very sticky and don't lift the paint off like the stronger masking tape adhesives do.

Start by masking one rectangle and painting the first small strip. Then use one Post-it note to mask the next panel and paint up to the previous painted one, then continue to the next, and so on all the way round.

By beginning at the front end and by brushing the panels in alternating directions, it does give the subtle impression of panel lines. You can just about make them out on the front section in the photo below. You'll notice I have also fitted the windscreen in place and that bulkhead isn't needed after all!

The fuselage, tail and rear wings are completed now and the whole fuselage is given a coat of Klear,

Incredibly, Brian achieved the final finish using a paintbrush! Humbrol Metalcote Polished Aluminium was the paint choice.

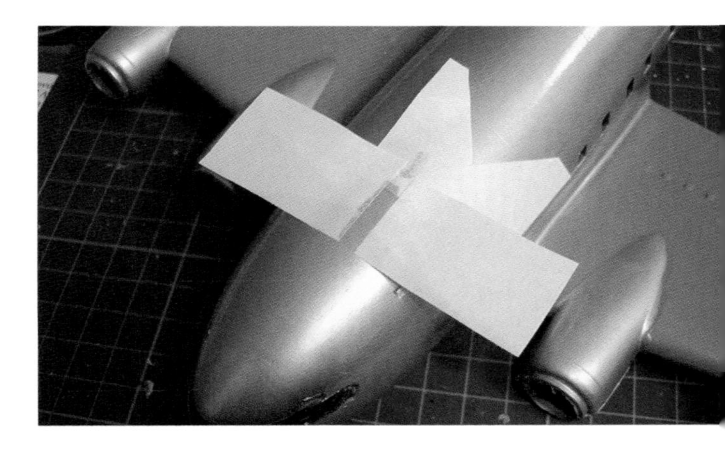

Post-it notes are used to mask off individual panels.

The low tackiness of the Post-it notes is ideal, as it will not harm the finish of the model.

The cockpit glazing in place.

The subtle variations between the panel colours can just be made out here.

The completed airframe is once again given a coat of Future.

The completed engines and propellers from the FROG kit.

although leave the wing fairings until the wings have been painted.

The engines are then assembled and the cylinders painted various shades of grey, which, once they are dry, are given a black wash to pick out the details. The propellers are black on the rear faces to prevent glare for the pilots and comfort for the passengers, but these are fitted at the very end.

The wings are painted in exactkly the same way as the fuselage and the control surfaces are painted in Humbrol H11 Silver. This is because on the real aircraft, they are fabric covered. This is a good example of where H11 silver should be used for the painting job, as it looks far more like a silver paint than metal.

The anti-icing boots to the leading edges now have the first coat of matt black: applied to them. They will then require a second coat of paint, followed by a little touching up of the silver colour around them.

DECALING

I mentioned earlier that the decals are incomplete and incorrect, but they are more incomplete and wrong than I had first thought! Not only is the blue colour too light, the decals are only good for the left hand side of the aircraft. As already mentioned, the titles should lean back towards the tail on both sides, and the wings of the 'Winged Globes' should flow back towards the tail. But if you look carefully the globes are the same, just in two completely different sizes! It would just look so wrong if they were applied as they are and, as if that was not enough, there are no 'Clipper Silver Cloud' decals or wing registration numbers and letters. All in all, the decals are pretty much un-useable!

But all is not lost as, although the kit originated from the days long before PCs and Macs, this is the twenty-first century! So, I scanned the original decals and using a photo editing software package, changed the colours to a much darker blue, in fact they were almost black. Next I 'mirrored' the globes so the wings pointed the correct way, but now the problem was that South America on the globes was back to front. To get around this I copied and pasted a couple of extra correct globes, with the wrong wings, which then had those trimmed off. The correct wings were then copied and pasted into place. At the same time I also made up some 'Clipper' titles. I was unable to find a way to make the 'Pan American' titles lean backwards though, but sometimes you just have to say 'I'll have to live with that!'

I've never made my own decals so I ordered some decal paper online and a decal sheet of suitable black numbers and letters for the wing registration numbers. When printing your own decals, do remem-

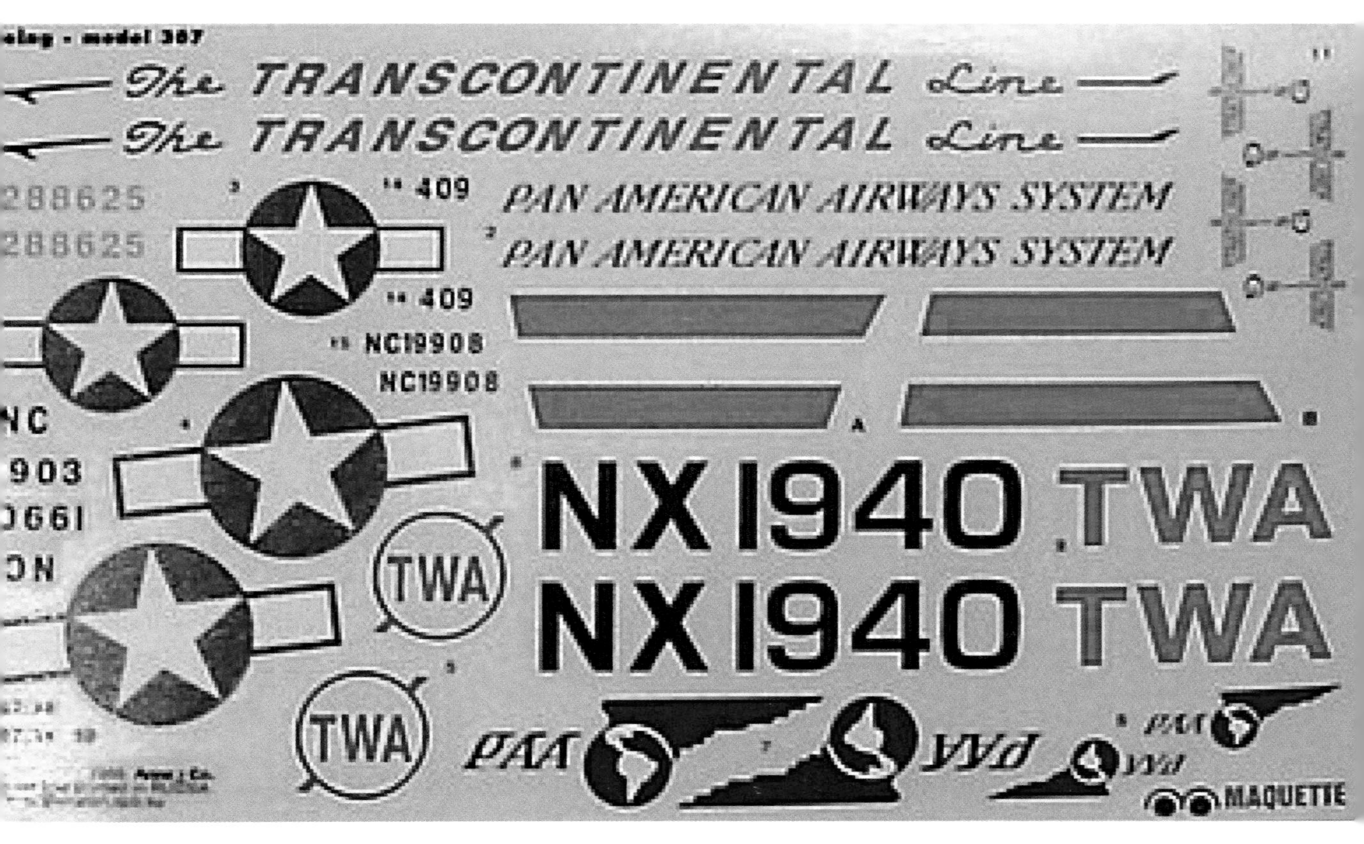

With the aid of modern technology, the kit decals are a good starting point to create the correct markings.

The finished Boeing Stratoliner, still showing some of her heritage as a former USAF bomber, but looking every inch a classic airliner design.

The finished Boeing Stratoliner viewed from the rear.

ber that once the decals are printed, they will need to be varnished, otherwise the ink will run when dipped in water. I tried both Johnson's Klear and a Liquid Decal Film on different areas of the sheet and, although I was extremely careful I still managed to get a little smudging.

The first set of decals printed off well, but I noticed that areas around the 'Globes' were quite yellow where I had scanned them from the original sheet. Therefore the sheet I made became the 'test shot' for experimenting. I re-ran the original scanned copy of the globes through a photo-editing programme again and 'filled' the yellowed areas with white and re-printed them. Perfect! All the yellowed areas had now gone.

As the first sheet had smudged I thought I'd try some automotive Clear Lacquer used for metallic paints. I did a couple of very light coats and let them dry. I built up about five coats of lacquer and let it dry between coats until the decals were nice and glossy before leaving them well alone to dry off fully.

Each decal was carefully trimmed, dipped in water and applied as you would any other decal. They went on perfectly! I did have a scare though as the first couple of decals were covered with Microscale setting solution which turned the

Brian's chosen theme of Pan Am aircraft has a highly personal element: here is the Boeing Stratoliner, alongside the B707 to which Brian is so closely attached.

'Kleared' Polished Aluminium a milky white. However after a few minutes it dried back to normal. I didn't use solution on any others; they didn't really need it anyway.

The windows are made by dipping a cocktail stick in Microscale's Krystal Klear and applying into the window hole with a circular motion. PVA glue can also be used and either starts off white then dries clear. The aerials are all fitted and painted and with the attachment of the propellers, she's now finished!

Patience and a lot of work resulted in this unique model of one of Pan Am's lesser-known aircraft. The learning curve was obviously steep in places but isn't that what we strive to do when we start a new kit? New skills were learned, not least the manufacture of my own decals, and here she is, certainly one that I am rather proud of!

CHAPTER 11

BRITAIN LEADS THE WAY

S&M MODELS 1/144TH VICKERS VISCOUNT

Never before have I been so excited about the impending release of a model kit! The Vickers Viscount is probably the most significant aircraft for me personally, as it became the very first multi-crew aircraft in my own flying logbook when I was recruited as a young and keen First Officer for British Air Ferries.

Up until S&M models released this lovely injected moulded model, the only option to create a replica of the Viscount was to build either the Glencoe or Welsh Models kits. However, the Glencoe model is actually the earlier Viscount 700 and being 1/96th is in a rather odd scale; the Welsh Models is a vac-form kit, so neither of them really fulfilled my own modelling wishes and no one had yet released a BAF decal sheet. Therefore, when S&M models announced that they were issuing an injected kit of the Viscount 800 in 1/144th scale, I was over the moon! But the release of the kit itself was almost overshadowed when TwoSix Decals announced the release of a range of liveries for this kit, including my own former employer's: this was as close as I had ever been to modelling heaven! So, with all this in mind, please allow me to indulge in a little diversion from modelling and let's take a look at the history of this wonderful aircraft.

When asked 'Who designed the turbo-prop engine?' would you ever think that it was a Hungarian? And if you're asked: 'What was the first turbo-prop aircraft to fly?' would you ever consider that it was actually a Gloster Meteor? Well, the Hungarian in question was György Jendrassik, whose efforts did not go unnoticed by the British. After World War Two he moved to London and a development of his design became the Rolls-Royce RB.50 Trent that was used to power the 'Trent Meteor' on her maiden flight in September 1945.

Meanwhile, back in 1943, an important committee had been formed to study the British Empire's future civil aircraft requirement. This was a defining moment in the history of British commercial aircraft production and The Brabazon Committee, as it was known, announced various design requirements. The Type II called for a: 'small-sized, medium-range pressurized aircraft, carrying twenty-four passengers up to 1,750 miles at 200 mph'. Vickers put forward their proposal, powered by four turbo-prop engines and this led to some debate amongst the members of the Brabazon committee. However they relented and agreed to split the Type II design into two sub-groups: Type IIA using piston power, with Type IIB being a turboprop aircraft. Vickers' proposal eventually won the Type IIB contracts and one of the most beautiful piston-engined aircraft of all, the Airspeed Ambassador, became the winner of the IIA design.

Initially called the Vickers Viceroy, the name changed to Viscount after India became an independent state and the name was, therefore, politically less provocative. The airframe design remained virtually unchanged, but the engines were changed a few times before Vickers finally decided upon four Rolls-Royce Darts. It was in this configuration that, on the 16 July 1948, at Wisley in Surrey, the Viscount became airborne for the first time. On landing the test pilots, J. 'Mutt' Summers and J. R. 'Jock' Bryce declared it was: 'the smoothest and best I have ever flown'. On presenting the aircraft to the press in December 1948, Chief Designer and Engineer, George Edwards was asked if they had ironed out the bugs, he replied: 'That's what's worrying us. We can't find any!'

The subject of this chapter is Vickers Viscount c/n 412, a V.806, originally built for British European Airways and first registered on 19 November 1957 as G-APIM.

On 2 November 1971, she was sold to Cambrian Airways / British Air Services and the next day flown from Heathrow, London to her new home at Rhoose airport in Cardiff, Wales. However, later in 1972 Cambrian Airways came under the control of the newly formed British Airways group, and, as this ultimately resulted in the merger of BEA and BOAC, G-APIM eventually returned to her original owners. On 12 November 1973, she was rolled out in full British Airways livery with small Cambrian Airways titles.

G-APIM had the distinction of serving British Airways for many years and was the last Viscount to be overhauled at the Rhoose engineering facility, as well as being the last British Airways Viscount to be retired from service. Her final flight with BA was from Kirkwall in the Orkney Islands to Glasgow, Scotland on 28 March 1982. She was stored for nearly two years before joining the fleet of British Air Ferries on 27 January 1984.

G-APIM was christened 'Viscount Stephen Piercey' on the 25 August 1984, after Stephan Piercey. Stephan was the chief photographer of Flight International but was tragically killed in a mid-air collision at the Hanover Air Show on 20 May 1984. An incredible photographer and avid turbo-prop fan, the decision to name G-APIM after him was unanimously welcomed amongst the community at Southend Airport, home to British Air Ferries.

Unknown to the crew who flew her on 9 January 1988, that would be her last flight as, two days later, on 11 January 1988, a Guernsey Airlines Shorts SD3-30 taxied into her. The Shorts SD3-30 was taxiing to the runway at Southend to depart when suddenly the nose gear steering failed. The aircraft entered an un-commanded left turn and collided with the stationary Viscount, damaging G-APIM beyond economic repair.

In her thirty-one years of Airline service, she flew a total of 39,757 hours with 42,210 total cycles/landings. I did not join British Air Ferries until late 1989 and so never had the opportunity to fly G-APIM, but anyone can now go on board her as she is a permanent part of the exhibit at the Brooklands Museum in Weybridge in Surrey, at the site where, in 1958, she

S&M Models was the first to release an injected moulded model kit of the Viscount in 1/144th scale.

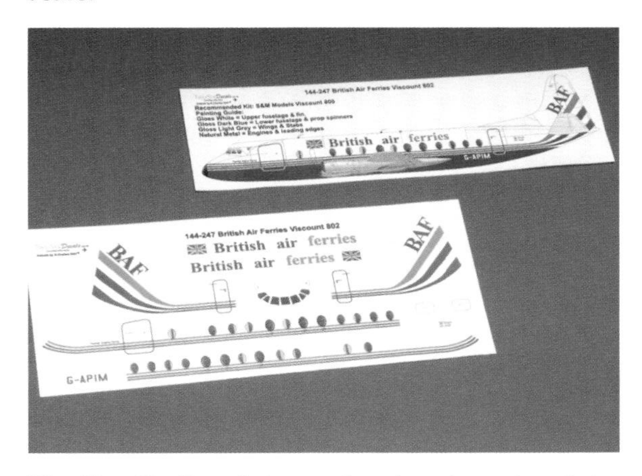

The TwoSix Decal sheet: showing the colourful and rather patriotic livery of British Air Ferries.

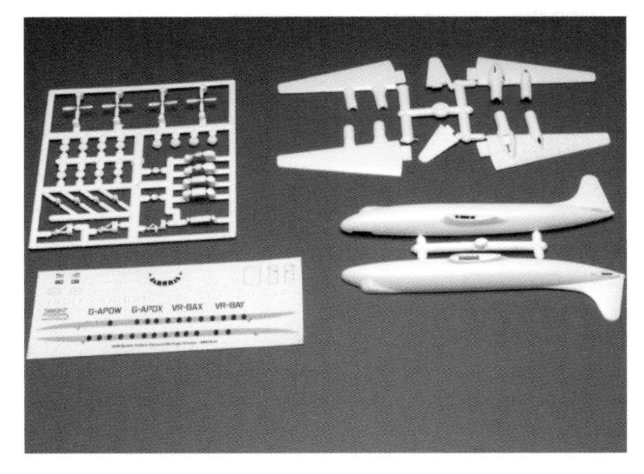

The box contents: with the supplied decal sheet, incorporating the livery for Eagle Airways.

After a very short time the model is unmistakably a Viscount.

The lower wing to fuselage seam is filled with thick superglue and after hardening, sanded smooth.

An overall coat of Halfords' Grey Plastic Primer – straight from the can.

was originally built. With my indulgence over, let's get back to some modeling!

The S&M Models kit is beautifully moulded in only a few pieces of white plastic and comes as standard with a set of decals for Eagle Airways. However, there are now a myriad of Viscount decals available from TwoSix Decals, including the subject of this build. The decals themselves are really very nice indeed and include such details as the correct pattern of window blinds, which were in two halves and closed over the window from each side, as opposed to the more common single downward sliding blind.

Start with the standard practice of washing the kit parts in warm soapy water, this cleans off any residue from the moulds. There are just thirty-nine parts and these almost fall together very quickly indeed! Assembly starts with the two halves of the fuselage. As the windows are all represented by decals, there is no detail to add to the interior and after the glue has dried, the wings are assembled and attached. Finally the tail planes are attached, making sure that the correct dihedral is achieved before the adhesive sets. And there, in no time at all and with just eight parts of the kit used so far, is the basic airframe of the Viscount!

At this point I reflected on having spent over 700 hours flying this classic aircraft between Aberdeen and the Shetland Islands, from Southend to Europe on behalf of various charters the airline had, and from Heathrow to Brussels on behalf of Federal Express where, one night, we parked right next to Concorde!

The only area that really needs a bit of extra work is the wing root area, where the wings join the fuselage. This is not an uncommon problem with much more detailed and expensive kits, but a simple smear of cyano-acrylate adhesive is applied, left to harden and then sanded smooth.

The airframe is then sprayed with an overall grey, in this case using Halfords' plastic primer scheme, which reveals a few areas that require further filling and sanding. This is an important step as often, especially on white moulded plastic, the small imperfections can go unnoticed until you start spraying the final scheme: this is obviously not the best time to discover a few gaps!

The leading edges of the Viscount's wings were left as bare metal on the real aircraft; this is represented on the model by spraying the leading edges of the wings, as well as the engine cowlings, with polished aluminium from the Alclad II range. After masking the bare metal areas, the wings themselves are sprayed light grey. I did try and search for the exact grey that Vickers used but had to settle with using Light Aircraft Grey from Xtracolour's range of gloss enamels. After this has dried and the masking has been removed, the colour appears to be a good match to the photos that I have of the original aircraft. As hard as I have tried to remedy the gap at the wing root, closer inspection reveals that the CA adhesive has sunk into the gap and there is still some work to do here.

The classic schemes of the 1950s and 1960s were almost always white above another colour and British Air Ferries kept this tradition with a white upper fuselage above a deep blue. This has the advantage of being an easy masking job and the white areas are sprayed with Halfords' Appliance White after being decanted into the airbrush cup. It is so tempting at this stage to try and remove the masking, handle the model and admire your handiwork. But if my years of modelling have taught me anything at all, it is that you are almost certainly going to stick a thumb into wet paint if you do not let it fully harden first! Resist the urge to start immediately on the next phase of painting, and leave the Viscount for a couple of days so the paint can cure completely.

Finding a correct shade of blue proved to be a difficult task but finally, after trying shades of dark blue from nearly every manufacturer, I settled on Revell's Lufthansa Blue. It is number 350 in their enamel range and is a very close match for the deep blue undersides of the BAF scheme, as well as matching the decals too.

Being a 1/144th model, the masked areas are not huge but it would be a waste of Tamiya's masking tape to mask everywhere using that, so I cut large pieces of a low tack masking film called Frisk Film (which is available at most good art stores, as well as on-line) and use these to cover the wings prior to spraying the dark blue. Once again, leave to dry for almost a

After the wings have been painted grey, the leading edges of the wings, as well as the engine nacelles, are sprayed with Alclad II.

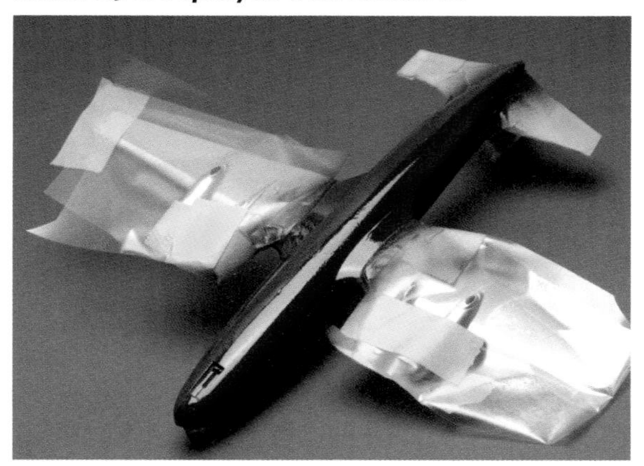

The closest match that I can find to the dark blue lower fuselage is Revell's enamel Lufthansa Blue, number 350.

It is tempting to continue, but the dark blue gloss paint needs to be left for almost a week to dry fully before the model is handled again.

week to avoid the fingerprints that will inevitably end up on the model if this isn't done.

The decaling process is an absolute joy when building airliners, as this is when the model truly comes to life. With the workbench cleared and tidied, the basic tools are all assembled and in no time at all the first of the TwoSix decals are applied. As the main part of the livery is printed as on piece, rather than in many smaller, individual decals, the BAF scheme takes shape very quickly indeed.

The decals handle wonderfully, with good colour density: they are neither too thin as to be almost impossible to use, nor too thick to conform to the model's contours. The one area where they do need some encouragement, with a good drop of decal softener, is where the fuselage cheat-lines wrap around the nose. The whole decaling session takes less than an hour to complete and once they are dry, the whole model is given a coat of Johnson's Future as a final gloss varnish.

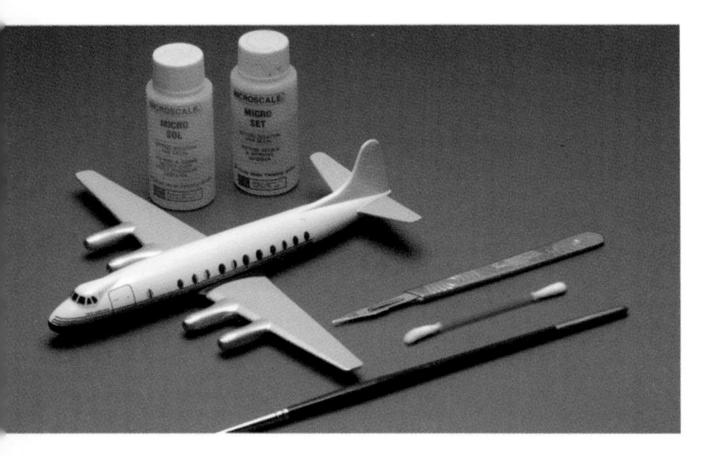

The main tools required when applying decals include: a scalpel, a brush, cotton buds and decal softening agents, such as Microset and Microsol.

The glazing is all represented by decals.

The acrylic floor polish takes only a day to dry fully and gives a nice shine to the model; however as this is somewhat unrealistic of a 1950s era airliner, albeit operating in the newer BAF scheme of the 1980s, something needs to be done in order to dull the shiny lustre down. But first, there are some tiny details to add.

It is often said that the difference between a good model and a great one is hidden somewhere in the detail that is added: the amount that you want to add is, of course, entirely up to you. I have learned, however, that the amount of extra work that I do on a model is almost directly connected to how well I know the subject and if I have had a personal involvement with the aircraft. In this case, I naturally wanted to add a few bits to really bring the model to life and, to my eye, there were a couple of easy fixes.

The wingtip navigation lights in many airliner model kits are simply missing, or at best represented by just moulded panel lines in the plastic. This is the case with the Viscount model and, after a quick swipe or two with a file the wingtip lights are cut out and replaced with clear coloured resin, cut from the moulding blocks of CMK's generic light sets. These are available in red, green, blue and clear, and are a good choice if you want to represent any aircraft light as they are cast in various shapes. The moulding block, as you can see, has also been put to good use here.

After the areas on the wingtip are cut out, red (left) and green (right) blocks of resin are cut and adhered with CA. These are then gradually sanded down and finally polished. Small, red, teardrop shaped lights are used from the red set to represent the upper and lower anti-collision beacons, which are a prominent feature of the upper fuselage.

The propellers and undercarriage are completed, painted and attached to complete the model.

The wingtip navigation lights are cut out and the area filed smooth.

The resin navigation lights by CMK Resin are certainly an item worth having in the workshop inventory.

A block from the resin runner that the small lights are attached to is used and, after gluing in place, is sanded smooth.

The anti-collision beacon, again from the resin CMK set of navigation lights.

Flory Models ready-mixed wash is a water-based wash that highlights panel lines.

The wash is applied liberally by brush and allowed to dry.

Once dry, the area is wiped clean with a slightly damp cloth or piece of kitchen towel, leaving the dried wash in the recesses.

The completed model really does capture the look of the original.

However, going back to the general look of the aircraft, she looks brand new and that is certainly not how I remember the Viscounts during my time flying them! After a look through some of the weathering techniques that can be used, I opted for a simple wash, using Flory Models' water-based weathering washes. These have a very fine pigment and dry quickly, leaving the pigment residue in the panel lines after the model has been wiped clean.

The technique in using these washes is simple but effective. The wash is brushed over the area and simply allowed to dry. Using a clean, damp cloth the wash is wiped away to leave nicely defined panel lines. This gives me just the right amount of dirtiness that I'm looking for and completes what is, for me at least, a highly prized model of an aircraft that was important, not only to the British aviation industry, but to me personally as it was with the Vickers Viscount that I began my career.

CHAPTER 12

NOW HOW DO YOU FOLLOW THE DAKOTA?

AIRFIX 1/72ND FOKKER F.27 FRIENDSHIP

The success of the Douglas DC-3 is in no doubt, with many examples still flying today. But during the 1950s it became apparent that a replacement design was going to be needed and it was with this idea that the Fokker designers turned to their drawing boards. The Dutch manufacturer assessed various configurations before finally deciding on a twin-engined, high wing design, powered by the successful Rolls-Royce Dart engine; a pressurized cabin would seat twenty-eight passengers.

The first prototype, PH-NIV, first flew on 24 November 1955 and established that a slight redesign was necessary. The second prototype and initial production machines were 0.9m (3 ft) longer, tackling the first aircraft's slightly tail-heavy handling and, as a by-product, allowing seating for an additional four passengers, bringing the total to thirty-two. The power plant was also changed to the more powerful Dart Mk 528 engine.

The first F.27 entered service in 1958 and its popularity quickly grew. With a cruise speed of 320 knots and a capacity of more than fifty passengers, the F.27 had twice the passenger capacity of the DC-3 and could get those passengers to their destinations at more than twice the DC-3's cruising speed. The dawn of turboprop regional airliners had arrived: to this day a number of cities are connected by the short haul air routes flown by the turboprop airliners.

According to sales figures, the F.27 was the most popular European-built turboprop airliner, with nearly 800 examples produced, as well as being produced under licence by Fairchild in the United States, as the US market would eventually become the largest user of the F.27 in the world. While this particular Fokker is now retired from the fleets of today's airlines, numerous examples remain in cargo service around the world today.

Airfix has suffered many trials and tribulations over the years and there have been quite a few occasions when it looked likely that this historical modelling brand might very well disappear altogether. But the ownership of the brand looks in very safe hands now, with Humbrol taking this brand (as well as other famous names such as Hornby and Scalextric) into the future with new development of kits, as well as a concerted effort to re-release some of the most sought after kits from the last century.

During the 1970s I was far more interested in building Spitfires and Phantoms than the airliners that I concentrate on today and the Fokker F.27 Friendship did not seem that, well, 'dangerous and deadly' to me at the time! It did not have guns nor could it carry bombs, so it was not until the recent

Since the purchase of Airfix by Hornby, the British company's huge portfolio of models is slowly being re-released. The new boxing of the Fokker F.27 is a welcome surprise and is a perfect starter kit for those wishing to venture into airliner modelling.

re-release of this wonderful 1/72nd kit that I had the opportunity to build it; and I am very glad that I did!

The open box reveals the familiar 1970s era sprues, with the light grey plastic parts attached to the sprues by rather large attachment points. It always took a bit of care to remove the parts, as well as requiring a bit more work than usual to clean them up. I did chuckle as I saw the two 'blobs' of plastic that represented the pilots. I remember clearly trying to attempt to paint the Airfix pilots and never once questioned their seated position, with both arms at their sides, not thinking how they were going to control the aircraft like that! They always seemed to be the same pilots too, regardless of whether they were sitting in a Messerschmitt or a Mirage. But that was the trend when the kit was released and it was not until much later that companies started to focus on reproducing the details far more accurately. Separate arms, that you could position so that the pilot could hold the control column, came much later!

But the basic shape is good and the decals provide alternatives for: TAA, Trans Australia Airlines, Turkish Airlines and Royal Dutch Airlines, KLM. The decals are really stunning and have an excellent colour density, with a nice shiny finish to them. I decided that it should be a TAA aircraft as my closest friend hails from 'down under' and prior to the infamous pilots' strike of 1989 in Australia, briefly flew for TAA. So, with the plan formed, it's time to start taking the parts off the sprues.

(Further information about the Australian pilot's dispute of 1989 can be found in this fascinating account by one of the pilots involved at the time: www.vision.net.au/~apaterson/aviation/pd89_document.htm.)

The fuselage halves are sprayed with matt black and left aside to dry as I start the cockpit. This area of the kit is actually quite nicely portrayed given the age of the kit: it was a pleasure to actually create a small replica of an airliner cockpit for a change, given that most 1/144th airliner models are completely devoid of anywhere for the pilots to sit!

The cockpit parts are removed from their respective sprues and the floor and instrument panel are sprayed grey, with the seats painted blue. I'm not too

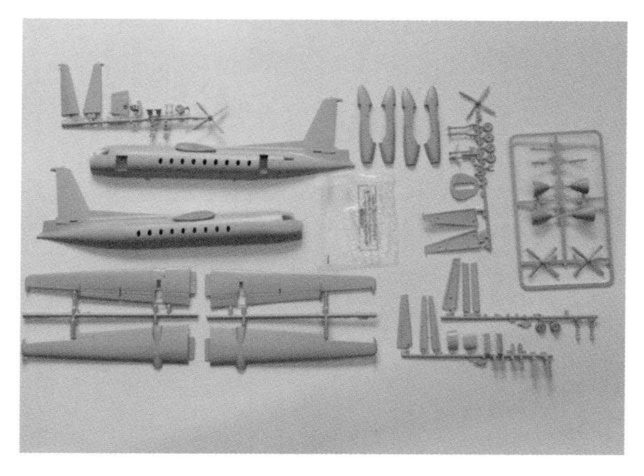

Originally moulded in a silver-grey plastic, the new release has been produced in a more user-friendly, light grey.

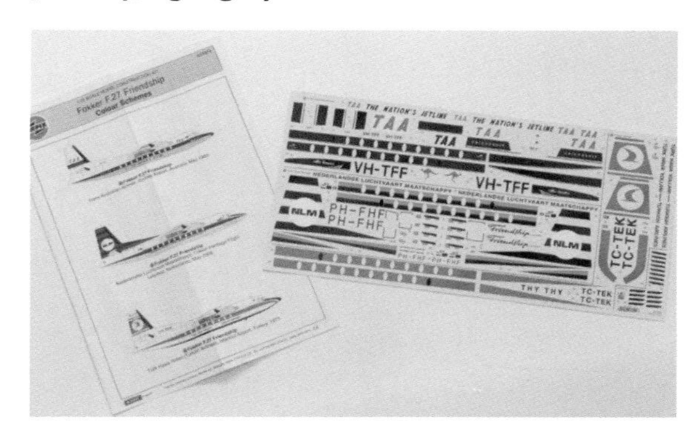

The decal sheet is one of the best I have seen from Airfix, with dense colours and a gloss finish; they really are very nice and include options for: Turkish Airlines, Nederlandse Luchtvaart Maatschappij (NLM) the Dutch Fokker heritage Flight and Trans Australia Airlines, TAA.

Since the kit is in the larger scale of 1/72nd, a cockpit area is included.

Some sink marks are evident on the fuselage halves: these will need filling and sanding smooth prior to painting.

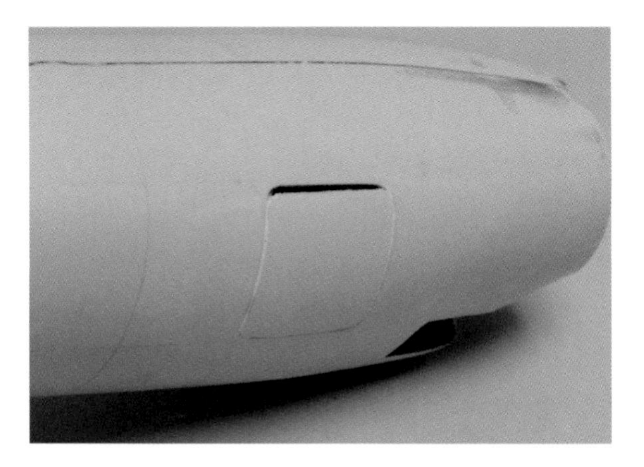

The front cargo door is slightly smaller than the opening in the fuselage; this gap can easily be filled.

The door is also too thin which results in it being recessed in the opening. To remedy this, small strips of plastic strip are added to the door edges to build it up and allow it to fit flush with the fuselage.

sure of the exact colour, but most airliner cockpit seats seem to have a blue cloth covering, so that is what I went with. To further adorn the cockpit, I have painted some masking tape matt black and cut strips to represent the seat belts. It is simple enhancements like this that get responses of: 'Wow! Look at that!' from those viewing your models and simple ideas like this make them stand apart. Of course, if you really want to go to town then please do! There are etched metal seat belt bucles available from various companies that would suit the F.27's cockpit, but on this occasion I have just used tape.

The instrument panel and centre console are represented by decals and once these are applied, the seats are attached to the cockpit floor and the whole sub-assembly left aside whilst work progresses on the main airframe.

Having previously painted the interior black, the windows are fixed in place with a strong PVA adhesive. This dries clear and does not attach to the plastic, so is perfect for gluing transparent parts in place. These are left to dry prior to the fuselage halves being test fitted together. The basic shape is ok, although the kit's nose does suffer from being slightly malnourished. There are also a few sink marks where the plastic had shrunk during setting. These are most prominent around areas where the plastic is thickest, notably on the outside surface where a locating pin is situated.

The model is covered with fine raised panel lines and when the various imperfections are filled and sanded, inevitably the panel lines are lost, but that is not a bad thing as the finish I want is of a clean airframe. The front cargo door is supplied separately and this is a fraction smaller than the opening, so some work is needed with some scrap plastic and filler to get a nice finish. The door itself seems to fall too far into the fuselage, so the edges of the door are built up with small strips of plastic strip from the Evergreen range.

Once the two halves are attached to each other, the cabin windows are masked with Humbrol Maskol, a PVA-based masking fluid that dries quickly and is easily removed once the painting has been completed. You can see from the photographs below that

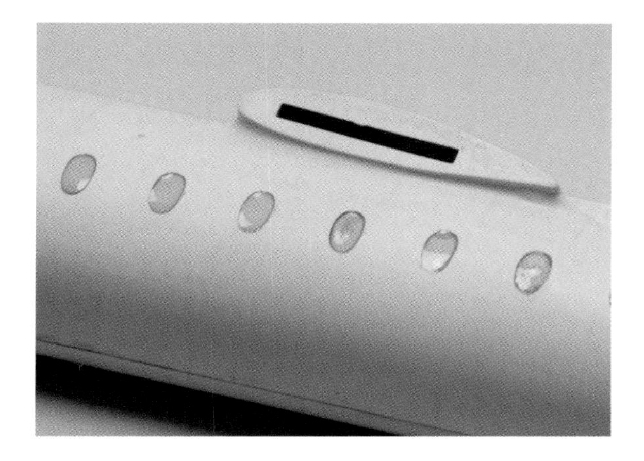

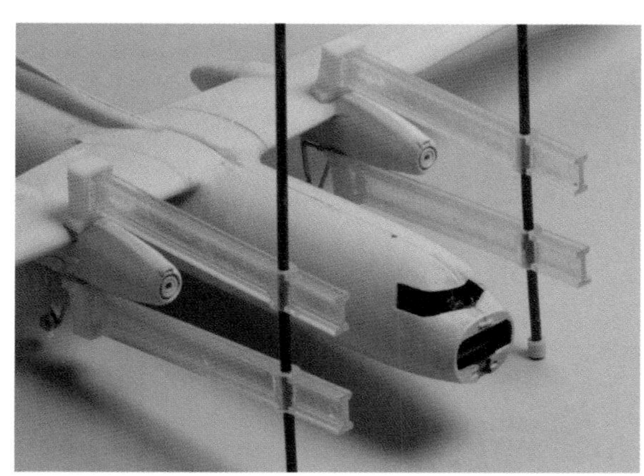

CLOCKWISE, FROM TOP LEFT:

Humbrol Maskol is used to mask the windows.

The upper and lower wing halves are assembled and the separate engine parts held in place with the Berna clamps as they dry.

The windscreen is a less than perfect fit and needs sanding at the edges with progressively finer grades of sanding sheets. A final polish and an application of Johnson's Future will restore the clarity.

The nose shape needs re-profiling; here Milliput epoxy putty is used as it dries to a hard finish and is easily sanded.

After the Milliput is sanded to the correct shape, the windscreen is masked ready for the first coat of paint.

the fluid dries to a semi-opaque, darker purple when dry. It is then perfectly safe to paint over.

The fuselage is now ready to receive the wings and, after these are assembled, they are attached to their respective wing roots. There are certainly lots of gaps and sink marks that need to be filled and these will receive attention as the build continues.

Once the wings have set firmly, the rear horizontal stabilizers and undercarriage are all cemented in place. At this point, the prominent rear inlet on the left rear side of the fuselage is thinned to give it a less toy-like appearance.

The fit of the cockpit transparency is not fantastic, but this can be filled, sanded and then polished later. With respect to transparencies, it is certainly acceptable to sand them, as it is quite easy to resurrect their clearness later by sanding with progressively finer grades of abrasive, before finally polishing to a shine with some toothpaste and paper towel. A final coat of Johnson's Future will then give the parts a perfect finish. So the cockpit glazing is sanded to give a better fit and then it is time to look at that odd-shaped nose.

The nose itself is a separate part and tapers in faster than the fuselage tapers, giving a rather odd look. So once the nose has been attached to the fuselage (and resisting the temptation to scratch build the weather radar!) the sides of the nose are built up with Milliput modelling putty. Milliput is a two-part, epoxy resin putty that adheres perfectly to plastic and dries hard, giving a perfect finish once sculpted and sanded. On the F.27's nose, the Milliput is simply smeared around the join to give a thicker profile that is then sanded to a more accurate shape.

With the nose area having received attention, next on the list to correct are the aileron hinges that are far too simple on the model. All it takes are a few small pieces of plasticard to represent this area correctly.

Finally, all other areas that need to be filled and sanded are finished off before the model is masked prior to painting. As the undercarriage needs to be fitted when the engine nacelles are joined, I find it easier to spray the undercarriage first, before attaching it and masking it off, rather than having to mask the surrounding area later and then spray-

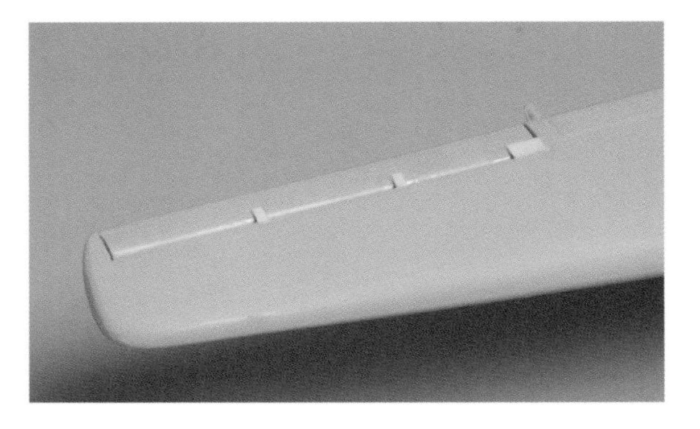

The aileron areas receive extra detailing in the form of small strips of plasticard, to better represent the appearance of the full-sized aircraft.

Masking the undercarriage readies the aircraft for the primer coat.

Halfords' Plastic Primer is used, straight from the can, to give the model an overall coat of grey primer.

Continuing with Halfords' aerosols, the F.27's fuselage is painted Appliance White, whilst the wings and tailplanes are painted using Xtracolor enamels.

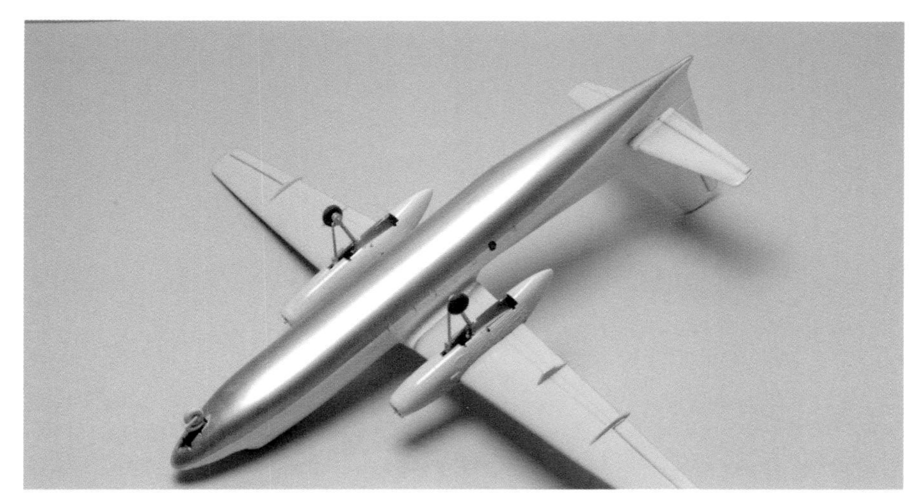

The lower fuselage is masked and sprayed with Alclad II Aluminium.

Masking larger areas can be done using Frisk Film, a transparent, sticky-backed plastic sheet.

This Fokker F.27 now sits in the study of a colleague, a former pilot for TAA.

ing the undercarriage. Once this is done, the model receives its first coat of primer. This is sanded back and another coat applied before a check to see if there are any imperfections in the finish that need to be attended to.

The TAA scheme is a simple white and silver fuselage with grey wings and this is easily masked off, given that the 1/72nd model is quite big. It doesn't take long to give the upper fuselage a coat of gloss white from Halfords' range, while the wings and horizontal stabilizers are painted light grey. These areas are masked once they have dried, before spraying the lower fuselage aluminium. Finally, the de-icing boots are masked off ready to be sprayed matt black.

Final painting includes the de-icing boots on the rear flying surfaces and the anti-glare panel on the upper nose. The decals are all put on without any problems at all and the undercarriage finally assembled with the, already painted, wheels and tyres fixed in place. The masking covering the cabin windows is now carefully peeled away with the help of a wooden cocktail stick in order not to scratch the clear plastic windows. The final details include the aerial, made from a strand of stretched sprue, which runs from the upper cockpit area to the fin.

TAA had a long history, having been formed in 1946 and changed its name to Australian Airlines in 1986. The airline was ultimately sold to QANTAS in 1996. It was a real treat to build this classic Airfix kit and I really do think she looks rather resplendent in the livery of a long standing, but no longer with us, Australian airline.

CHAPTER 13

BRITAIN LEADS THE WAY – AGAIN!

AIRFIX 1/144TH DE HAVILLAND COMET 4B

On the 27 July 1949, powered by four de Havilland Ghost turbojets, the de Havilland DH106 Comet prototype thundered down the runway at Hatfield and became airborne in what would have been a cacophony of noise. At that moment Britain entered the age of jet powered air transport!

Another product of the Brabazon Committee, the de Havilland Comet was an exceptionally clean looking aircraft, with the four turbojets installed within the wing roots and with a pressurized cabin allowing smooth flights at altitudes in excess of 30,000 feet, well above most of the weather. Commercial success was forecast with load factors as low as 43 per cent; the passenger advantage was the greater comfort and higher speeds that the Comet had over the range of other piston and turbo-prop aircraft of the day. In fact the Comet was over 50 per cent faster than the DC-6 on the same routes. Entering service in 1952 with BOAC, the Comet was the first jet-powered airliner; G-ALYP departing London for Johannesburg on 2 May, after being the most exhaustively tested airliner yet designed. However, joy soon turned to sadness as a number of incidents and fatal accidents harmed the Comet's reputation and in 1954, the aircraft had its certificate of airworthiness revoked and BOAC grounded their fleet.

A court of enquiry was set up under Lord Cohen to establish the cause of the accidents that plagued the Comet's early life and under Sir Arnold Hall, Director of the Royal Aircraft Establishment at Farnborough, began looking at metal fatigue as a primary cause. After the court of enquiry the basic design was deemed to be sound, but de Havilland started refitting aircraft with thicker gauge skin sections and, importantly, changing the window design from that of square to oval shaped. Inevitably, the lessons learned at de Havilland's expense were used to benefit other manufacturers and the Comet's commercial viability suffered greatly.

The Comet did not resume services until 1958, by which time the American manufacturers Boeing and Douglas both had four-engine, jet transport aircraft either in, or imminently due in service. Vickers was soon to introduce the VC-10 and BOAC replaced the Comet on its premiere routes with their recently ordered B707: the last BOAC Comet revenue service being in 1965.

All was not lost for the Comet though, as some charter carriers and other, smaller carriers took delivery of the used aircraft from BOAC. Notably Dan-Air, at one point, owned all Comet 4B aircraft then currently airworthy and it is here, in this chapter, that we take a look at representing the Dan-Air Comet 4B from the almost antique 1/144th kit by Airfix. I say 'antique' slightly unfairly, but the kit itself hails from a time when The Beatles were yet to feature in the music charts, JFK was the President of the United States and I was still three years away from even existing!

I do, however, have a fond connection with this simple kit as it was amongst the first models that I built, after having seen the real aircraft on the ramp at Gatwick. It was with those memories that I turned to the computer and was astonished at how much these are now selling for on that popular on-line auction site! It is best that I state now never to let yourself get lured in by the tag 'rare' when looking for kits online. These kits are certainly not sitting in every model shop, but neither are they rare enough to be worth quite the sums that some go for. Sit tight, be patient and you should be able to pick one up for less than £10.

The clean lines of the De Havilland Comet are captured by the Roy Cross artwork on the Airfix box.

On opening the box of my particular kit, a 1970s release, the parts looked in good condition and were all there. The first thing that you should check when buying from an auction site is that what you are buying is what you expected, and that naturally means that all parts are present in the box.

The kit comes together very quickly and the nose area is filled with solder, wound tight to fit into the nose and then cemented in place with cyanoacrylate. The windows are blanked from behind using strips of plasticard, as these are going to filled and represented by the decals.

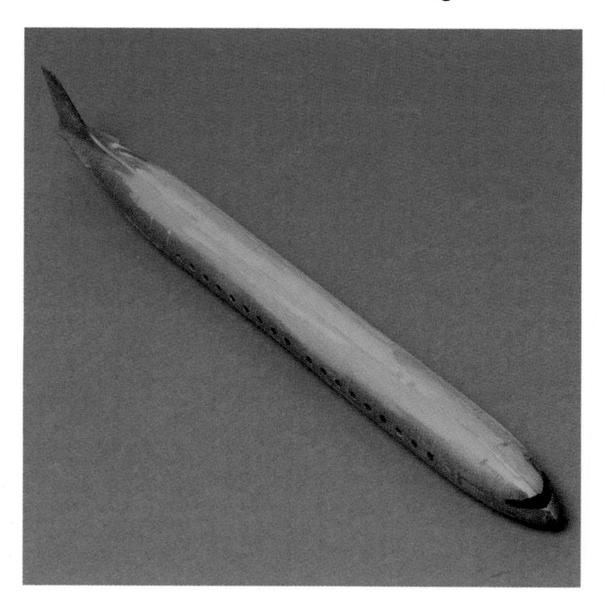

The silver-grey plastic certainly reminds me of my youth – although I never bothered to fill the gaps back then!

Berna clamps in action again!

The clamps are very versatile and once the fuselage halves have set, they are utilized again to hold the wing firmly in place.

The fuselage halves are clamped together during their assembly to allow the adhesive to set and create a good join; likewise with the wings when they are attached to the fuselage. It is important to produce a solid assembly, as this model will be handled quite a lot during the filling and sanding process.

You can see from the three photographs below how the lower fuselage join needs masking on each side to allow a neat application of filler to be spread along the join line. After drying the area is sanded and polished before the final coat of paint.

The upper surfaces of the Comet are sprayed with Halfords' Appliance White, decanted as usual into the airbrush cup, rather than being sprayed directly from the can. The lower surfaces are Light Aircraft Grey

The top of the fuselage requires extensive filling and a lot of work is needed to sand the joins smooth.

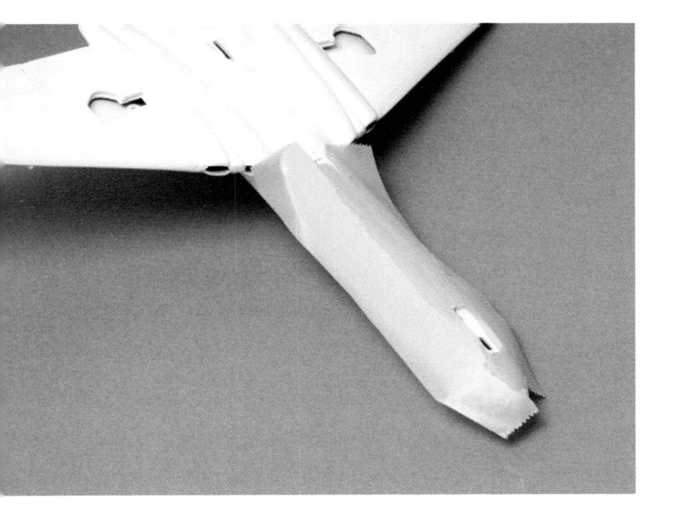

CLOCKWISE, FROM TOP LEFT:

The lower fuselage is masked either side of the seam line and an application of filler is smoothly applied along the join.

The filler is gradually sanded smooth.

The lower surfaces are sprayed Light Aircraft Grey from the Xtracolor range.

When fully dry, the grey areas are masked off prior to the metallic paint being sprayed.

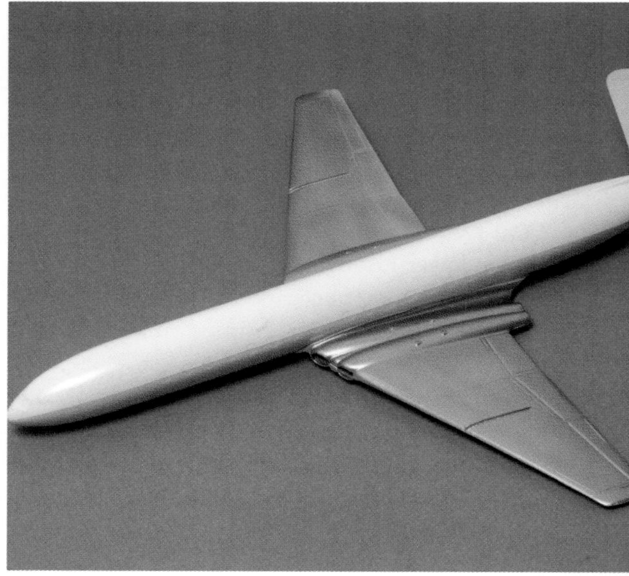

The Comet is now ready for the decals. The livery is an easy choice!

from Xtracolor and the model is left for a few days to allow the paint to harden.

The lower, outer wing sections are masked using Tamiya masking tape, as is the fuselage, prior to spraying the wings with Alclad II Polished Aluminium.

The model is certainly looking rather sleek by now; it just needs some subtle shading on the wing surfaces and engine nacelles, using differing shades of Alclad II metallic colours to break up the rather toy-like appearance of a single, metallic shade.

This is something you can practice on scrap parts in order to create more realistic, natural metal finishes. Start by applying a gloss enamel coat, preferably black or a dark grey. Although I have used the light grey finish here, Alclad II does seem to give better finishes when sprayed over a dark gloss finish. Then, gradually build up the metallic coat to give a uniform finish. Let this dry, only about five minutes with Alclad II, then you can experiment with the application of other shades as you wish. Refer to photos of the actual aircraft and you'll soon be able to copy the way that the natural metals on the real aircraft display different hues. Finally, the tail is painted red and then left to dry before starting to put the decals on.

The decals again come from TwoSix because, although they represent the same livery as the kit's own decal sheet, the Airfix ones had aged beyond use and the TwoSix decals are certainly of far better quality. Just like the Viscount, these decals quickly bring the model to life and the Dan-Air livery soon takes shape.

The undercarriage took an hour to clean up and assemble, before painting and finally attaching to the model. I had been a bit worried that I had not put enough nose weight in, but a quick check by placing her on her wheels for the first time allayed any fears that I had.

I must admit to feeling rather sentimental about Dan-Air. An ever-present sight at Gatwick, Dan-Air were the first airline to offer me a job (I was offered a position as First Officer on the H.S.748, but elected to join British Air Ferries on the Viscount instead) and how the landscape changed on the ramp at London's second airport when, in 1992, Dan-Air was sold to British Airways for the sum of £1.

But regardless of airline politics, the Comet still looks so very sleek and slender and totally resplendent in her Dan-Air livery. I am so glad to have, once again, a de Havilland Comet in my collection.

What modeller of 'a certain age' could forget the stands supplied with nearly all kits in the 1960s and 1970s?

Although we've started talking about jet powered commercial aircraft in this chapter, the 1960s were a cross-over period where many airlines still operated large, turbo-prop powered airliners on routes that were later to be the domain of the jet. The next chapter looks at one such aircraft and is in the much larger scale of 1/72nd. This particular model is an absolute beauty to see 'in the flesh' and I was very pleased that the owner and builder, Simon Lind, offered to write about the construction of her for this book: and the aircraft in question? Bristol's 'Whispering Giant', the Britannia!

CHAPTER 14

THE WHISPERING GIANT

AIRWAYS 1/72ND BRISTOL BRITANNIA

BY SIMON LIND

G-AOVT is probably the most well known Britannia surviving today, as she is the one at the Imperial War Museum at Duxford in Cambridgeshire. But a little research shows that she has also had a very interesting career and this is the subject I've chosen to model, using the Airways vac-form kit in, naturally, 1/72nd scale. Why naturally? Well, I'll leave the answer to that question to the very end!

'VT was built at Bristol's Filton works in 1958 for BOAC and flew for the first time on 17 December that year. She is a 312 series aircraft developed for the trans-Atlantic run but, by the time she was delivered to BOAC, on the first day of the following year, the jets were dominating the lucrative North American crossing so she was relegated to African service, the run the Britannias were actually originally designed for.

Needless to say the advent of the jets, particularly the Boeing B707, ensured that 'VT, along with the rest of the BOAC Britannia fleet, would only last a few more years in front-line service before being snapped up by independent and charter airlines.

Incidentally, I opted for 'VT as a subject as her life mirrors my own; her early years were spent in Africa, and then she came back to England only to tour Europe and Australia, before finally settling in Cambridgeshire! Aside from that she also wore the colours of both Eagle and Monarch Airlines, and it is in Monarch's bright and distinctive scheme that I've chosen to portray her.

The Airways kit that I made this model from is the second-generation version, as it came with white metal undercarriage and propellers (although the latter were useless) and an A3 sized instruction leaflet. The original kits, of which I have one too, didn't have the detailed undercarriage but did have better packaging and a much more informative instruction booklet. Two sheets of vac-formed white plastic contain all the parts needed. The only additional items I bought were replacement propellers from Aeroclub and some resin wheels.

I won't go into detail about the build, save to say that it is a typical vac-form process as outlined elsewhere in the book. The basic structure is cut out, the parts are sanded and a wing spar is installed (in my case a firework stick) as well as some fuselage bulkheads. I added some nose-weight and glued the lot together! As usual with my own builds, I did add a little more by building a detailed cockpit, opening the doors and building the entry and galley areas. I also opened the baggage hold doors and offset the rudder, detailed the undercarriage and engine intakes, and added aerials etc.

However, a few general comments are in order. The 'rivet counter' will find the panel lines a little

With larger scale kits, it is quite an easy task to open doors and cargo bays.

The nose wheels come from a 1/72nd kit of the Hawker Typhoon.

The doors are easily removed as, being a vac-form kit, the plastic is much thinner and easier to work with.

crude and inaccurate; I filled the most glaring mistakes but can happily live with the rest!

Aligning the engines is very hit and miss: no guidance is given and the scribed lines are of no help. I think I've got it almost right, though, and just by rack of eye, a little luck and care. There is no engine intake or exhaust detail and little to help model this. Fortunately I have good references and as I don't live too far from Duxford I was able to take many detail photos.

Finding a set of wheels is almost impossible if you want to use flattened resin wheels. In the end I used 1/48th Hawker Typhoon wheels that I reduced in diameter. They are still probably a little too large but don't look too bad. They are a definite improvement on the kit offerings, though. The nose wheels are also Typhoon wheels, this time in 1/72nd!

Other factors to consider if you are going to attempt this kit are as follows:

- Use Aeroclub propellers!
- The wing tips need reshaping.
- Check the dihedral; I don't think I've given it enough but very little is required.
- The airframe at Duxford has obviously been weatherproofed; the wings have been painted but I think should be natural metal as I've depicted on my model.
- Cutting accurate circles in plastic card is not easy; getting perfectly circular engine fronts is almost impossible. Getting them all the same size is also difficult; thank goodness for a mini-drill and sanding 'wheels'. I also used plastic drinking straws as the engine exhausts: the nearest things to scale thickness!

Building the interior is also not difficult, it is just time consuming and largely hidden. I covered the galleys in bright Bare-Metal foil so that they do at least show up in photos! Fortunately, the fuselage is mostly circular and the plastic quite thin, so that cutting bulkheads of the correct diameter is not difficult. The doors on the real thing slide rearwards into the fuselage so I had to make sure I left room for them; adding them in last was an interesting exercise but they do look the part. The one advantage of the Airways vac-forms is the thinness of the plastic; when the doors are cut out the walls look about the correct thickness for the apertures.

I had decided quite early on that I wanted to model an aircraft with an interesting history and was initially going to do it in BOAC colours, to go alongside all my other BOAC liveried aircraft. While reading about the development of Britannias in Frank McKim's excellent book Whispering Giant, the Story of the Bristol Britannia published by Scoval, I came across several pictures of 'VT in different guises so studied her a little further.

She was built for BOAC, but shortly after entering service on the Johannesburg route, via Nairobi and Salisbury, she was leased to East African Airways Corporation. In 1961 she helped out BEA when that airline found itself a little short for the summer holiday season, but before long she found herself wearing Nigerian Airways titles when she joined them on lease. However, by 1963 BOAC and its associated airlines had no further use for her so she was sold to British Eagle Airways and named 'Enterprise.'

When an over extended Eagle was forced to cease trading, she stood for a while at Heathrow facing an uncertain future. Fortunately, the wait was short-lived as Monarch came to the rescue in August 1968 and bought her, along with several other Britannias. After many years of sterling service with Monarch, including periods spent on trooping contracts and on lease to Invicta Airlines, she was donated to the Duxford Aviation Society and made her last flight, to Duxford, on 29 June 1975.

The Monarch colours of the 1970's are quite striking and I've not, to date, seen any other model in those colours, least of all a Britannia. With my model nearing completion my mind was made up; it was definitely going to Monarch, but only if a friend of mine could do the stylized 'M' on the tail and the titling as a decal. True to form my friend, Neil, came through with the goods and so it was out with the Halfords' Appliance White and let the spraying commence!

The yellow is the most difficult to do as the Humbrol colours are very translucent. An undercoat of Halfords' filler primer, which is very yellow, solves that problem and this time I haven't tried for a highly polished, natural metal finish as all the pictures I've seen of the Monarch aircraft show them to be quite dull. So I've used shades from the Humbrol Metalcote range and sealed that with Johnson's Klear; personally I think it has turned out quite well!

The Britannia on display at ScaleModelWorld 2008, held in Telford.

My Britannia made its first public appearance at ScaleModelWorld in November 2008 (I was putting the finishing touches to it the day before!) and was the centre-piece of the newly formed 1/72nd Commercial Aircraft SIG (ca72sig.webs.com/). So there you have it, the reason for choosing the larger scale was simply to comply with the newly formed, Special Interest Group (SIG) and I cannot recommend highly enough the advantages of joining the IPMS and signing up with one or more of the SIGs that you feel are close to your own personal areas of interest. (The IPMS (UK) hosts many special interest groups and full details of these are available directly from the IPMS (UK) website.)

The stylized 'M' and airline titles are all custom-made decals.

The Bristol Britannia certainly looks very attractive in the 1970s Monarch scheme.

CHAPTER 15

THE QUEEN OF THE SKIES

AIRFIX 1/144TH VICKERS VC10

Built by Vickers-Armstrong (Aircraft) Ltd and first flown in 1962, the Vickers VC10 is one aircraft that I hold in high regard due solely to the aesthetics of the design. There is no doubt that the VC10 is a graceful and elegant aircraft; sharing the rear four-engined layout with the Russian Ilyushin Il-62, she was the last of the long-range British airliners and primarily designed to operate on the longer, intercontinental routes and also be capable of operating from hot and high airfields, such as Johannesburg. Well known for her civilian airline operations with BOAC (later British Airways) the VC10 also served with, amongst others, Gulf Air, Ghana Airways, East African Airways and Nigeria Airways. As of 1 June 2010, thirteen VC10s remain in service as aerial refuelling and transport aircraft with the Royal Air Force.

AIRFIX SKYKING

As has already been mentioned, Airfix concentrated their initial airliner releases under the SkyKing banner and this kit, of 1964 vintage, proudly has the SkyKing logo emblazoned across the box top. The kit itself has long been out of production and as the moulds were re-tooled to enable the military K.Mk.2 to be kitted, the original civil VC10 therefore sells for quite high prices through the on-line auction sites. The only other release of the VC10 in 1/144th scale has been the vac-form kit produced by Welsh Models and, despite the trickier assembly, builds into a much more accurate representation than the Airfix original. But this chapter will be concentrating on the Airfix kit, but enhanced with some extra detail to overcome the model's most glaring shortcomings.

Before I go any further though, I did read with interest an online debate regarding the range of modeller's feelings towards the accuracy of a given kit. (www.britmodeller.com/forums/index.php? and follow the links.) On the extreme left you have the 'Rivet Counters': those who would not accept anything other than an exact representation of a subject, while on the far right you have the: 'That Looks About Right' team. I make no apologies for this particular kit tending towards the right! In the end it is about how you, as a modeller, perceive your own work and if it looks about right to you, then who can argue with that!

It has been suggested that Airfix based the initial tooling of their kit on a pre-production example and therefore have not included the two large wing fences, so prominent on the inboard section of the wing on the original aircraft. The engines are also mounted on slightly misshaped pylons, being too flat on the under surface. The latter is quickly solved by the replacement of the kit's engine's with the superior resin set from Bra.Z Models and surely, as this book assumes a degree of modelling competency, you should be able to add a couple of scratch-built wing fences! A quick cut with a razor saw, some plasticard and a bit of filler: now how easy is that?

On opening the box I was confronted with the musty smell of a long stored kit and the decals were certainly showing the extreme signs of age. Having discoloured quite badly and looking extremely brittle, the plan to do this kit completely OOB (Out Of the Box) was not looking good.

Most modellers will have some form of 'stash': be it a collection of unmade kits, accessories, decals or a combination of all three! After a brief search through my own stash, I discovered one set of decals for the VC10 representing an aircraft of Air Malawi; I had no idea at all that I even had these! However, in my own humble opinion, there is only one scheme for a VC10: that of the British Overseas Airways Corporation, BOAC. So prior to starting the kit, a set of these was ordered directly from TwoSix decals and the Air Malawi decals would have to wait for another day.

It is always a good idea when building any kit to test fit as you go, but especially so with older kits, it's also a good excuse to see what the finished aircraft is going to look like and, I know I've said it before, but aesthetically the VC10 is just so right! There really is no other airliner that has the sleek look and the elegance of this classic Vickers' design. I therefore could not resist taping a few parts together!

Having decided the scheme in which the aircraft will be painted, the initial assembly starts with the adhering of the forward bulkhead to one side of the fuselage. Preparation of the parts is a little more critical and after the parts are removed from the runners, they are given a good clean up with subsequently finer grades of abrasive. I have found that the four-sided sponge nail cleaners, that are available from the beauty sections of department stores or from chemists, are superb as they have four varying grades on each side and make a quick job of cleaning up the parts.

Once this is done the complete interior of both halves is painted, in this case with a dark grey from the Vallejo Acrylic range. This water-based paint sprays very well when thinned with plain tap water, to a consistency just slightly thicker than milk, and dries very quickly. This enables me to move onto the next stage, joining the two fuselage halves and here things became, well, slightly interesting!

The kit, as we have seen, is old: in fact, being a 1964 kit, it is exactly as old as me! The plastic fuselage halves are far from straight and the whole of one side is twisted, the other bent like a banana! The only way that I could get each half of the fuselage to adhere to the other was to do it gradually, over the course of a few days. Starting with the nose, the two halves are glued together along the first 4cm of its length. After that has fully dried, small tabs are adhered along the remaining length and gradually, over three days, the remainder of the fuselage glued together, bit-by-bit. As this is being done, after each part of the fuselage has been glued together, the section is taped and held

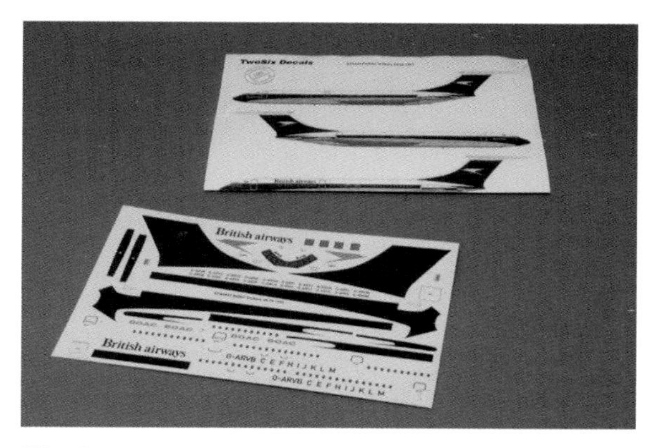

The 'classic' BOAC scheme was my choice for this aircraft, with the livery provided in decal form by TwoSix decals.

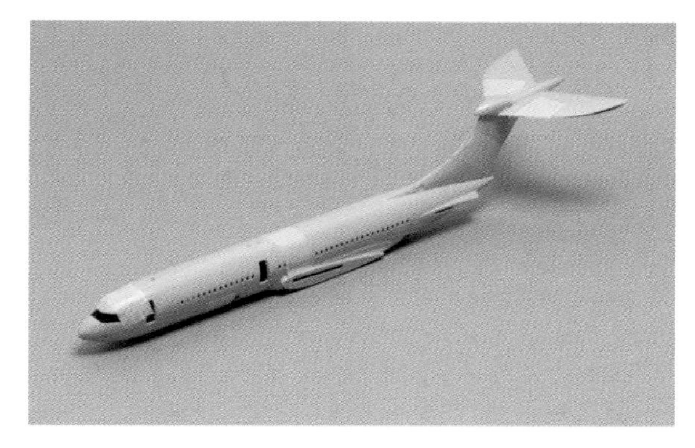

Airfix always issued airliner kits with separate doors and quite often a separate kit of the apron stairs, allowing a diorama scene of passengers embarking up the stairs and off on that dream holiday!

Another feature of the 1970s era airliner kits from Airfix was the inclusion of bulkheads, to give the larger fuselage assemblies extra strength.

The cockpit bulkhead in place: this has the benefit of adding strength, whilst also stopping a see-through effect from the cockpit glazing into an empty fuselage.

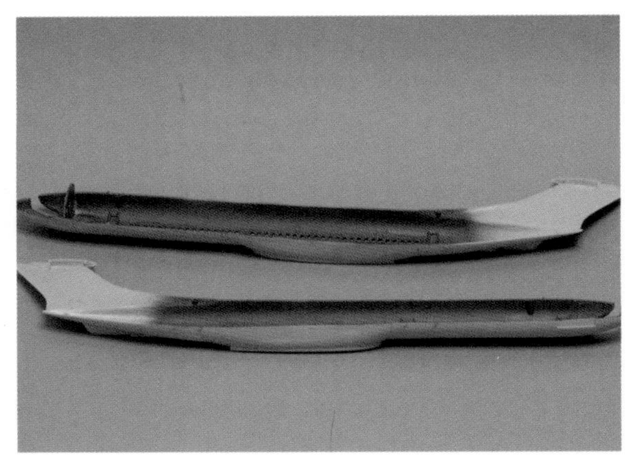

The interior of the fuselage halves is sprayed matt black, although this is really unnecessary, as the window apertures will be filled.

together by a mini clamp, ensuring that the section does not move whilst the glue cures. This process is well worth it as the result is a completely straight fuselage!

The resultant seam is filled with Tamiya's model putty and then, after drying, sanded back and finally polished with very fine grades of sanding stick, followed by a final buff with the polishing stick. Next come the wings and the aforementioned wing fences need to be made, prior to the aircraft receiving her first coat of primer.

The wing halves themselves are detached from their runners and cleaned up, taking care to thin the trailing edges of the wings as much as possible. Older kits tended to have both upper and lower wing halves identically sized, whereas the newer mouldings have their trailing edges moulded complete with a section of the lower wing; this gives a much finer edge. I did measure the trailing edge of the VC10 here and without thinning, when scaled up, the wing edge would be nearly 20cm: hardly aerodynamic!

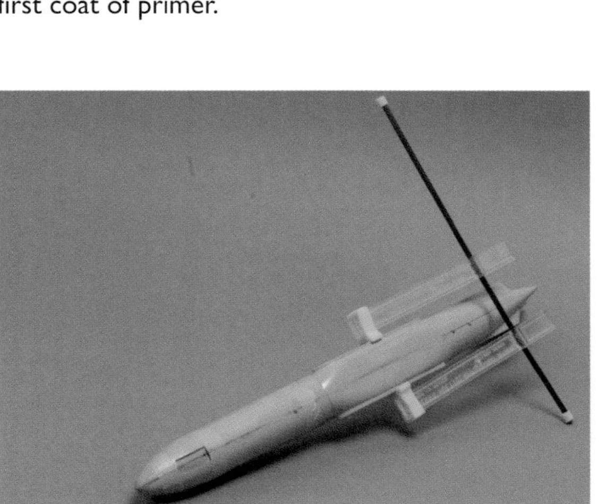

The fuselage halves need careful attention as the two halves are quite warped.

The wing trailing edges are thinned with sanding sheets to give a much better representation of the thin rear edges of the wings.

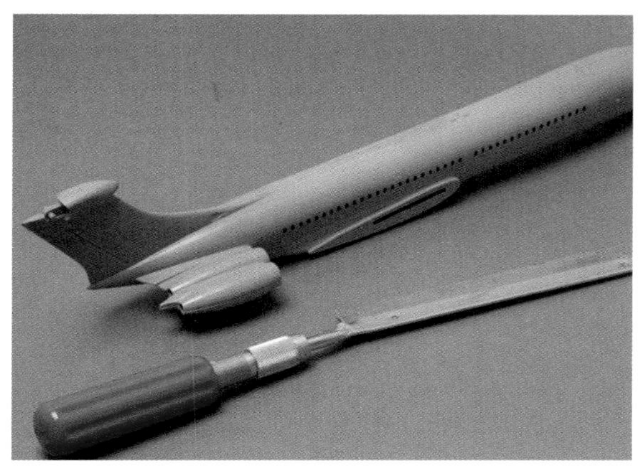

CLOCKWISE FROM TOP LEFT:

I intend to use the superb resin engines from Bra.Z, so using a razor saw, the kit's engine pylons are cut off.

The engine pylons now have to be sanded back, flush with the fuselage, in order to receive the resin replacements.

The rear engine pylons have now been completely removed and a quick dry-fit of the wings reveals the need for more filling and sanding later.

Just prior to attaching the wings to the fuselage, I cut the rear engine mounts off, as these will be replaced with the resin engines from Bra.Z. This is a relatively simple job with a razor saw and the remaining plastic is cleaned off with some careful sanding.

The wings are attached to the fuselage without a problem, other than the need to fill the rather prominent gap along the upper join. This is done with Tamiya plastic filler and the whole assembly is given a coat of white primer to highlight any areas that need attention. Now it is time to look at the missing wing fences and the exact position of the fences is ascertained, using references from the Internet. The position is marked initially with some Tamiya masking tape, before the exact lines are pencilled onto the wing surface. As a guide to where to cut and to make sure the cut is accurate and straight, small strips of Dymo labelling tape are finally laid next to the pencil lines.

Two thin cuts are then made in the upper wing surface, one in each wing, in order to accept the thin fences, which will be cut from a sheet of plasticard. The cuts are then cleaned up using a scriber and a small strip of plasticard, slipped in to see whether the fit would be good.

It was not an easy task to find detailed references of the exact shape of the fence and it was suggested that, in fact, there were different sized fences on different airframes. Sometimes the task of investigating references can throw up more mysteries than it solves! But one good photograph of the preserved airframe at Duxford's museum provided me with the side view I needed and this was used to get the profile right.

After a few practice dry runs, the fences are finally inserted and glued in place, after which a little filler is applied to the sides where they meet the wings to hide the original cuts. This is, of course, a little more

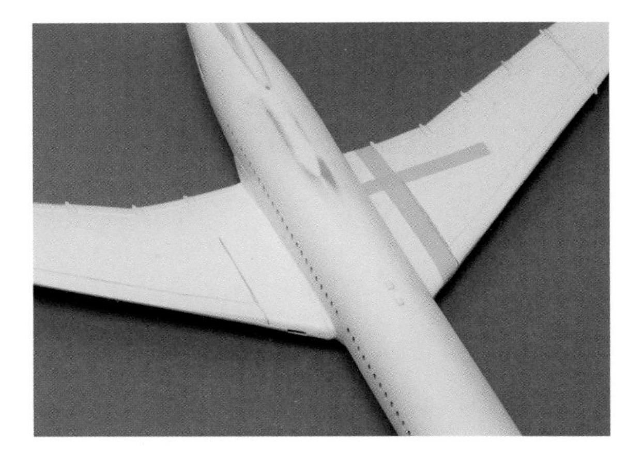

Following reference drawings and photographs, the position of the fences is marked on the wing with masking tape.

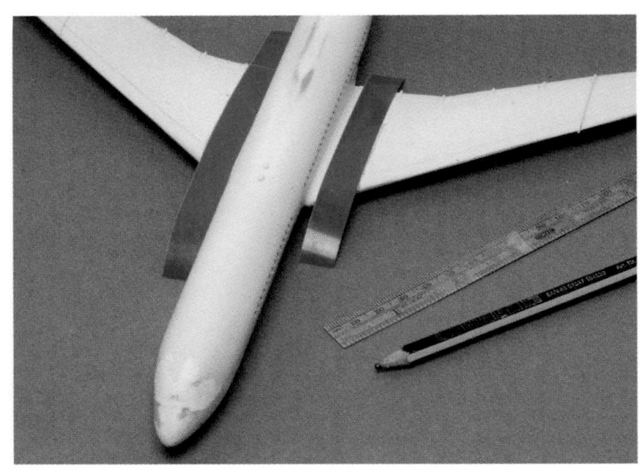

The position is now defined by Dymo tape, which acts as a stencil to scribe against.

The razor saw is used to complete the cuts in the wing.

Prior to cutting the wing fences from the plasticard, a dry-fit of the sheet shows that the cut is wide enough to accept the plastic fences later.

work and over and above that required to build the kit, but it is far more rewarding to know that the model is just that little bit more accurate now.

The engines are assembled next and, although their basic shape isn't bad, the replacement resin engines by Bra.Z are way ahead of the kit's engines in terms of shape: being solid they also do not have any hard-to-fill and sand seams on the inside of the engine intakes. In addition the engine's front fans are much better detailed than the Airfix originals.

But after the new engines are removed from the resin-pouring block, the question arises as to how to actually fit them to the fuselage.

After a few moments thinking, I looked through the spares box and decided to fix some plastic tubing to the fuselage and cement pins into the engine pylon ends; that way not only creating a well defined attachment point for the engines, but also a strong support for them too. Although relatively small, the resin is somewhat dense and they do weigh quite a bit, so simply butt-joining them to the fuselage

The shape of the fences is traced onto the plasticard and then cut out. A small application of filler is needed after the fences have been attached to the wing.

The model is given a quick coat of white primer in order to see if there are any major areas that need filling and sanding again.

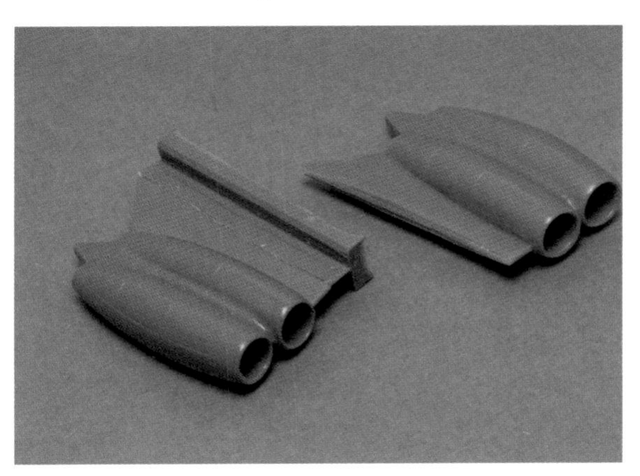

Bra.Z have really carved a niche in the market for replacement resin parts for airliner models. The Rolls Royce Conways are much better representations of the originals than the Airfix parts.

Rather than butt-fit the resin engines to the fuselage, in order to give more strength to the join, brass tubing attached to the engines, slides into plastic tubing adhered to the fuselage.

would almost definitely see them falling off at some point. Therefore, once the original engine attachment areas have been cut off, these being part of the engine pylons, the result is a hole on each side of the fuselage, perfect for accepting the length of plastic tubing, which is inserted and set in place with some cyano-acrylate.

Into these tubes are cemented some brass tubing to represent the 'male' part of the assembly, inserted into holes drilled into the end of each pylon. Care must be taking when doing anything like this to get the geometry right and many dry runs should be attempted before finally committing the engines into place with some cyano-acrylate. Again, some filler is applied to the join and smoothed over with some Tamiya lacquer thinner, using a cotton bud. There is something extremely evocative viewing a VC-10 head-on and seeing the four Rolls-Royce Conways sitting in close formation at the tail of the aircraft!

The windows are masked, top and bottom, with Tamiya tape and then the cabin windows have a thin

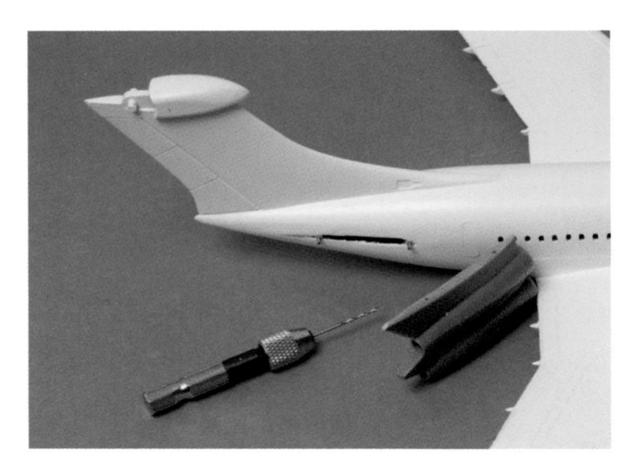

A pin vice and small drill bit are used to drill holes in the resin parts where the brass tubing will be attached.

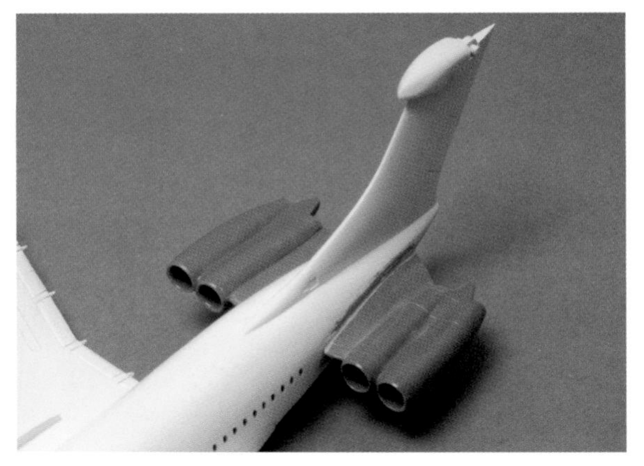

The engines are adhered in place with CA and the gaps filled and smoothed down with a cotton bud soaked in Tamiya's lacquer thinner.

line of filler applied, which is pressed into the window holes. When this has dried, another layer of filler is applied and, once dry, is sanded smooth. This is just one way to fill windows and gives a smooth finish to the fuselage sides, ready for the window decals later.

The whole fuselage is rubbed back with gradually finer grades of wet and dry. When sanded wet, the finish is much smoother, not to mention healthier in terms of the dust released into the modelling room! And so, after a complete coat of Tamiya's Fine Surface Primer, the VC-10 is left to dry before being sanded back to a very smooth finish. She is to display the BOAC colour scheme and this requires the fuselage to be painted grey and white. Xtracolour's RAF Barley Grey is the closest match to the BOAC grey, with the white areas being painted straight from the Halfords' Appliance White spray can.

As previously mentioned, Halfords is the United Kingdom's chain of bicycle and car spares stores, and in recent years their range of acrylic spray colours in aerosol cans have been a big hit with modellers. Their Appliance White is an excellent alternative to 'modelling' paints: it gives superb coverage over a primed surface, dries very quickly and, being a very bright white, is just perfect for airliner models.

The next job is to apply the livery and the TwoSix decals are perfect in representing the, almost regal, livery of BOAC. The blue tail is represented as a decal, although the gold 'Speedbird' logo, proudly worn by airliners from 1932 to 1972, is supplied separately if you decide to paint the tail fin instead. Although I had doubts about the large blue decal, I need not have worried as it beds down beautifully onto the tail surface.

The remaining decals are placed on the model without any problems at all and the main airframe is, essentially, complete. Once again I decided to use a decal for the windshield as the kit part requires a lot of filling and sanding to get it to fit correctly, so this is just cleaned up and painted over and the decal applied.

Whilst the decals are drying, the undercarriage parts are painted, along with the wheels and tyres. The wheel wells are masked and sprayed a dark aluminium and, once dry, the separate undercarriage legs are cemented into their respective wheel wells.

A few smaller decals are applied and the model is then given a coat of Johnson's Future to seal the decals and give a good base for the Flory Models wash, the same as that used on the Viscount model, in order to highlight the hinge lines of the control surfaces. It does look a bit of a mess when applied, but after being wiped off with a damp piece of kitchen towel, leaves some nicely defined lines where the pigment of the wash has settled into the recesses.

A little treat, long since forgotten by the manufacturers, is the inclusion of a set of steps for the diminutive passengers to board the elegant jet. This

The windows are masked, top and bottom, with Tamiya masking tape.

Tamiya filler is used to fill the holes: after drying a second application is made; however, the putty doesn't have anything to press against as I have left the holes open instead of closing them up from behind.

The filler is held firmly in place as it is sanded.

Halfords' Appliance White is used for the upper surfaces.

The grey proves more difficult to match and after comparing references, RAF Barley Grey is chosen from the Xtracolor range.

A view that always reminds me of seeing the VC-10 at airshows as a youngster.

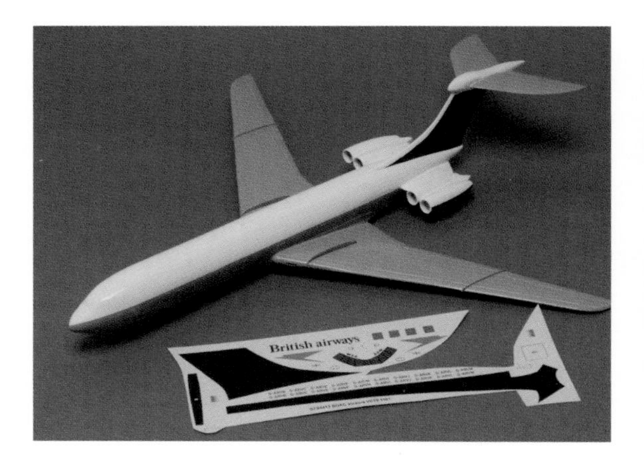

The TwoSix decals perform flawlessly, despite the large size of the fin decal.

The decals are left to dry whilst work is carried out on the undercarriage.

Tamiya tape is used to mask off the undercarriage bays.

With the undercarriage in place, she needs to sit upside down for a day to ensure the parts are fully dry before letting her sit on her wheels for the first time.

tiny model is constructed and painted in its own right in an appropriate scheme and, although the top of the stairs is far above the level of the entry door of the model, more appropriate to boarding a Boeing 747 than a VC10, they are a welcome inclusion. The VC10 is now finished and alongside my BOAC Junior Jet Club badge, still kept after my very first passenger flight on a BOAC B707, looks just as elegant as I remember.

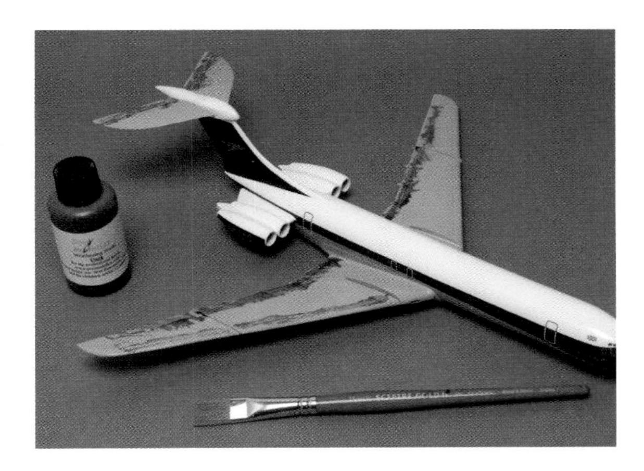

Flory Models' wash is used to create depth to the panel lines and control surface hinge lines.

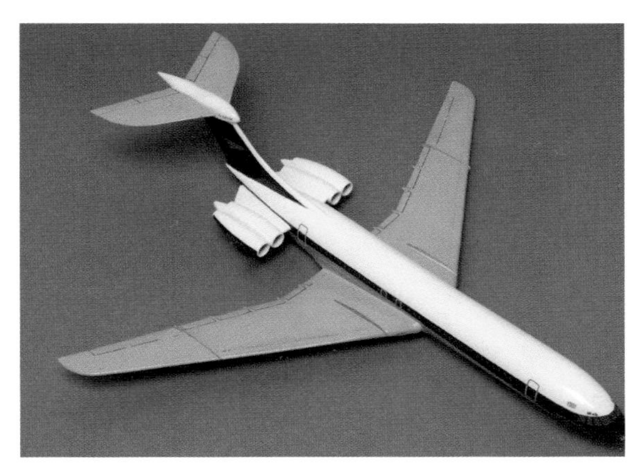

Having been weathered slightly with the wash, the model becomes more animated and less like a toy.

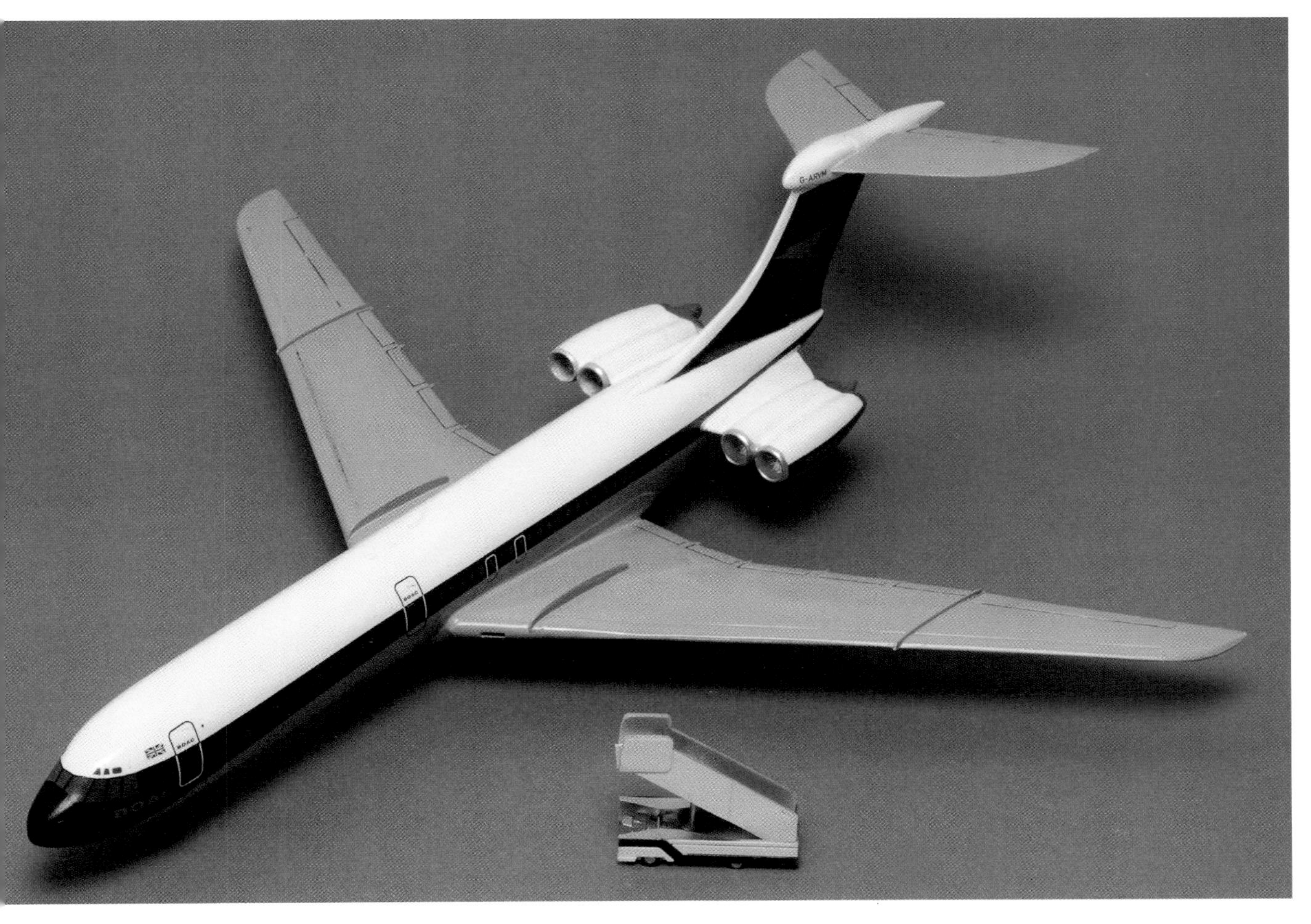

Having completed the model I cannot resist constructing the steps, although they are slightly bigger in scale than the kit itself.

CHAPTER 16

THE RUSSIANS ARE COMING!

ZVEZDA 1/144TH TUPOLEV TU-154M

It is the mid-1960s, the Cuban Missile Crisis, having happened just three years earlier, is still very much a recent memory; the world nearly was plunged into a horrific nuclear confrontation and the new vocabulary being discussed, really did include such phrases as: 'Mutually Assured Destruction'. Had I known anything about what was going on, I am sure that it would have been a frightening time to be growing up! Fortunately I was ignorant of the politics and, as the years passed, the spy movies certainly made up for my lack of knowledge with, what I was certain, was the absolute truth! Yes, there was an enemy and not very far away!

In 1981 I went on an overseas camp with the Air Training Corps to RAF Gatow, the airport in the British sector of Berlin. I saw Checkpoint Charlie and the no-man's land between the wire fences, making up the wall in the areas away from the centre of the city; I saw the turrets housing armed guards who were ordered to shoot anyone trying to escape to the west; I saw the concrete wall itself that made up the barrier within the city, and the memorial crosses at the side of the riverbank near the Reichstag building, commemorating those that had died near that very spot, trying to cross the river to a cherished freedom that they had only ever dreamed of.

To me the Cold War was a strange period as, whilst I fully understood the east versus west philosophy in Europe, I was also fascinated at the machinery that Russia was producing to sustain the military forces, particularly the aircraft. Yet they were all so very secret; it seemed that even wanting to take a photograph of a Russian airliner was a dangerous act, but they were so exciting to see as they just seemed so very different from the airliners of the west.

I joined the Royal Air Force in 1983 and during our own 'war games' there were two sides, Blue and Orange and we were left in no doubt that, had it not been such a sensitive topic, the opponents to the Blues would have been the Reds! So Blue and Orange it was. But gradually the Cold War thawed and the respective nations all shook hands and the former USSR divided into many, smaller countries. Now, once the domain solely of Russian aircraft, the livery of the Russian state carrier, Aeroflot, can be seen adorning Airbus and Boeing aircraft. The carrier also has orders placed for the Boeing 787 Dreamliner, how things have changed in such a short period of time! But the era when Aeroflot operated a fleet of Tupolevs, Ilyushins and Yaks, to me at least, all seemed to be so much more interesting.

Powered by three Kuznetsov NK-8-2 turbofans, the first Tu-154 made her first, noisy take-off on 4 October 1968. She became the main workhorse of the airlines of the USSR, as well as those within the Soviet BLOC. Over half of all Aeroflot passengers would have flown on a Tu-154. As well as being exported to many non-Soviet airlines, the Tu-154 was also used by many air forces and has remained the mainstay of Russian domestic routes until as recently as the mid-2000s.

Looking at the Tu-154 you will immediately notice the anhedral wings, as opposed to the more usual dihedral wings that most western built airliners have. This anhedral configuration was a common feature of Russian airliners built during this period. She was also very fast, and indeed still is, with only the Convair 990 beating her in the subsonic class; obviously nothing beats Concorde!

The undercarriage configuration is also of note as the main undercarriage legs each held a triple bogie of three pairs of wheels, each of the six wheels being equipped with low pressure tyres. This made the aircraft suitable for operating off rough landing strips and the operating envelope varied incredibly with operations to hot and high airfields, as well as those well within the Arctic Circle.

The engine configuration is similar to the contemporary Boeing 727 and Hawker Siddeley Trident and is a true workhorse indeed. Despite Aeroflot having now ended operations of the Tu-154, the type is expected to continue service with other carriers until 2016.

Yet, despite the popularity of the aircraft, we have only recently seen a good model kit in 1/144th, released by the relatively new Russian company, Zvezda. When I opened the box I discovered the exceptional runners of parts, all moulded in a mid-grey with a slight matt texture. The detail is of a very high standard and, on dry-fitting some of the parts together, I knew that this model was going to be a joy to build. The undercarriage parts are extremely fine and even the unusual green wheel hubs can be correctly painted, as Xtracolor has the correct shade, number X628 in their range and conveniently called Soviet Wheel Hub Green. In fact the wheels were started first as I just wanted to see how they looked with the green hubs!

The kit is supplied with a very nice decal sheet depicting three aircraft. Two Aeroflot liveries are included, one from the 1980s, the other the new current scheme and the third is one that was used by the Yuri Gagarin Cosmonaut Training Centre. My choice was the current scheme as it is such an attractive livery that does not seem out of place on this 1960s era jet.

The wheels are the first pieces off of the sprue and these, all fourteen of them, are attached to a cocktail stick prior to painting. When it comes to wheels I have two secret weapons; firstly a large blob of plasticine and secondly, a draughtsman's circle template. The former can be found at any toyshop and serves as a holder for the cocktail sticks to be stuck into; however in these days of computer aided design, the draughtsman's templates are becoming more scarce, but if you go to a good office supply company you should be able to find one or, alter-

The dramatic box art of the Zvezda kit also shows the three versions available on the decal sheet.

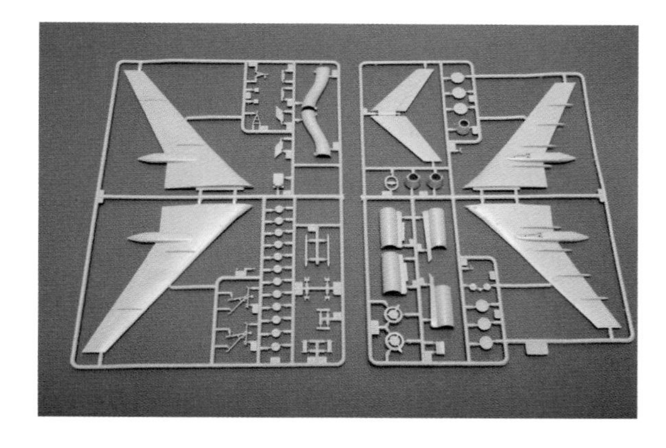

The trailing edges of the wings are exceptionally thin and the small parts exhibit a lot of detail for this small scale.

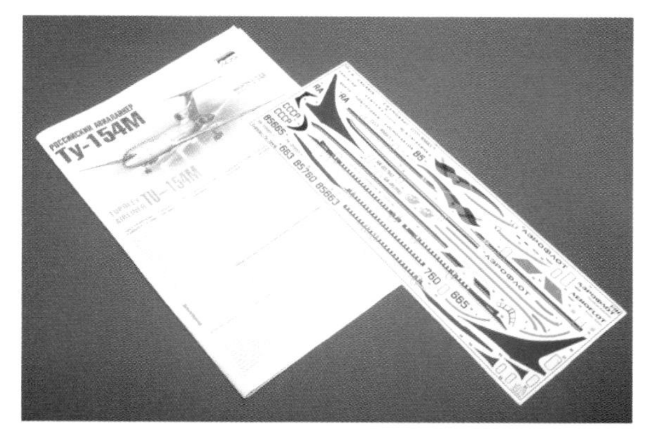

Three versions are available on the supplied decal sheet, although the after market manufacturers now offer many more options to choose from.

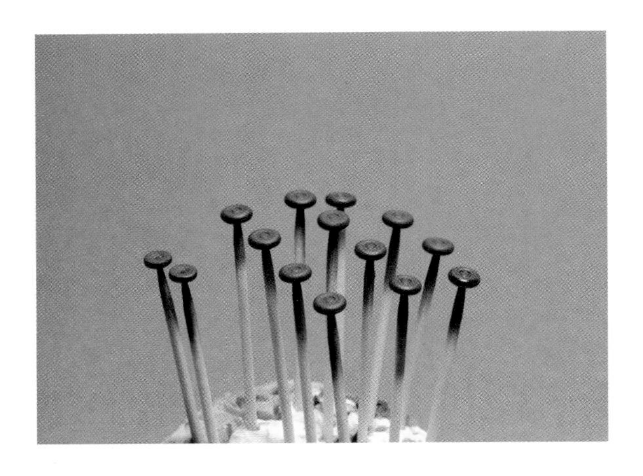

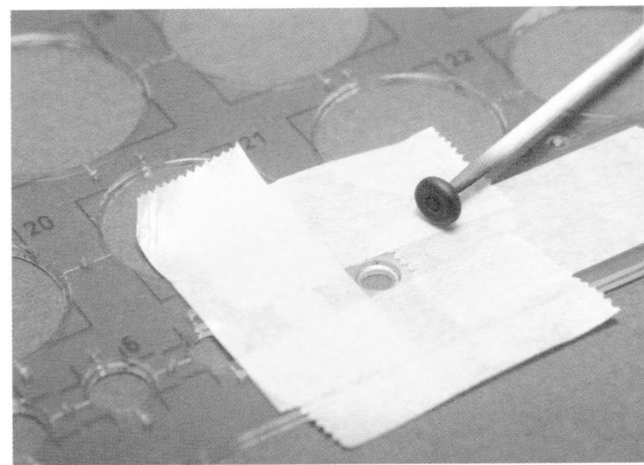

CLOCKWISE, FROM TOP LEFT:

The fourteen wheels are supported by cocktail sticks held in plasticine, ready for painting.

A draftsman's circular template is used to paint the wheel hubs.

Small plastic clamps are used to hold the two wing halves together.

All leading edges are masked and sprayed silver. The wings are shown here with the silver leading edges masked off ready for the main colour to be applied.

All rear-engined airliner models will be 'tail sitters': in order to avoid this, nose weight must be added before the fuselage halves are joined. Solder is used here and the entire fuselage interior is sprayed matt black.

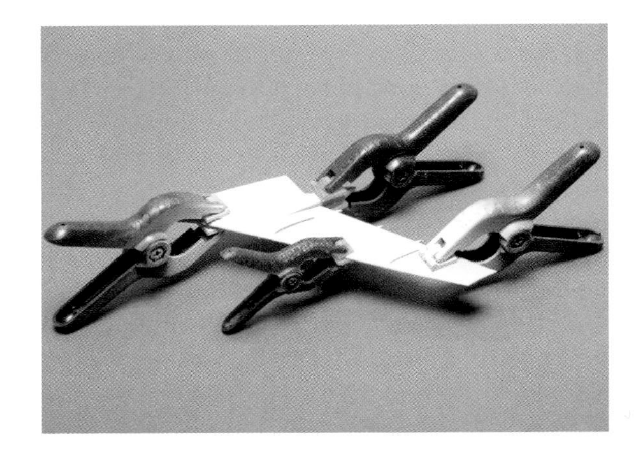

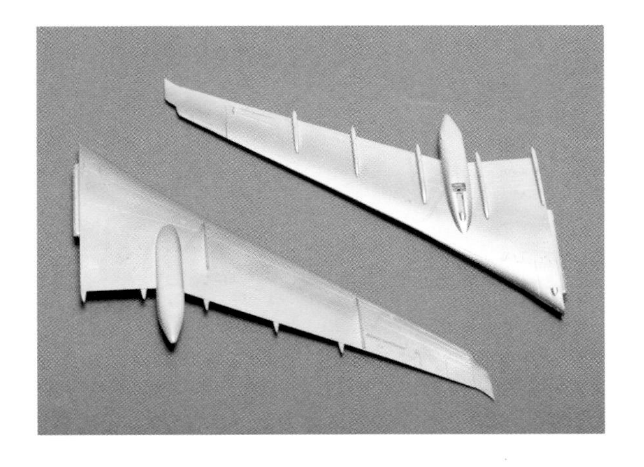

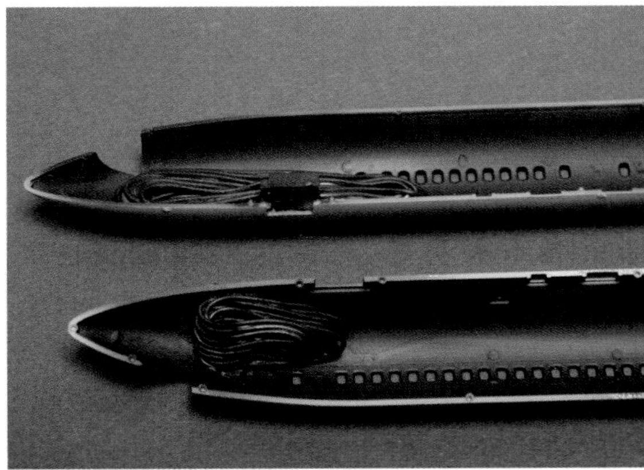

natively, look online. Rotring do a range and I would recommend getting the largest you can and with as many sizes of circular holes as possible.

The technique in painting the wheels is quite simple. Firstly spray the whole wheel a dark grey, representing the tyre. Never use black as the rubber is not that colour to begin with, if you don't believe me have a look at your car or bike! As the wheels have been attached to the cocktail stick, this makes it easy to hold them as you spray them, then, once finished, they are simply pushed into the plasticine to allow them to dry before the hubs are sprayed.

Once the paint has dried on the tyres, each wheel hub is carefully sprayed through the circular template. I always mask the area around the correctly sized hole and the wheel is taped to the rear side of the template, before spraying the green. This does give a neat finish and is a relatively quick way of achieving the desired result. After the hub colour has dried, you can then dab a small amount of highly thinned black paint into the wheel rim. This will naturally flow around the rim and give a nice tidy finish.

Having followed a few model builds so far, you will not be surprised to learn that this model assembles in exactly the same way. The wing halves are assembled, clamped together while they dry and then the correct wing tips are attached. Zvezda very thoughtfully provides the two different styles to represent an early or late Tu-154M.

The wing leading edges are sprayed aluminium prior to being masked to allow the rest of the wing to be painted light grey. The same process is followed for the horizontal stabilizers.

Although Zvezda includes the windows on a few clear strips of polystyrene, I had another idea: in preparation for the fuselage halves being joined, the interior is sprayed black and some solder wound tightly and adhered in the nose to act as a weight. The rear engine duct halves are assembled and this is then placed in the rear fuselage. This is such a great idea as the centre engine of many tri-jets is represented by nothing at all, just a gaping hole! So, full marks to Zvezda for providing a nice depiction of the inlet. Once the minimal interior work is complete, it is time to join the two halves of the fuselage and these

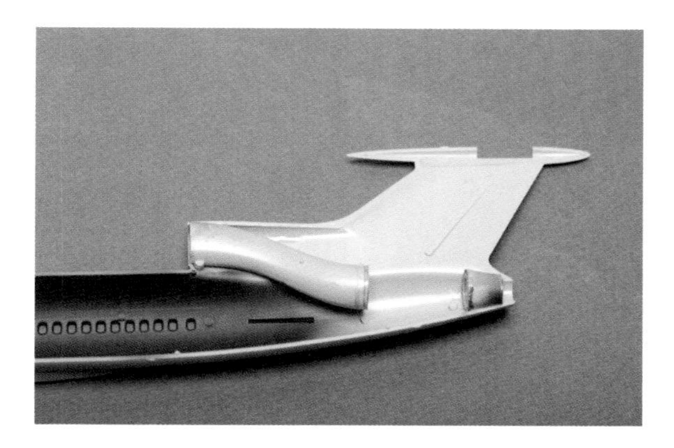

The centre engine intake trunking is supplied in the kit: a very nice touch.

The fuselage halves are joined using thin liquid cement and held together with the Berna clamps.

Similar to the Minicraft idea, Zvezda supplies the cockpit glazing as one large piece that can be masked, or not in my case!

With the extreme wing sweepback and those pods for the landing gear to retract into, she looks fast just standing still!

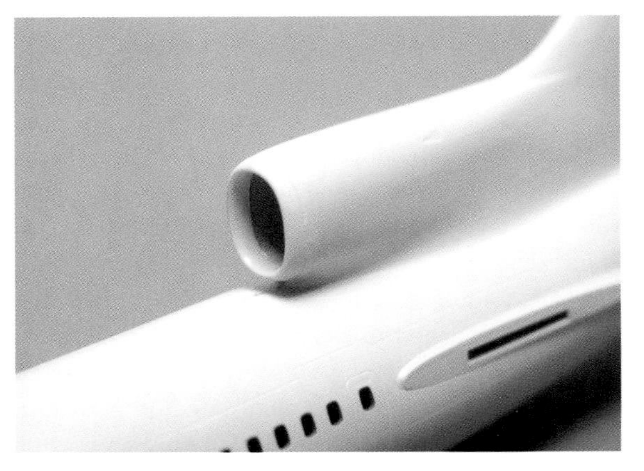

The completed centre engine, with the lip as one piece, doesn't need any further cleaning up.

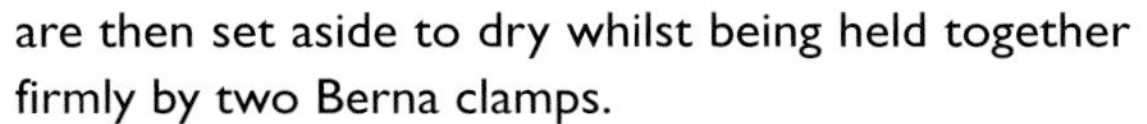

are then set aside to dry whilst being held together firmly by two Berna clamps.

In a similar manner to the earlier build of the Boeing 377 Stratocruiser, the cockpit windows are provided on one large, clear part. This is attached and left to dry and, with the wings test fitted, along with the horizontal stabilizer, the fact that this is one of the world's fastest airliners is evident by the sleek lines.

The centre engine inlet has already been mentioned, but the intake lip, being in just one piece, really does look nice as there are no apparent joins around the circumference, as there would be if the parts were supplied in two halves.

The new Aeroflot is very striking, being a dark blue fin and lower fuselage, with an almost pearly dark silver on the upper fuselage. Alclad Dark Aluminium is a good match for the metallic area, but the blue is a harder match. On searching through the paints in my cabinet, I found a very dark blue, produced by JP enamel, their number 15 Night Blue and this proved to be a good match to the photos of the original, as well as the Airbus A320s that are currently wearing the scheme.

The whole airframe is sprayed with Tamiya's white primer and when dry, is sanded smooth in preparation for the dark gloss blue, which itself would be a suitable undercoat for the Alclad II. The engine inlets are each masked with a small piece of sponge after which the spraying can commence with a vengeance! The air is thick with blue paint spray and the importance of a good, tight-fitting mask cannot be stressed enough. The model is then left aside for a day for the paint to fully cure and harden.

However, it turned out that a day was not enough! The paint was still tacky and so the model was left for a further twenty-four hours but the following day, the paint had still not hardened! In fact it took another four days before the paint had dried sufficiently and was hard enough to withstand handling and even then I did so very carefully! I hadn't been that careful though and I will always own up to my mistakes! In my hurry to spray the fuselage, I had forgotten to mask the cockpit windows and so these were irrecoverably painted over with primer! So another idea had to be thought of, but that would have to wait until later.

After the seemingly endless wait for the blue paint to dry, the next item on the agenda was to spray the upper fuselage. The decals supply the orange and red cheat-lines and the large tail fin flag conveniently separates the silver and blue, but there is quite a complex curve that needs to be masked correctly. So using the decals as a guide, masks are made from Tamiya masking tape and these are placed on each side of the fuselage. Once in place

The blue finish is achieved using JP Enamel's number 15, Night Blue.

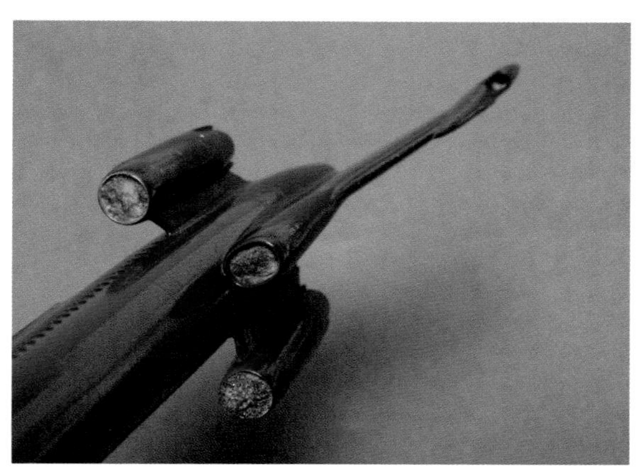

Although the blue is a good match to the original, it takes ages to dry! After it has eventually hardened, the engine intakes are masked off in preparation for their intakes to be sprayed with Alclad II Chrome.

The curve of the cheat-line is carefully masked.

The forward section of the fin and centre engine, along with the upper fuselage, is sprayed using Alclad II Dark Aluminium.

the Alclad II Dark Aluminium is sprayed, firstly in light dusting coats, before a final coat to give a nice even finish.

The metallic shade takes much less time to dry and decaling can commence the same day, with the masked line between the two colours matching the line of the decals perfectly. Finally the engine intake lips are carefully masked with thin strips of Tamiya masking tape and sprayed Alclad II Chrome.

The final details are soon all attached in place with the six-wheeled, main undercarriage looking particularly nice. I now decided to attempt a different technique to reproduce the windows.

Zvezda does supply the windows as clear parts, but masking these prior to painting would be a long and tedious job. There are a number of ways to depict fuselage cabin windows in the small scale of 1/144th, one of which is just to leave them open. But

All the decaling takes place over two days and is divided into left and right hand sides of the model.

The intake lips can be seen here after being sprayed with Alclad II Chrome.

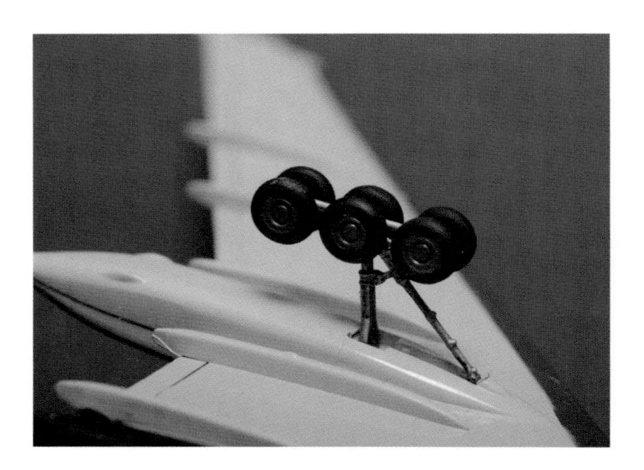

All six wheels on each of the undercarriage legs need to be attached very carefully to ensure that they all sit on the ground.

There is certainly enough nose weight added, as she sits firmly on the nose wheel and, rather miraculously, all fourteen wheels do meet the ground.

if you do want them glazed over, you can be assured that it does look better. There are various products available, all PVA-based, that are suitable and for this model I used a product specifically manufactured for the purpose of representing model window glazing. This product, called Formula '560' and produced by Pacer, a name more often associated with radio-controlled modelling, is a thick PVA adhesive that dries to a clear finish. This is perfect for placing in the window openings with a cocktail stick; you may be worried, as I was at first, that the white blob of glue will not become clear; however, give it a couple of hours drying time and you'll be impressed with the finish that you've achieved.

Having made a mistake with the cockpit windows, failing to mask them prior to spraying them, I decided to mask each window individually and spray them black. A tiresome job, but it was my own fault! The result, though, was worth the work and I am quite pleased with the outcome.

The final details are now added, including the undercarriage doors and the two prominent aerials

Applied by cocktail stick, the adhesive is initially opaque…

… but dries to a clear, almost transparent finish.

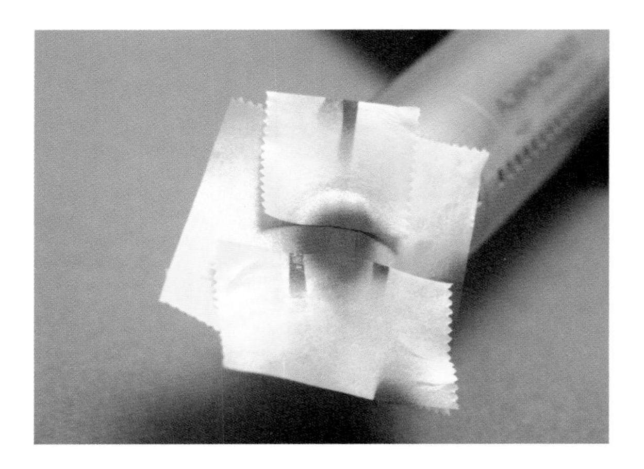

In my rush to complete the model, I've forgotten to mask the canopy glazing! So the individual glass panels are masked off and sprayed black.

After each window has been individually sprayed, I'm quite happy with the result.

on the top of the fuselage, which are made from thin plasticard. The aircraft now looks factory fresh and ready for its first flight, but that is not quite the effect that I want to achieve. With the help of Flory Models dark wash, the panel lines and control surface hinge lines are all highlighted and given a more used look. The Flory Models washes are water-based, brushed on roughly and then, after a few hours to allow the wash to dry fully, the resulting sludge is wiped off with a damp tissue, leaving the residue in the recesses. A messy start, but don't worry, the results are worth it!

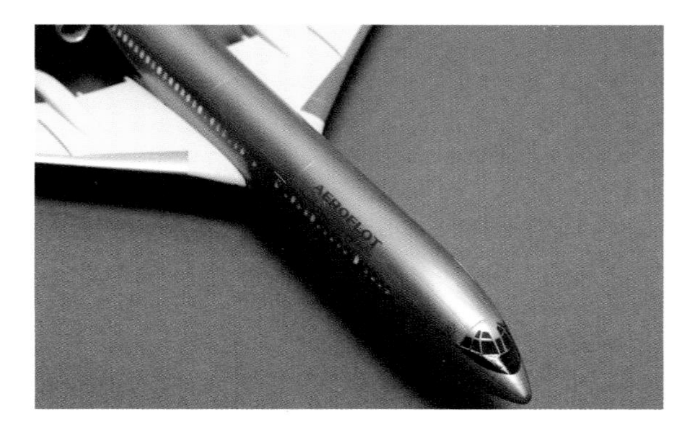

The cockpit windows after painting.

Dirtying up the kit with Flory Models' wash.

A simple base is chosen to photograph the model on. This is from the Verlinden range and is technically in 1/48th scale, but I think it contrasts nicely with the finished Tupolev.

And so with a roar of those Koznetsov turbofans ringing in my ears, the Tu-154M is finally completed and departs the modelling desk, bound for the display cabinet.

Zvezda have subsequently produced more airliner kits, including the best Boeing B767 in 1/144th scale. They have also notably been licenced by Boeing to produce the first model kit of the Boeing 787 Dreamliner. These are really lovely kits; do not be put off if you have never heard the name Zvezda before, I'm sure that in the near future the company will become synonymous with quality airliner models. In fact, the Boeing B787, produced by Zvezda, has now been added to the Revell catalogue, so you can be assured that these are superb kits.

If the Tu-154M was the mainstay of short to medium haul travel in the Soviet Union and the Soviet Bloc countries, then the equivalent in western skies must surely have been Boeing's small, twin-engined jet, which first flew a year earlier than the Tu-154, in 1967. Entering into service in 1968, the Boeing 737 has been a major success and is still in use today with many airlines around the world. So, let's take a look at the history and development of Boeing's baby jet, before taking a look at the aircraft in 1/144th scale and applying a most unusual livery on her.

CHAPTER 17

THE BEST SELLER

SKYLINE MODELS BOEING B737-300

When deciding which models to build for this book, there were so many choices I knew immediately that I was not going to be able to cater to everyone's interest; there were just too many models to build and not enough time, a perennial problem of mine! So I had to think of a way to incorporate as many historically important aircraft as possible, as well as different, lesser-known aircraft; which is where the idea of a timeline, a chronology of the history of commercial aviation came from. But even then, there were so many important aircraft that have made a significant impact and to include them all would be beyond the physical size limitations of this book. But as planning commenced, I immediately knew a few of the aircraft that would definitely be represented: the Douglas DC-3 was one of them and later I shall be looking at Concorde. Both of these, for very different reasons, have left their own mark on the history of aviation, as has this aircraft.

Boeing's single-aisle, twin-engined airliner is not particularly fast, neither is she very pretty, to the extent that there have been many unattractive nicknames given to the world's best selling airliner. Incredibly, the Boeing 737 is still in production today, forty-five years after her very first flight. Over the years, the B737 has changed in both performance and appearance, to the degree that she can almost be called a new type of aircraft. With high-bypass fan engines and blended winglets, the B737 almost looks quite handsome now, sitting on the apron amongst the more modern designs. Certainly the elegantly extended wings and longer fuselage have detracted from one particularly rude nickname! Nevertheless, that unmistakable, pinched nose (also seen on the B707 and B727) always gives the game away. Yes, she's forty-five years old, but still going strong.

The B737 was initially conceived in 1964 and it was just three years later, on the 9 April 1967, that the first variant, the B737-100, achieved her maiden flight. Entering airline service with Lufthansa in February 1968, the number of delivered Boeing B737s now exceeds 9,400 making the type easily the best selling airliner ever produced.

The history of the development of the B737 can easily be divided into four main versions. The Original Series were powered by the Pratt & Whitney JT8D engines and were mounted in long, thin nacelles, almost on the wing itself. These were the -100 and -200 aircraft and the last -100 was retired from service, with Peruvian airline Aero Continente, as recently as 2005. Only thirty of the -100 series were produced with the massive bulk of the 1,144 produced Original Series being the -200. The -200 was

The colourful box containing Skyline Models' Boeing B737-300.

so popular and successful that production continued for four years into the production of the -300. There are still many -200s operating, but noise restrictions mean that they are a rare sight at the modern and environmentally aware airports of today.

The next main variants looked very different to the Original Series. The second main group of variants, the -300, -400 and -500 aircraft, especially the -300 were the aircraft of choice for the more cost conscious airlines of the 1980s. The obvious difference to the earlier versions was the use of the CFM-56 engine, and with a much larger circumference cowl meant that ground clearance was an issue. With some modifications, including moving the auxiliary gearbox to the side of the engine and a reduction in fan diameter, the engine was enclosed in a new cowl that has a very distinctive, non-circular inlet with a flattened bottom lip. This series of the B737, destined to become known as the Classic Series, can still be seen everywhere as, between 1984 and 2000, 1,988 aircraft were delivered, with most of those still in service today.

It was the European manufacturer, Airbus and the serious threat imposed by their A320 series, that prompted Boeing to review the design of their aircraft and once again, a new, more efficient B737 was soon being developed. This series of aircraft, again numbered in ascending hundreds, the -600, -700, -800 and -900 was certainly the most significant upgrade of the aircraft as many major changes took place. These included an increase to the wing area by over 25 per cent, resulting in a greater fuel capacity and, when combined with newer and more efficient engines, enabled the B737 to fly trans-Atlantic services for the first time. Known as the Boeing B737 NG, or Next Generation, these aircraft now have optional blended winglets and advanced avionics packages and although, technically, a new aircraft design in many ways, the B737 NG retains many common features with the earlier versions.

But the story does not end there; the B737's life is far from ending with Boeing announcing the B737 Max Series that will be named the B737-7, -8 and -9. Once again it was the announcement by Airbus of a new generation of A320 aircraft, the A320neo, which prompted Boeing to look once more at developing a new twin-engined airliner. Initial studies did include a brand new type, known internally as the Boeing Y1, however it was decided to further develop the B737. The new CFM Leap-1 engine will power these aircraft and an initial order by Southwest Airlines for 150 confirmed, and a further 150 options, almost guarantees the success of the B737 Max Series for many years to come.

So, be it an Original, Classic, NG or Max, the B737 offers so much scope for the modeller in terms of airframe and airline schemes. The latter is well catered for, with an absolute plethora of airline schemes available as decals, but there have been only a few kits of the B737 that, given the huge success of the original aircraft, have not really done the subject any justice.

Airfix has a very old kit of the -200 Original Series. This can, of course, be converted very easily to a -100 with a few millimetres removed from the fuselage. This is definitely an Airfix 1960s release, as can be seen on the raised panel lines on the silver/grey plastic preferred by the British manufacturer. The model is essentially accurate for converting to a -100 and an early -200, but for the majority of operators, the wider engine pylons were used. So these need fixing, or after market engines using instead, such as those released by Bra.Z and, if you really want to be pedantic, the -100 and some early -200 also had stairs incorporated into the lower door frame. These extended out and down and were also fitted to the rear, left-hand side door of the B737-100. The result is that the rear left door of the -100 is slightly larger and this can easily be corrected, it just depends how you want to represent your own model.

The more recent series of the B737, the NG Series, has received attention from Revell, but despite the fact that the kit is a relatively new release, there is one glaring mistake: thankfully this can be easily corrected. As described earlier, the Classic Series has a distinctive engine profile with that flat bottom lip, but on the NG Series the engine cowl is round and that has not been depicted in Revell's kit, with the German manufacturer incorporating the Classic Series engine onto their NG kit. The competent modeller can easily re-profile the engine cowl, with some careful application of plastic strip, filler and some hard work sanding the cowl to shape. The lazy modeller (in which group I would probably count myself!) has the availability of a new resin engine from Contrails Models. So after-market or scratch build, the choice is yours in order to get an accurate NG Series model from Revell's kit.

But now, what of the Classic Series? It was in 2001 that Minicraft released their kit of the B737-300 and, whilst it did receive some good reviews, I always felt that airliners in general were not being treated to the same degree of care as the military aircraft were by the model kit manufacturers. This kit is a relatively simple build; however there is a slight, upward cant to the engine nacelles that makes the finished model look a little odd. Once finished she certainly looks like a B737 Classic, but I always felt that Minicraft could have gone a little further in producing a much more detailed model of such an important aircraft.

SKYLINE MODELS

Danny Coremanns might well be known to some modellers, but take the first two letters from his forename, add that to the first two of his surname and you get DACO. I am certain that now many more of you will be familiar with Danny, as DACO decals are amongst the very best and are certainly good enough for Revell to have chosen DACO to research and supply decals for more than seventy of their kits. On the civil side, DACO has produced beautifully designed and printed decals for exceptionally complex airliner subjects, such as Revell's Airbus A340 flown by Austrian Airlines in their Wiener Philharmonic scheme. It was not too long ago that subjects like this would never have been considered and we are certainly lucky that, with companies such as DACO, the more interesting schemes are available for us to model. But how best to display some of these stunning decal sheets when there is not a great kit of the subject to do them justice? Simple, release your own!

Thanks to the Belgian airline SABENA, Danny was given access to measure and record almost every component of the full-sized Classic Series of B737. Entering that data onto a computer to produce a 3D modelling programme, enabled the tooling to be made to produce an accurate injected plastic model. Skyline Models, a subsidiary company of DACO Products, released the B737 Classic Series family, comprising the -300, -400, and -500 variants but hurry, there are not that many left! The three kits are all very similar; it really is just the fuselage parts that are different, being different lengths depending upon the actual aircraft within the series.

The kit box is a quality item in itself, exceptionally sturdy and easily capable of protecting the finely moulded parts inside. There are many reviews of this kit online but one in particular calls this: '...an exquisite effort and a very valuable addition for the airline modellers' collections. This is a labour of love...' and I whole-heartedly agree.

The detail incorporated into these kits is at the same level that many manufacturers include in a 1/48th scale model, not one in the relatively diminutive scale of 1/144th. There is very good detail in the wheel wells and even the pitot tubes, essential on the full-size aircraft and actually quite prominent and noticeable on a modern airliner, are included on the sprues of tiny plastic parts. Confusingly the size of each B737 variant does not increase with the type numbers: to explain, the -500 is the shortest, the -300 is the middle one and the -400 the longest. But my chosen version was dictated by my choice of decals and these can only have come from the artwork of Danny Coremanns!

WESTERN PACIFIC AIRLINES

During the mid to late 1990s, the sky over Colorado Springs was bursting with colour. The 'logojets' of the short-lived Western Pacific Airline used the Colorado airport as their hub and, although they were not the first to use their aircraft as advertising boards, they were certainly the airline to do it on the largest scale! Normally we associate an airline livery with a splash of colour on the fin, maybe a cheat-line of matching or contrasting colours. But when you see a Boeing B737 with a half-naked lady adorning the fin and 'Sam's Town Casino' emblazoned in red along a gold fuselage, well, wouldn't anyone take notice? There were less exciting companies that advertised, such as Thrifty Car Rentals, but all of these aircraft certainly brightened up the airport apron wherever they parked. There were over fifteen of the Western Pacific logo jets painted up in the advertising of the aircraft's sponsor. My own favourite amongst these was that sponsored by Fox Studios, featuring the cast of the TV show, *The Simpsons*.

So now you probably know where we are leading to with this, as DACO have in their collection of airliner decals many of the logojet schemes worn by Western Pacific in their brief existence and yes, there is a Simpsons sheet. Not only is there a sheet of the WP Simpsons aircraft, but Xtracolor have also released the correct shade of yellow enamel paint. Now I have no excuse not to start this project!

KIT, PAINT, DECALS AND.... ACTION!

Despite this being somewhere towards the end of this book, it was actually one of the first models that I made; I was that excited about getting this one finished and I simply could not wait!

The kit is superb. There is nothing more to add really and this was recognized by the model receiving the 'Model of the Year, 2006' in the civil airliner category by the German model magazine, ModellFan. The plastic parts are very well moulded and show some lovely detail with fine and restrained panel lines. There is an option with the windscreen as this is moulded as an integral part of the fuselage or, if you wish, you can cut out the marked area and replace the solid plastic with a clear part that includes the windshield.

Of special note are the engines; these are made up of six separate pieces, with the fan and turbine areas being very nicely moulded. But the real treat here is that the engine cowl lip is moulded as one piece, along with the front interior lining of the cowl. It is hard to describe, but you should be able to see what I mean on the photograph, it means that there are no visible join lines in areas that are traditionally hard to clean up.

On the clear sprue are all the navigation lights, as well as the landing lights. As there are so many decals available for the B737-300, Skyline has just included a comprehensive decal sheet of stencils and generic markings, allowing you the choice of main livery.

There are no surprises at all in the basic steps to follow when building one of the more modern airliner kits: there are no interior details and following a simple process will allow you to quickly see the aircraft taking shape. This model is no different, with the exception that the wheel wells are separate parts and really do look much better than simple representations of this area.

Once the wheel bays have been installed the fuselage halves can be assembled together and, after an application of Tamiya's thin plastic cement along the fuselage seams, the two halves are clamped together and left until the join is solid.

In the earlier photo of the kit parts, you might be able to see that the wing 'tongues' that fit in the slots on each fuselage side have a 'jigsaw' type end. This allows each wing to lock into the other inside the fuselage and produces a very secure join. It also allows the wings to be attached after painting the fuselage has been completed, which is the next stage.

The fuselage is completed with the addition of the lower wheel bay and both main and forward gear bays are sprayed white; after drying they are plugged with small pieces of sponge prior to spraying the fuselage.

The main fuselage colour is, of course, a very bright shade of yellow, which is a notoriously difficult colour to paint on models: coverage tends to be poor and there is a tendency for it to be quite dull after drying. I don't know why this should be the case for different colours, obviously it is due to the pigments used, but yellow has always been a little challenging to get right. But, if you follow the next few steps carefully, then you should get a great result.

Firstly, it is important that the plastic parts are free from grease and mould-release agents. A simple soak in warm water with some washing detergent will achieve this; the parts need to be rinsed off and left to dry completely before any painting can begin. This is best done straight from the box, prior to any

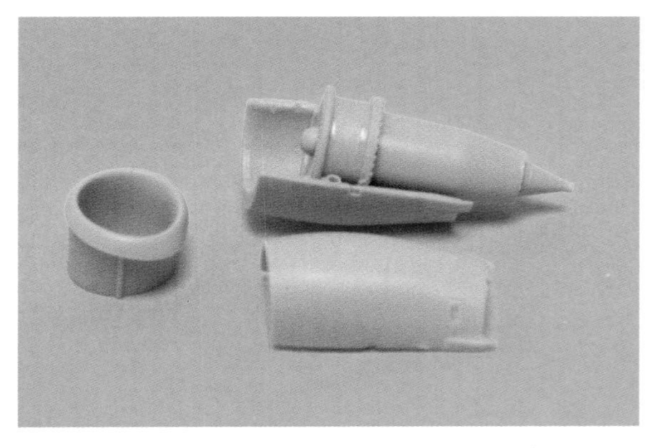

The multi-part engines are almost a kit in themselves.

The landing gear bays are supplied as separate parts.

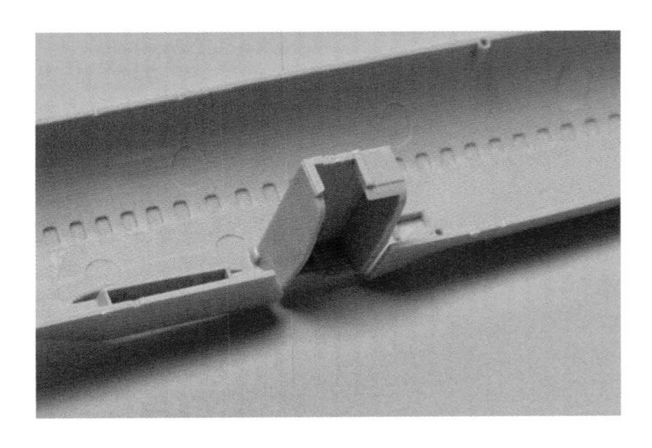

The partially complete airframe is very sturdy and strong once assembled.

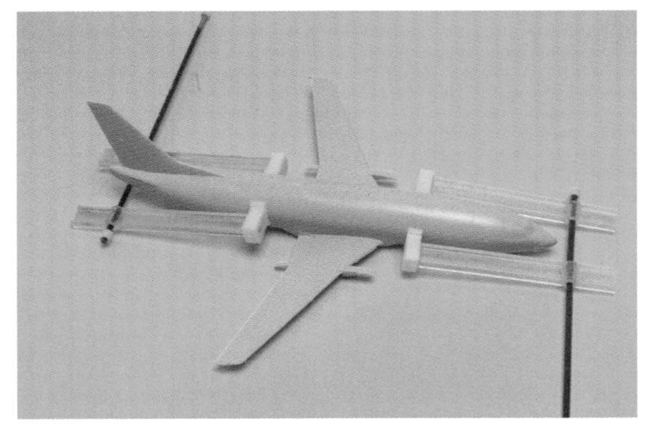

The partially complete airframe is very sturdy and strong once assembled.

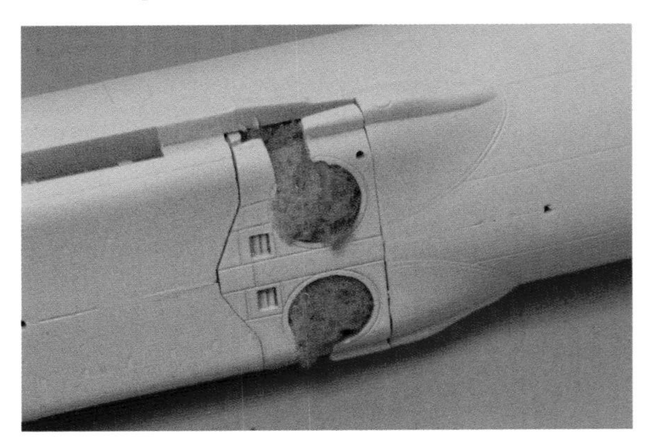

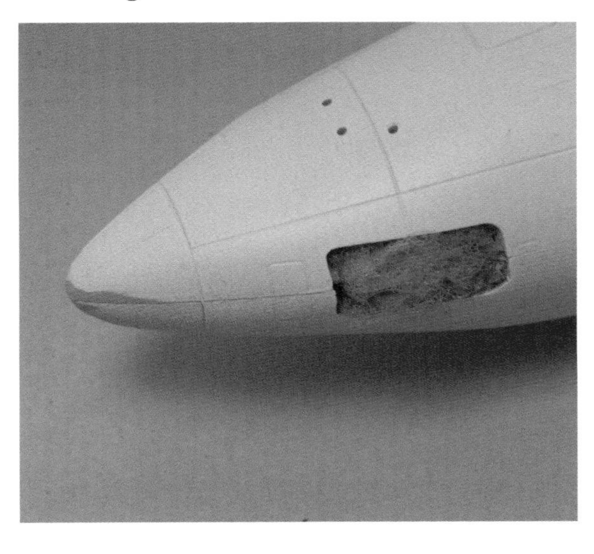

ABOVE AND ABOVE RIGHT: ***All the landing gear bays are masked off with small pieces of sponge.***

parts being assembled. When spraying any large area, a good primer coat is necessary and I use Tamiya White Surface Primer decanted from the spray can to the cup of my airbrush. White was chosen as, beneath the yellow, this will allow the top coat the best chance of a vibrant finish. Start by using extremely light strokes, just misting a little of the primer onto the plastic. Now leave this to dry a little before going over the model again, once more just dusting the surface with light coats of the primer paint. Finally, a slightly heavier coat will give a uniform finish that should be left overnight to fully harden. This process gives the subsequent coats of paint a better grip and the secret, as in any modelling really, is patience. By leaving the model overnight, the primer will be hard and fingerprint marks will not ruin your pristine finish!

Check over the model and make sure that there are no blemishes or runs, which should be sanded and re-sprayed with primer prior to the yellow topcoat being applied. On the nose area of my model, the join between the fuselage halves needed some attention so this was sanded smooth and primed again and left another night before being handled again.

The Xtracolor X316 Simpsons Yellow tinlet is given a good shake and then stirred thoroughly using a small, electric, hobby paint mixer. This is extremely important and the enamel paint is mixed, approximately 50:50 with Hannants' own brand of Xtracolor thinners.

Follow the same technique as when priming the model's fuselage: lightly dust coat first, allowing each coat to dry a little and build up the yellow finish slowly. Be very careful when handling the model now as the wet paint will show up any small fingerprint, so hold it between a pair of tweezers, mounted in a large chunk of plasticine and handle it as little as possible.

Patience and care give me the results that I am hoping for and, as tempting as it would be to dry fit the wings and see what she would look like, the model is put away, under the cover of a large plastic tub, similar to a Tupperware tub, and left for a few days before the next stage of assembly and painting can begin.

After about five days the paint has hardened sufficiently and is ready for those great Simpson decals. These are produced as individual characters and wrap around the lower fuselage. The whole process is relatively easy, but care, patience and some decal softener all play a part in getting the decals to sit correctly in place.

The first decal applied is the windscreen, followed by the main *Simpsons* characters. Once these are all finished, with Marge taking pride of place on the fin, they are left to dry again before the second decaling session begins, this time to apply the windows and stencils to the fuselage.

The wings and horizontal stabilizers are painted Boeing Grey, again from the Xtracolor range, and

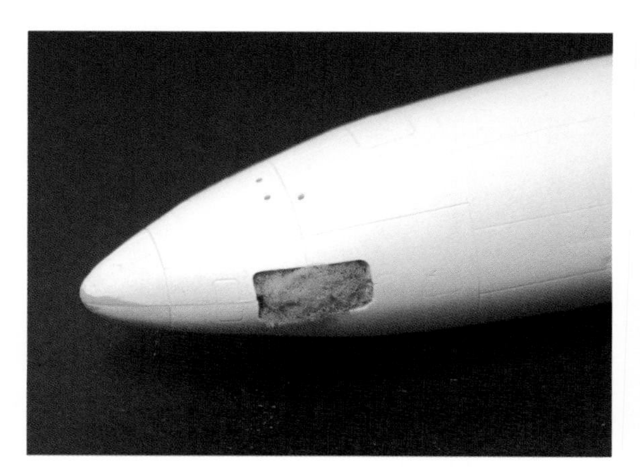

The nose area requires some extra work prior to painting.

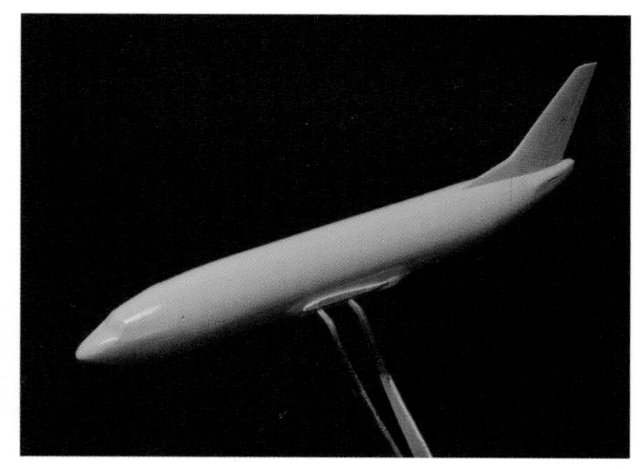

Having been first painted with a white undercoat, the yellow really is quite bright!

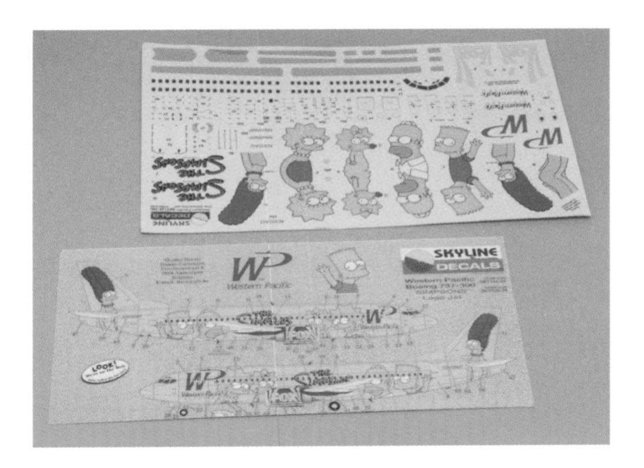

The exceptional decal sheet is quite daunting initially.

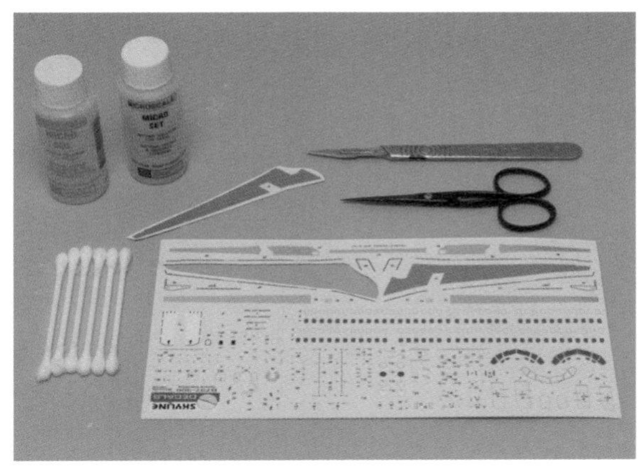

The upper wing Corogard areas are supplied as decals.

the leading edges sprayed using Alclad II Aluminium to represent the bare metal of the full-size aircraft. The bare metal areas are left unpainted on the full-sized aircraft, as they are areas of the wing that get heated by bleed air from the engines; this is so that ice does not form on the critical areas. Once the aluminium paint has dried, the inner wing panels are covered with the 'Corrogard' decals that are supplied with the kit itself. 'Corrogard' is a polyurethane-based, anti-corrosion coating that is applied to the wings and sometimes the horizontal tail surfaces. It most often looks like a darker, metallic shade than the wing itself, although it can be tinted different colours. The area of a model wing can be masked off and sprayed with Xtracolor X331 Corrogard, but many decal manufacturers supply the correctly shaped decal for a number of airliners. It is certainly easier to use the decal on a smaller model, however on a larger model kit I would probably prefer to spray the area.

After the decals have dried, the thin black walk lines can be applied along with the relevant stencils. I certainly find this a much easier way to build the model, having the wings separate from the fuselage makes them much easier to handle.

The decals are all applied using the Microsol / Microset decal softeners and, after all the decaling has been completed, it is time to have a look at the engines and smaller sub-assemblies that will complete the model.

As mentioned before, the engines are beautifully moulded and the fan cowl, being a single part, makes life very easy when it comes to cleaning up the seams.

The engine core and fans are painted in appropriate metallic shades and the interior of the engine cowl is sprayed dark aluminium, again from the Alclad II range. The engine cowl itself is a dark blue and proved hard to match from my own stocks of paint. I therefore went to the local hobby store and selected a few blues from the huge range of Vallejo acrylic paints on display. The chosen paints dry to a matt finish, but after a coat of Finish gloss acrylic floor polish, the desired result is achieved. It is just a case of selecting the right colour from the selection of blues: not as easy as it sounds. By matching swatches of the dried and varnished paints with the blue from the decal sheet the right shade was eventually found. To save you all time if you choose to make this model, I can confidently say that Vallejo 70930 Dark Blue gave me the best results. There, surely it was worth buying this book just to find that out!

With the engine cowlings sprayed blue and then sprayed with a coat of Future, these are left to dry before being assembled together with the front engine cowl. The fan blades themselves are dry-brushed with a lighter shade of metallic colour and then given a wash of highly thinned, dark grey oil paint, just to bring out the detail a little more. The overall result is very good indeed and far exceeds what can be achieved from most of the current other airliner models.

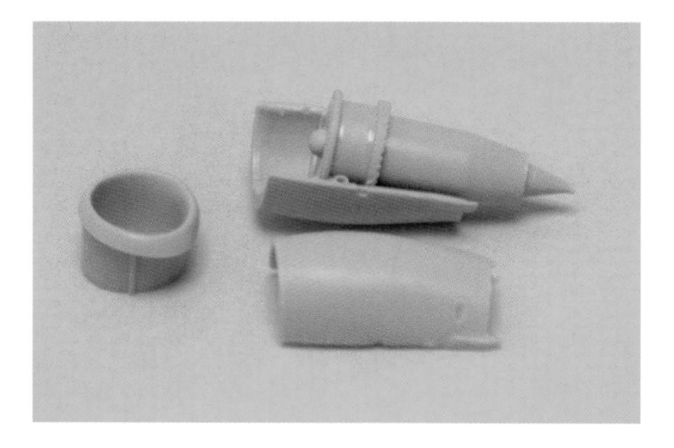

The multi-part engines really are almost a kit in themselves.

The engine fans and cores are painted prior to installing them in their respective cowlings.

The finished engine cowlings are masked with sponge before painting.

The Vallejo 70930 Dark Blue is a good equivalent to the original colour scheme.

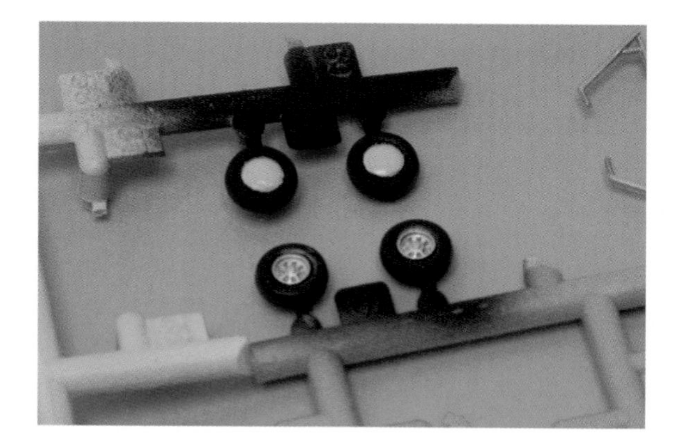

The wheels and tyres are painted in situ on the sprue.

The underside showing clearly how the Simpsons characters wrap around the fuselage.

The Skyline model kit includes such fine details as the pitot tubes.

At the same time, the wheels are painted. The B737 is unusual amongst jet airliners in that the main gear is exposed; there is no main gear door to cover the wheel and tyres, so the wheels are painted carefully in the correct colours, which are steel or magnesium for the inner wheels, whilst the outer wheels have yellow hubs to match the fuselage undersides.

At this stage we are very nearly there: the model sub-assemblies are all complete, the wings are attached, the horizontal stabilizers are adhered in place and the engine and landing gear are all completed and placed correctly on the model. The little and very colourful B737-300 is now ready to have the final details, such as the aerials and pitot tubes, attached.

This was a highly enjoyable build and a thoroughly recommended model kit to add to your own collection of airliners. Skyline Models and Danny should be congratulated on the release of this fantastic model: certainly one of, if not the most important airliner in the history of commercial aviation. It only makes me want to complete the rest of Western Pacific's colourful fleet of logojets!

CHAPTER 18

CORPORATE AVIATION

REVELL 1/48TH DASSAULT FALCON 10

One area of aircraft modelling that seems to be less well catered for is that of General Aviation, incorporating private and executive aircraft. Few companies have ventured into this market, with only a very small number of kits of light and business aircraft being available.

Minicraft, of the United States of America has produced some light aircraft; notably the single engined Cessna training aircraft, the C150 and its bigger brother, the four-seat C172. The Piper PA-18 Super Cub, a tail wheel touring aircraft from the late 1940s has also been produced. This was a development of the earlier J-3 Cub and can still be seen at many airfields today.

Airfix has released some aircraft kits, mostly in 1/72nd scale, that would attract the interest of the light civilian aircraft modeller. The British manufacturer has released kits of the Piper PA-28 Arrow and, although they are military trainers, the De Havilland Chipmunk and Scottish Aviation Bulldog have both been flying on the civilian register under private ownership. Venturing up to slightly larger aircraft, Airfix has also released the Handley Page Jetstream and Hawker Siddeley H.S.125 Dominie. Again, these are military aircraft kits but both aircraft have been civilian registered. One much loved British aircraft is the Britten Norman Islander and this too has been released as a 1/72nd kit by Airfix.

A new company from Yugoslavia, Gremlin Models, has very bravely ventured into the light executive, piston, twin-engined aircraft model arena with releases of: the Cessna C335 and C340, the C411, C414 Chancellor, C425 Corsair and the C441 Conquest. Along with the Piper Cheyenne and Mojave series, these resin kits will certainly look very attractive and very different amongst a collection of jet airliners!

Catering for the business jet modeller, there are fewer kits available. The H.S.125 has been mentioned already, but just a small number of other business jet aircraft have been kitted over the years, with Hasegawa releasing the Lear Jet, Cessna Citation and Falcon 10. Revell has reissued these kits and it is the latter kit, the Dassault Falcon 10 that provides the main subject for this chapter.

The Dassault Falcon 10 is just one of a number of executive aircraft that just look so very sleek and aerodynamic. In service with numerous private individuals, corporations and some military services, the Falcon 10 was developed out of numerical sequence from the larger Falcon 20. Two Garrett TFE731-2 turbofans, developing 3230lb thrust each, power the Falcon 10 which was first produced in 1971. Production ended in 1989, although the aircraft is apparently highly sought after on the used market.

Revell's release of the Dassault Falcon 10 in 1/48th scale.

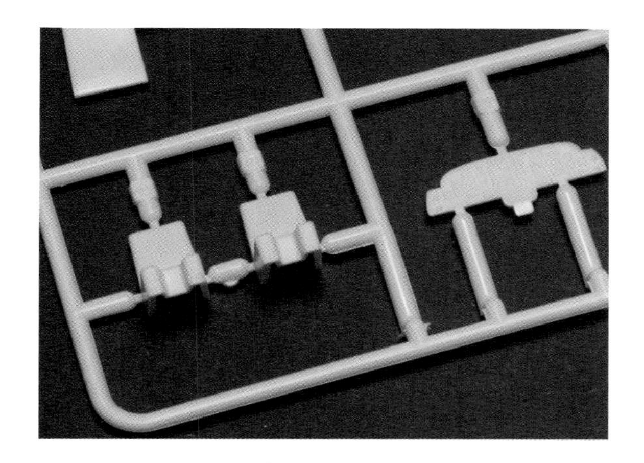

A cockpit is included amongst the parts.

The parts count of this particular kit is not very high at all and just fifty-four parts are presented on four sprues. The main parts are moulded in white polystyrene plastic and the clear parts are nicely represented in a slightly smoke-tinted, transparent plastic. Although this kit was of an older generation of Hasegawa tooling, with raised surface details as opposed to the more modern recessed panel lines seen today, the detailing is exceptionally fine. The kit has a simple, but nicely detailed interior that, with only a little enhancement, can be made into a very nice replica of the original.

While the kit provides colour recommendations for the interior, it should be noted that the interiors vary significantly, as third party companies often carry out the refitting of interiors, based upon the owner's criteria. Whilst you could do some research on the correct appearance of these aircraft interiors, you could also have just as much fun colour coordinating the interior as if you were the new owner of your very own business jet!

Getting back to the kit, the interior provided includes the flight deck and seating for six in the main cabin. One interesting error in the instruction booklet has you install the cabin bulkhead (part A6) at the front of the main cabin. In the next step, they have you putting the second bulkhead (part A7) into the same spot. But it's a simple remedy as part A6 includes the cockpit door, so that is the one that goes at the front of the cabin, with part A7 going at the rear of the cabin.

The exterior of the kit is also nicely detailed with the only option available being the main cabin door, which can be modelled in either the open or closed position.

MARKINGS

As with any business jet, there are a wide range of colour schemes you could apply to this model, ranging from the factory supplied finish, to the more exotic individual liveries. The kit provides two interesting examples:

- Falcon 10, N59CC, Dallas TX, Dec 2003 (the subject of the box art).
- Falcon 10 MER, #129, French Navy, Landivisiau, 2003.

What I especially like about the newer Revell/Germany releases are their decal sheets. These tend to have more options and more interesting subjects than their original Hasegawa issue counterparts. This is especially true in this case and the quality is assured as DACO Products of Belgium manufactured these decals.

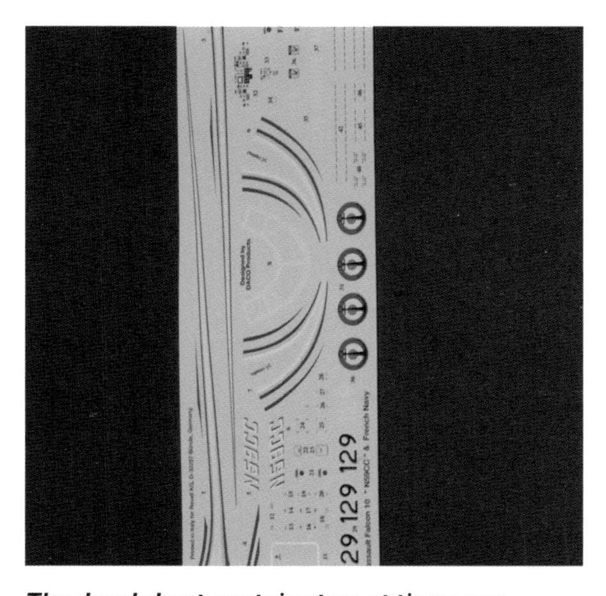

The decal sheet contains two options: one civilian aircraft, the other operated by the French Navy.

INITIAL CONSTRUCTION

The interior of the aircraft is constructed first and, as already mentioned, includes the cockpit and a six-seat interior. When completed, this will all be enclosed within the two fuselage halves and therefore a lot of extra work in super-detailing this area is wasted, as it will never be seen through the relatively small cabin windows. But after painting the respective parts and assembling them together, the seats could certainly benefit from the addition of some seatbelts, made simply from strips of masking tape that have been painted matt black.

I decided to give the cabin area cream leather seats with a deep red carpet, the flight deck being the 'standard' grey and blue. The instrument panel is supplied as a decal and the cockpit receives a small extra addition in the form of the throttle quadrant, which is missing from the centre console. This is made by sandwiching two very small strips of plastic together and then cutting two slices off of a piece of plastic rod, approximately 0.5mm in diameter. This tiny sub-assembly is then stuck to the forward section of the centre console and painted. It may not be visible through the cockpit transparencies, but I know it's there!

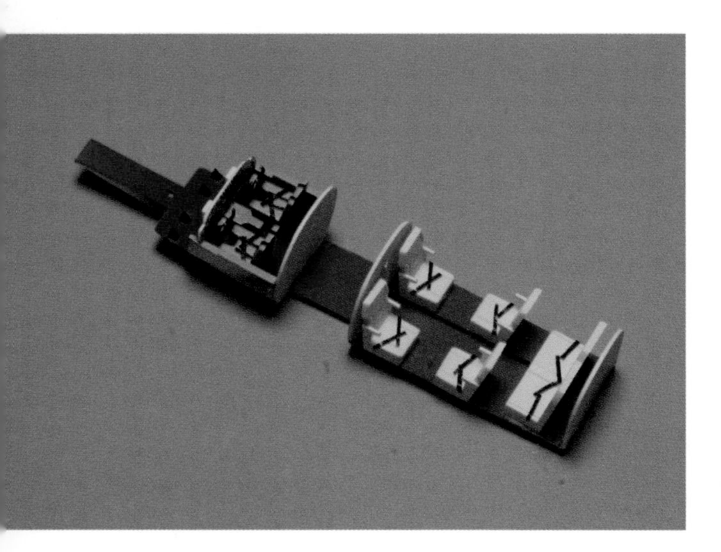

The interior can be further detailed with the addition of seatbelts made from black painted masking tape.

GETTING AN EVEN FINISH

The interior of each fuselage half is sprayed a cream colour, giving a fresh and airy feel to the interior, and the windows are adhered using very small drops of cyano-acrylate, or superglue. When using these adhesives with clear plastic parts it is essential to allow plenty of ventilation and use the glue very sparingly, as the fumes given off by the adhesive as it sets will fog the clear parts. The clear window strips are masked off on the inside, prior to spraying with the interior colour.

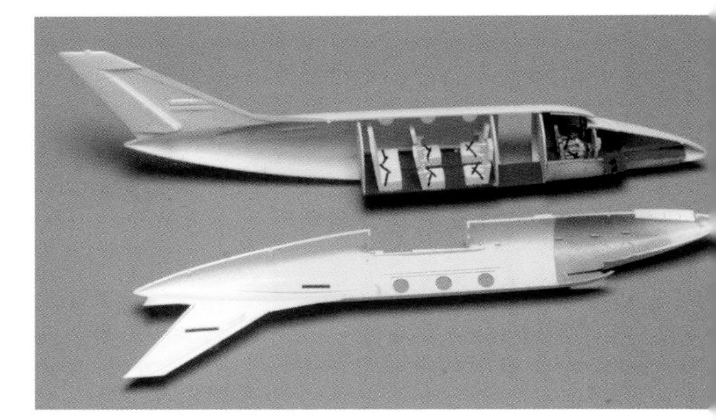

The interior colours owe a lot to 'artistic licence.'

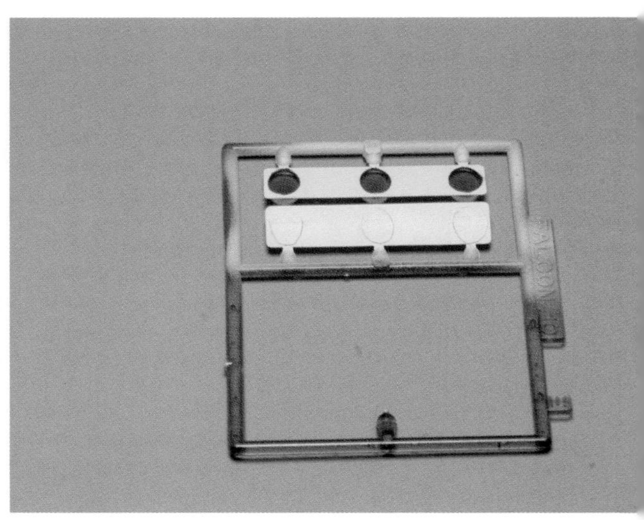

The interior of the cabin windows needs painting to match the interior colours.

After the parts have dried, the masking is removed from the windows and the result is exactly as I had hoped it would be.

With the two fuselage halves and interior complete, it is time to join the halves together but before doing so, some lead shot is super-glued into the nose area to stop her sitting on her tail once she has been completed. As always, it is at this stage that the kit starts to look like a replica of the original and, as she is going to be an overall white finish, the wings and horizontal stabilizers are all attached and the window areas masked before spraying begins.

The main area that I want to highlight with this kit is the careful application of the exterior colour. Being a private jet, she would have been kept in pristine condition and so the exterior is painted, first with a few coats of Tamiya White Surface Primer and allowed to dry before spraying the model aircraft with Halfords' Appliance White, straight from the can this time. Whilst this might appear to be a touch of overkill, with careful spraying and fast movements of the can as you go from nose to tail, allowing each fine coat to cure a little before applying another, you can achieve good results with the Halfords cans. Again, care and patience are your best friends here: do not allow the paint to build up too much when it is wet, otherwise you will definitely get runs and pooling of the paint.

After the final coat of white has been applied, the model is placed under a plastic container to allow it to dry fully and I can now turn my attention to the undercarriage. The wheels, being in 1/48th scale, are more detailed than the airliners that we have seen so far, and a little extra care to get the painted rim nice and neat against the dark tyre really pays off. I tend to use an artist's or draughtsman's circular template when painting the wheels and the technique is quite simple. Firstly the tyres are painted very dark grey and, once dry, are stuck to one side of the draughtsman's template, against the correctly sized hole for the wheels. The wheels themselves are painted by spraying through the hole and once the wheel has dried, a highly thinned black wash is allowed to run around the wheel rim. This gives a very neat finish and, of course, this technique is easily carried over to any type of modelling: be it military aircraft or vehicles.

The draftsman's template: in use again.

After the wheel has been painted very dark grey (tyres are not black!) the correctly sized hole is found, adjacent holes masked off and then the wheel is sprayed through the template.

The DACO produced decals are flawless in use.

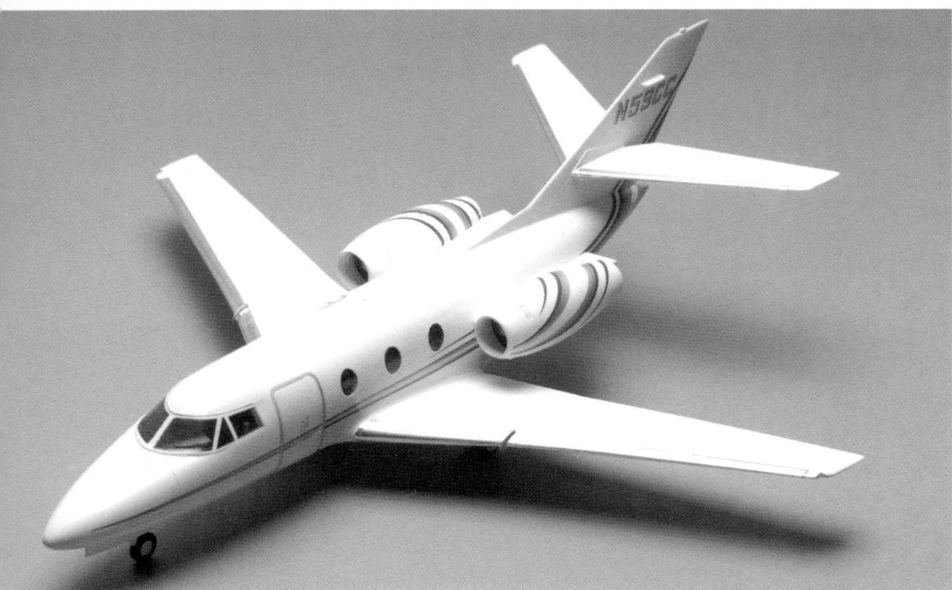

This is a very simple, but fun build of the Falcon 10: in the larger 1/48th scale the model can easily be detailed well beyond the basic kit.

DECALS AND FINAL DETAILS

As already mentioned, DACO are behind the decals and although the sheet is relatively small, the quality is excellent. It takes no more than an hour to get all of the decals placed and the little jet looks as pristine as I had hoped. A final coat with Future varnish gives the aircraft the realistic highly polished look she would have.

The masking is peeled off carefully and the undercarriage attached. Concerns that there was not enough nose weight to avoid the aircraft sitting on her tail, proved to be unfounded as she sat firmly on all three sets of wheels.

CONCLUSIONS

This kit was released in 2003 by Revell Germany but it is still readily available. I found this one on the sale rack of my local hobby shop recently. As Hasegawa continue to reissue their kits, normally with different decals, and Revell are re-boxing many Hasegawa kits as their own, finding the Falcon 10 in one form or another should not be a problem.

If you're looking for a nice aircraft subject that will actually test your scale automotive painting skills (gloss colours), and look really nice in one of those contest categories that see few entries, here is an excellent opportunity!

CHAPTER 19

SHE ROLLS... AND 002 FLIES!

REVELL 1/144TH BAC / AEROSPATIALE CONCORDE

One aircraft, above all others, remains right at the top of my list of those that I wish I had had the opportunity to travel on. I could ramble on forever about the sheer beauty of this aircraft; how elegant the design still looks and at the sheer power felt as the four Rolls-Royce / Snecma Olympus 593 engines, with full afterburner, accelerated the aircraft along the runways of Heathrow, Paris and New York. No, I was never lucky enough to fly on Concorde but, just like anyone else with a passing interest in aviation, this aircraft excited me like no other airliner could.

I last saw Concorde as I was taxiing an Airbus A330-200, operated by Emirates Airlines, on to Heathrow's Runway 26R, prior to departing for Dubai. The British Airways Concorde was behind us and I glanced back and thought how small she actually looked compared to the B777s and B747s that were also in the queue. But she had an elegance that the wide-bodies did not. I mentioned it to the Captain that I was flying with and we agreed that we'd donate a kidney to be able to be sitting where those two British Airways pilots were sitting. The date was 24 July 2000.

The following day I had a call from a friend who had heard news of an accident at Charles de Gaulle airport in Paris. We met and had an extremely sombre lunch watching the sad events of the 25 July unfold. An Air France Concorde had crashed on departure from Charles de Gaulle. A piece of metal had been flung up into the fuel tank by the main wheels as the aircraft departed. With fuel gushing out of the tanks and into the engine exhaust, this was quickly ignited and the aircraft, engulfed in flames, became uncontrollable.

The rest of the Concorde story is well known and this most graceful and historic airliner was retired by Air France on the 27 June 2003 and by British Airways on 24 October 2003. The final flight by Concorde was between New York's JFK airport and Seattle's Boeing Field on 5 November 2003, where G-BOAG joined the Museum of Flight's permanent collection.

However, in happier times Concorde created aviation history by becoming the first commercial airliner to fly supersonic: on 9 April 1969, Concorde 002, the 'British' Concorde became airborne for the first time. Brian Trubshaw was the aircraft's Captain and had already flown the 'French' Concord, 001. Raymond Baxter was the BBC commentator at the time: "And she rolls... Concorde accelerates... 50 knots perhaps... And Trubshaw has said that if all goes well he will turn a high-speed taxi run into a take-off... Rotate... All's going well and she's airborne... 002 flies..."

Thirty-two years later, in 2001, Jock Lowe was talking to the BBC and said he had vivid memories of the inaugural test flight from Filton: "It was on my twenty-fifth birthday. I was watching television, I had a private pilot's licence but I had not really decided to go into aviation. I saw that Concorde flight and thought, well, that wouldn't be a bad job." That has to be one of the greatest understatements in the history of aviation, ever! Of course, Jock Lowe ended up not only becoming the Chief Pilot of the Concorde fleet, but also British Airways' Director of Flight Operations.

There are many memorable anecdotes relating to Concorde, but possibly an insignificant one to many is one that I always remember. A television journalist was asking about Concorde and her significance and the interviewee mentioned that as an aircraft, she was referred to simply as Concorde, not The Concorde. No other aircraft that I can think of has had that privilege. We talk about the Boeing 747 Jumbo Jet, the Airbus something or other, even the Spitfire or the Lightning. But Concorde will always remain just that: Concorde.

MODELLING CONCORDE

As with the Boeing B737, such an important airliner has not really held the interest of the model manufacturers, with Airfix and Revell being the only two main companies that have produced kits of this supersonic airliner. Airfix have released a couple of versions of their 1/144th kit over the years, the prototype and the production aircraft. Revell have a very nice kit of the production aircraft that is quite a bit more detailed than the Airfix one and it is this kit that I have used for this chapter. The Japanese manufacturer, Doyusha, released a 1/100th scale model kit but it was based on the prototype and, although it seems to make a lot of money on Internet auction sites, is probably best avoided. Of special note is the 1/72nd release by Airfix of Concorde.

This is a big kit! I do have one in the collection of unmade kits, often referred to by us avid model collectors as 'The Stash', but I have seen these made up at various shows and competitions and they look superb. So, if you don't mind sharing your living room with a large model kit, then the 1/72nd Airfix Concorde is readily available. The kit is large enough to include features not normally seen in the smaller 1/144th scale airliners, such as a full cockpit, including the Flight Engineer's seat and panel. The fuselage is so long that the kit supplies this in three sections: the nose, middle and tail cone and the size can be seen when compared to the small tinlet of paint in the photograph.

However, we are sticking with 1/144th scale for my particular Concorde, but she is a very special Concorde indeed. First let's have a look at the contents of Revell's box, which, as you will have learned by now, is quite a standard format for Revell of sprues full of nicely detailed, white plastic parts. The larger components consist of the wings and fuselage sec-

Airfix has released a Concorde in both the 'standard' airliner scale, as well as this release, in the much larger 1/72nd scale.

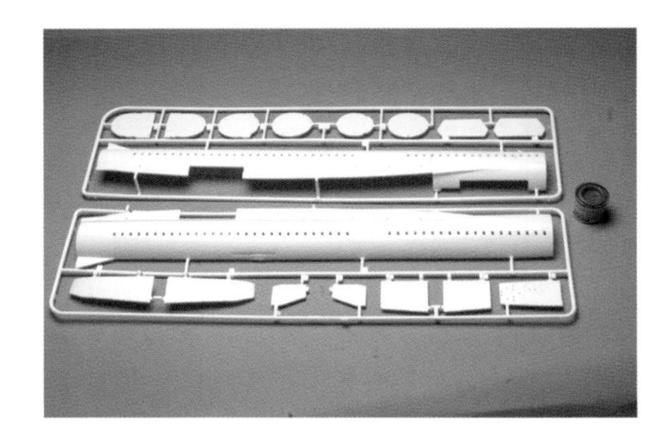

The fuselage in the 1/72nd kit is so long that it has to be split into three sections!

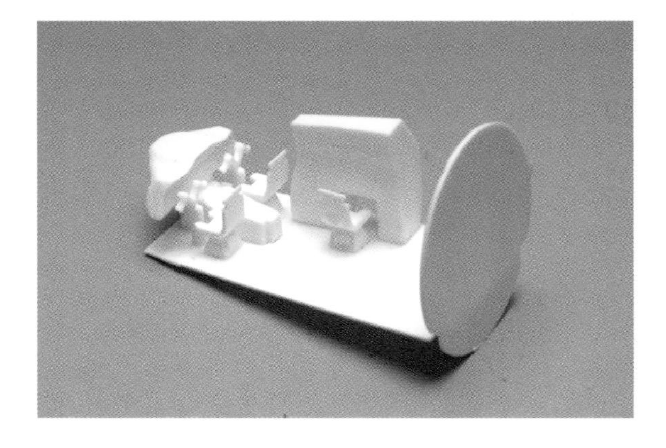

A nicely detailed cockpit is also included in the large model.

Revell has also released Concorde as a 1/144th scale model and this kit is the subject of this chapter.

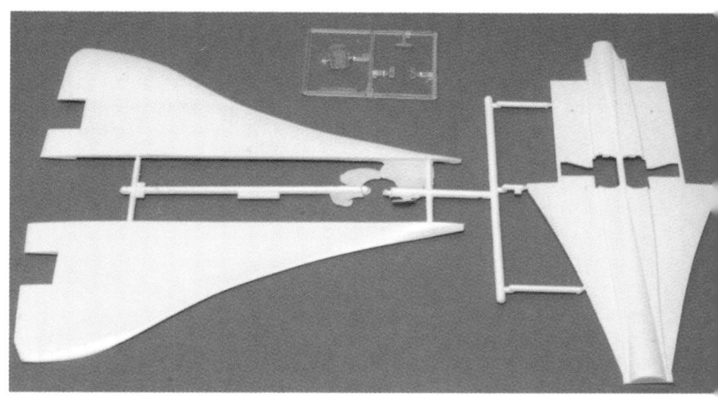

The Revell parts are moulded well, although there is a lot of flash to clean up prior to commencing building the model.

tions, with the remaining smaller details, such as the engine and undercarriage parts, all on a single sprue.

There are not that many parts to this kit, just sixty-seven in total, but I did want to make the best job I could of this kit and ordered the replacement engines from Bra.Z, which are a better representation of the Olympus engines.These resin parts simply slot into the nacelles provided by Revell and greatly improve this area. The decals include two British Airways schemes, the final Chatham Dockyard scheme as seen on the current BA fleet and the 'Landor' scheme, which to me is the definitive BA scheme. But my Concorde was going to go back a little further in time, in fact to the very late 1970s when British Airways flew a code-share route to Singapore via Bahrain.

A CONCORDE IN ANOTHER LIVERY?

Concorde is immediately associated with her two operators, British Airways and Air France. However, during her career she was actually operated by one other carrier. In January 1979, Braniff International leased Concorde from British Airways (thrice weekly) and Air France (twice weekly) on the Washington Dulles to Dallas Fort Worth domestic route. Although the aircraft were never branded in the Braniff livery, they did change ownership after arriving at Dulles and the aircraft were temporarily re-registered with sticky registration decals over the British or French registrations.

During her development she did attract interest from other carriers, with British Caledonian planning on acquiring two aircraft, representing the only other British carrier to have shown interest in the supersonic airliner. But significantly in her career, and for a short while in 1977 and between 1979 and 1980, British Airways (BA) and Singapore Airlines (SQ) entered into an early type of codeshare scheme on the route between London Heathrow and Singapore, via Bahrain.The flights were operated by G-BOAD and although the flight crews were from British Airways, the cabin crews were split fifty-fifty between BA and SQ. The aircraft was easily identified, as on the starboard side she retained her BA livery, but on the port side Concorde -AD was adorned with the livery of SQ.

This is my chosen scheme and, as modellers, we are so lucky to have a fantastic 'cottage industry', producing after market detail sets and decal sheets for subjects that the mainstream manufacturers are unlikely to cover. This is the case with the BA/SQ Concorde and, once again, it is TwoSix decals that have produced the scheme in, not only 1/144nd, but also in 1/72nd for the large Airfix kit as well. An interesting addition on the sheets is the inclusion of the American regis-

The decals are of the high standard associated with TwoSix and the colour density is superb.

trations that the aircraft wore when 'owned' by Braniff International on the US domestic sectors.

With the kit chosen, the Bra.Z engines on order and the decal sheet in my hands, it's time to start building the kit and, as you would expect, she goes together very quickly indeed. The nose area is assembled and sandwiched in between the two fuselage halves. I want to represent mine with the nose and visor up, so this is where the nose is glued in place. The two halves are assembled and the seam is given an application of Tamiya's thin plastic cement. Running along the seam via capillary action, the plastic soon

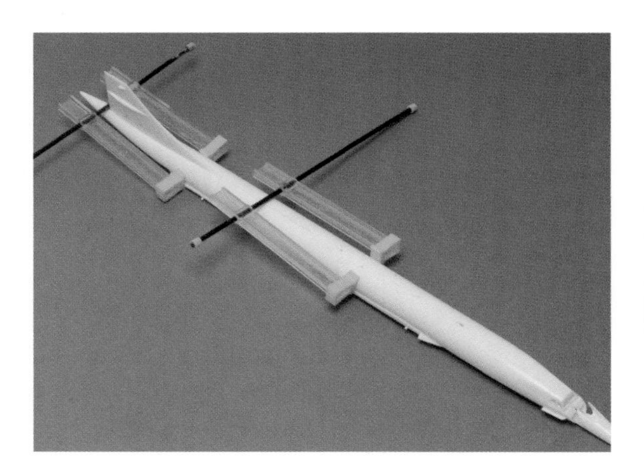

The fuselage is assembled in sections, first the rear, then the front, rather than attempting to do the whole seam in one go.

melts together and the fuselage halves are clamped together and left to dry for the rest of the day.

After the parts have dried, the wings are assembled and along with the windshield are attached in place on the fuselage. The upper fuselage seam is not perfect and needs a bit of filler along the length of it; once again it is the Tamiya products that I use in this case. Tamiya's plastic putty is fast drying and sands

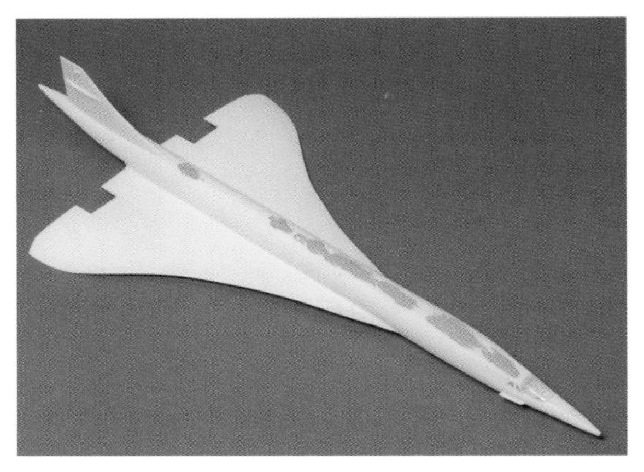

Revell's kit fits together very well, but to ensure a totally smooth finish, Tamiya filler is applied along the seams and sanded smooth.

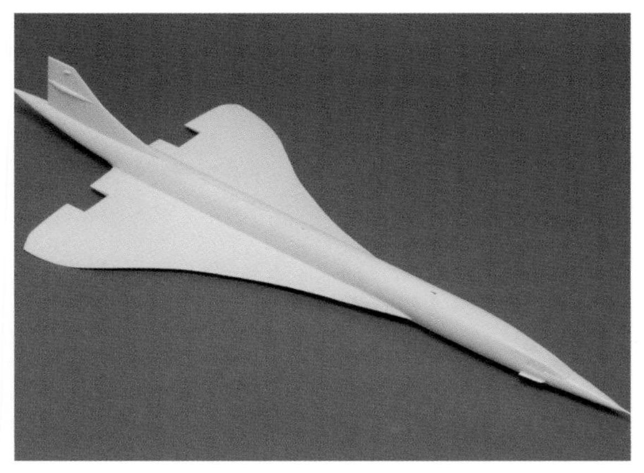

The basic airframe after a coat of Tamiya's White Surface Primer.

and polishes very well and is perfect for cleaning up gaps along any seam that needs attention.

Once the filler has dried thoroughly, it is sanded down using consecutively finer grades of sandpaper and given a final polish with a nail polisher. After inspecting the complete airframe for any other imperfections, she is given a fine coat of Tamiya White Surface Primer, which is followed by slightly heavier coats before a uniform finish is achieved. The final coat is once again the ubiquitous Appliance White from the Halfords spray can range. I say 'ubiquitous' as this spray can colour from Halfords really does seem to inhabit every airliner modeller's toolbox.

While the model is left to dry I turn my attention turned to the undercarriage and engines, which all come together very well, with no problems with the fit at all. The undercarriage could do with some extra detailing with fuse wire to represent the brake lines, but I will leave that level of detailing for a future chapter; however, straight out of the box, the wheels are not that bad at all.

Normally I would use the circular template to spray the wheel hubs, however on this occasion I am using an alternative method of spraying the hubs first, then masking them with circular pieces of masking tape before spraying the tyres. This also gives a neat finish, although I do find that the task is more tedious than using the template.

Prior to the final assembly I want to decal the aircraft, as the repeated handling will almost certainly knock the wheels off! When working with long lengths of decal strip, such as the cheat-lines on Concorde's fuselage, it can be quite hard to get the decals straight. One method to avoid the decal wandering all over the place is, prior to the application of the decals, to place a length of low tack masking tape along the area where they will go. This acts as a guide and helps to keep the decal nice and straight.

By working carefully along the fuselage and keeping the masking tape as a guide, the rest of the cheat-lines are applied relatively quickly and with a little help from the Microsol / Microset decal softeners, the decals settle down onto the painted plastic extremely well.

Revell's undercarriage components on all their 1/144th kits are very well moulded and nicely detailed.

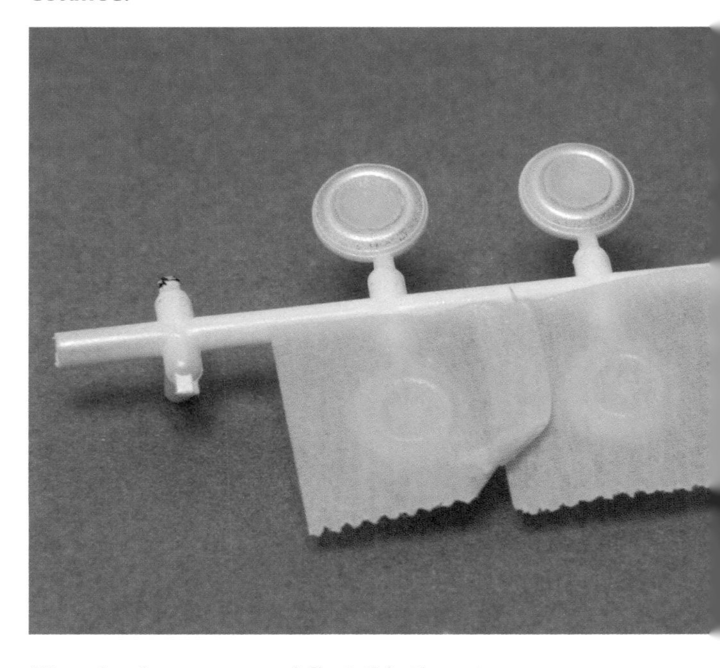

The wheels are sprayed first this time, to illustrate an alternative to using the circle template. Here the wheels are masked with circles of masking tape and then the tyres painted very dark grey.

The starboard fin; with the British Airways livery being applied.

The Singapore Airlines cheat-line is now nicely straight along the fuselage, thanks to the masking tape guide.

With the Singapore Airlines side of the aircraft complete, I simply turn the model round to work on the starboard side, with the British Airways decals looking superb, as they always did when seen on Concorde.

The only task that remains is to add the engines to the lower wings, glue the landing gear in place and carefully attach the nose mounted pitot tube. A final wash of the whole model is applied and for this I use the Flory Models light grey wash; this highlights some of the finer panel lines, without making them look ridiculous. Flory Models has a large range of model weathering products and they are so simple to apply: all you do is brush them on, let them dry and then wipe the surplus off with a damp piece of kitchen towel. But again, we'll look at more advanced techniques in a later chapter but for now, and after not very long at all, the model is complete.

Those that have seen my Concorde have always made comments about the dual livery; certainly very few of my friends and colleagues had any idea that this aircraft existed. It has also started discussions about the aircraft: her history and what could (maybe even should) have been, had Richard Branson's offer to buy the aircraft from British Airways on her retirement been accepted. And that is certainly a good subject for a 'what-if' build of this lovely kit!

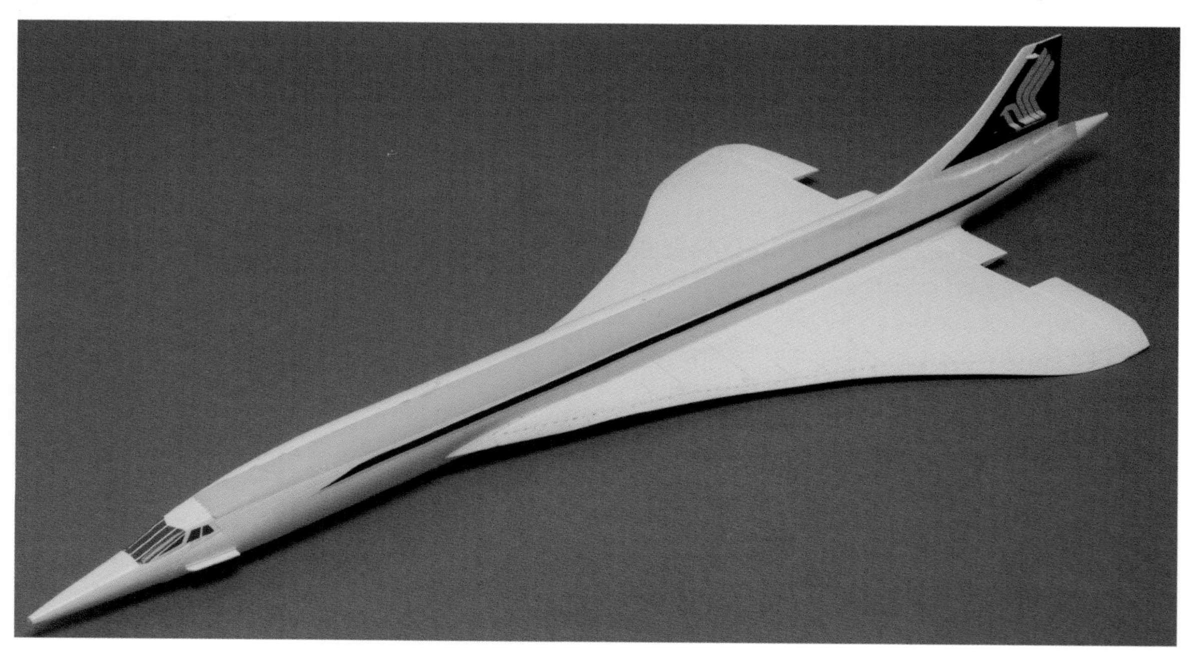

There are not many choices when it comes to Concorde's livery schemes, but this is certainly one of the most interesting: but then there's always the Pepsi sponsored one...

CHAPTER 20

A REGAL REGIONAL JET

REVELL 1/144TH FOKKER 100

This chapter contains a little more personal indulgence I'm afraid! When I take a look back at the airlines and aircraft that I have flown, probably the most significant step in career terms was when I boarded a rather bright, yellow and white, Boeing B767-300ER at London Heathrow airport. With a fourteen-hour flight ahead of me, I can still vividly recall the anticipation I felt: I was off to the Sultanate of Brunei to join Royal Brunei Airlines (RBA) as a First Officer on the Boeing B757 and B767 fleet. After three years flying around Europe with British Air Ferries on the Viscount turbo-prop, it was with incredible excitement that I contemplated, not only the countries that I would be visiting, but also the challenges ahead.

I spent nearly three years flying the wide-bodied B767 and the single-aisle B757 and had a fantastic time visiting, not only most of South-East Asia, but also the Middle East. Dubai became almost a second-home, as the long haul flights to London operated by the B767's all went through there. But I was spending more nights in a hotel room than at home and, although there is a perceived 'glamour' with long-haul flying, the truth is that it is extremely tiring and the jet-lag seems to be a continuous feeling; I would be coming back from one trip away and then recovering from the time zone changes, just in time to go away on another trip!

At that time, RBA operated a regional fleet utilizing the Fokker 50, the updated version of the Fokker F27. But, as the scheduled routes that this fleet operated increased in both numbers and distances, the company elected to source a small, regional jet. Swissair were disposing of their Fokker 100 fleet and it was not too long before there was a 'Notice to Crew', asking for volunteers to join the new Fokker 100 fleet. I decided that the lifestyle of being at home, more than being away, would suit me and just six weeks later I was once again a passenger on a B767, this time bound for Zurich.

Swissair's training was superb and we all quickly felt comfortable with the differences between the Boeing philosophy and Fokker's. The course, involving ground school and simulator 'flying', lasted eight weeks and, clutching my new type rating, it was time to get back to Brunei and start flying the real aircraft. Although the fleet lasted a very short time, just two years, I have very fond memories of flying the Fokker 100 around Borneo and beyond. It was great to go to work and be home for tea! The F100 itself was a delight to operate and as soon as Revell released a kit of the aircraft, I knew that I had to have one in the collection, although finding decals for the RBA

Revell has really cornered the market in modern European airliners. Here is the subject of this chapter: their 1/144th scale Fokker 100.

livery would be a problem, well, at least I thought it would be!

I cannot remember when or where I was, but I was looking through the range of decals in a model shop and there, amongst the usual airlines, was a set for the Boeing B767-300 in Royal Brunei livery! The set was produced by Flight Path decals and I immediately bought the sheet. On handing over my hard-earned cash, I commented that I would have loved a set for the Fokker 100, as well as the B757-200, to complete the RBA fleet. 'Hang on a minute...' the shopkeeper exclaimed as he disappeared behind the counter. Two minutes later he came back clutching the sheets that I had asked about. I left that shop with the widest grin on my face ever!

The Flight Path decals are very nicely printed and contain the relatively complex cheat-line, made up of four differing thicknesses of black and yellow stripe, separating the yellow undersides from the white upper surfaces. On the fin is a white circle containing the Brunei royal crest in a dark burgundy colour. The livery is striking to look at and represents a huge

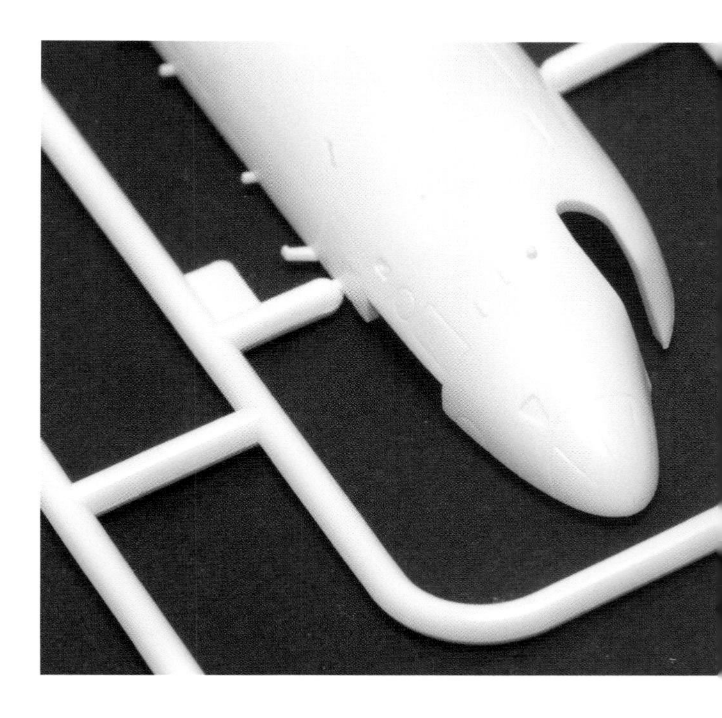

Revell has moulded the various antenna and probes in place on the fuselage halves.

A simple dry-fit shows how the final model will look.

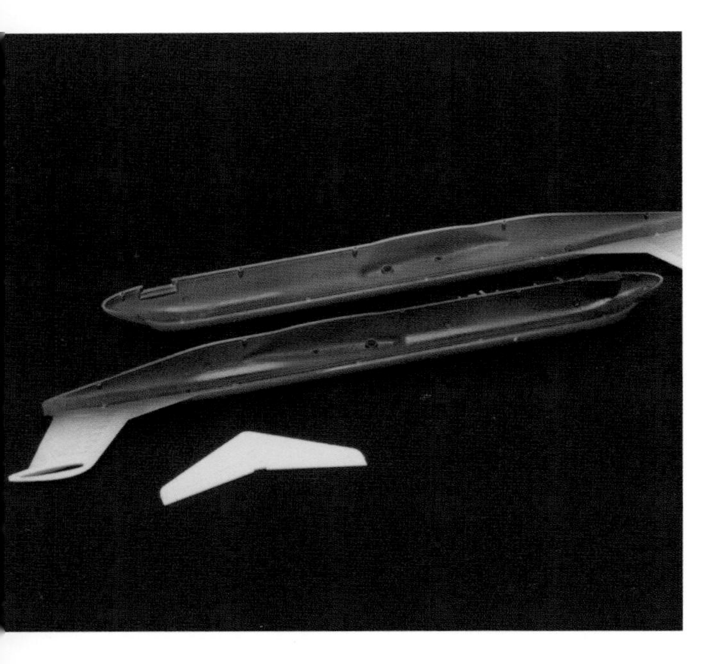

As usual, the nose weight is added and the interior sprayed black.

The window transparencies are easily masked prior to spraying.

improvement over the original scheme, worn by the leased Boeing B737-200s that were operated when the airline started. Incidentally, that original scheme is available on a sheet from Runway 30, should you want to create a complete model history of the airline.

But when is a Royal Brunei aircraft not a Royal Brunei aircraft? There have been many photographs online showing the different aircraft of RBA. But beware the fakes! The airline operated the B737-200 when it first started and the other aircraft that have been operated are the B757-200, B767-300ER, Fokker 50, Fokker 100, Boeing B777-200ER and the Airbus A319/320. There are photographs of a Boeing 767-200 and an Airbus A340-200 in the RBA livery, however these were operated by the royal flight and, in order not to appear too ostentatious, these aircraft were painted in the livery of the national airline, rather than in the individual schemes seen on many private jets. It did not take too long before the deception was uncovered and everyone in Brunei knew the real identity of these expensive royal family toys!

So, back to the model and this lovely kit of the F100 from Revell is in keeping with all of the manufacturer's modern airliner kits. Produced in white plastic, the parts are crisply moulded with fine details and the fit is excellent. A quick, dry-fit of the main airframe parts shows that this kit will fall together very quickly and the basic airframe is completed in less than a day. After the interior of the fuselage parts have been sprayed with an acrylic black-grey, this time from the Vallejo range, they are assembled and, once completely dry, the upper and lower seams are sanded and polished smooth. The model has some nose weight added and the windscreen is adhered in place. As I do not have a windscreen decal, the clear windscreen is left as it is, with just the clear panels being masked prior to the whole assembly being given a coat of Tamiya white surface primer. Once this has dried the whole fuselage is sprayed with Halfords' Appliance White and then left for a few days to fully harden.

The black and yellow cheat-line separating the two colours follows a straight line from the nose to the front of the engines, after which it turns upward in a curve up the fin. This line would be quite difficult to mask and Flight Path have, thoughtfully, supplied a paper copy of the cheat-line that can be cut out and tacked to the side of the fuselage in order that the correct position of the line can be achieved.

The model is first covered with masking tape, along the estimated position of the cheat-line, and then the paper copy is placed on top of the masking tape. The line is carefully followed with a scalpel, cutting into the masking tape. The lower part of the tape is then peeled off to leave the area that needs to be sprayed yellow clear. It is quite difficult to explain this process in words, so I hope that the photograph below shows exactly what I mean.

When spraying any two colours like this, it is a great idea to first spray along the masking tape in the original base colour. This seals the masking tape against any bleeding of the second colour and gives a very sharp finish. So, after a light coat of Appliance White has been sprayed along the masking tape and allowed to dry, a light dust coat of Tamiya's TS-47 Chrome Yellow is sprayed through an airbrush, having first been decanted from the spray can. Carefully building up the colour gives a dense and uniform bright yellow and, once fully dry, is unmasked to show a nice, neat demarcation between the two colours.

Prior to any further assembly, the decals are applied to the fuselage and this is done carefully aligning the cheat-line with the demarcation of the colours. The airline titles and national flag are applied, along with the registration mark.

The engines are assembled after painting the interior front fan and rear turbine areas and the nacelles are sprayed, first with the Tamiya surface primer and then Appliance White. After drying fully, the front cowl is masked and sprayed aluminium, with the rear 'hot' area of the cowl being sprayed, first magnesium, and then a light coat of stainless steel from the Alclad II range. The wings themselves are grey and, after looking for references as to the exact shade, I elected to use the Airbus Grey from Xtracolour.

With the undercarriage assembled, all that remains to be done is to attach the horizontal stabilizer, the wings and the undercarriage. The aircraft is given a light coat of Johnson's Future and, once dry, all masking is removed from the windshield.

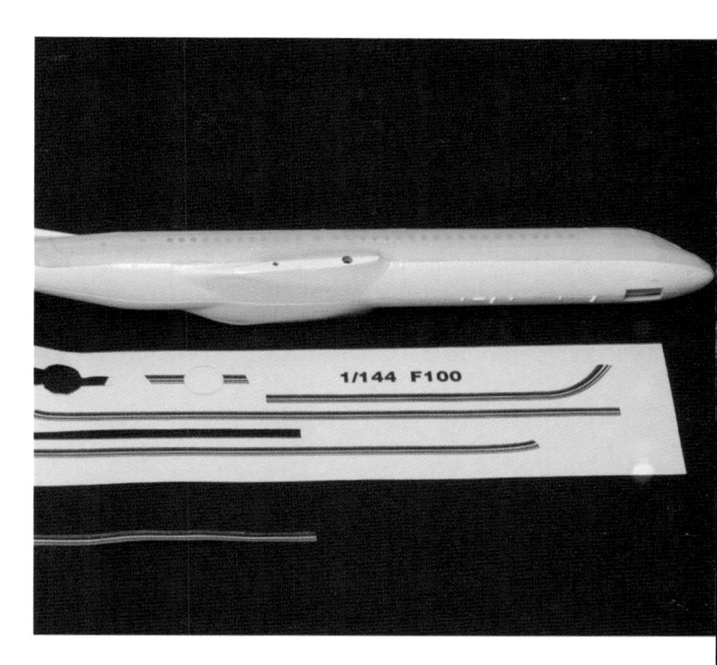

The cheat-line of Royal Brunei Airline's livery extends up the fin in a sweeping curve and needs to be masked carefully.

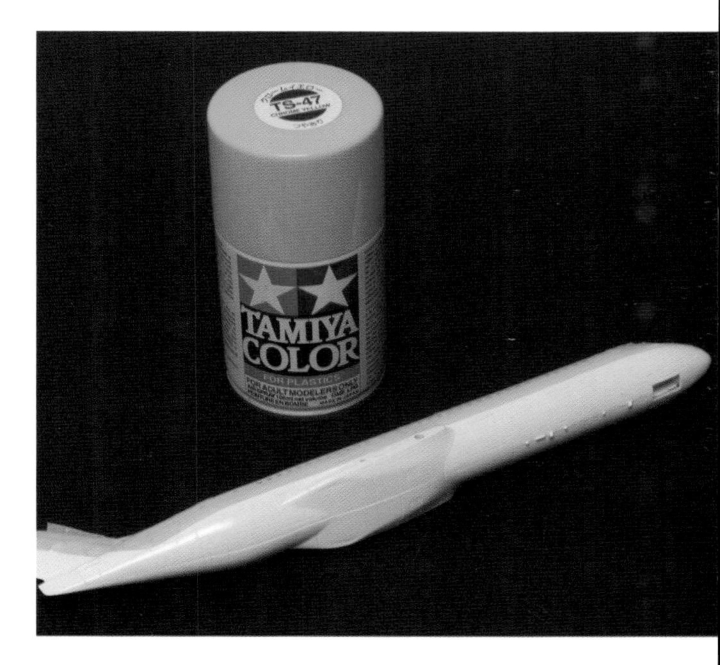

Tamiya TS-47 Chrome Yellow is a very close match to the original livery.

With the main painting complete, the model is ready for the decals to be applied.

Starting with the cheat-line, care and patience are needed in abundance!

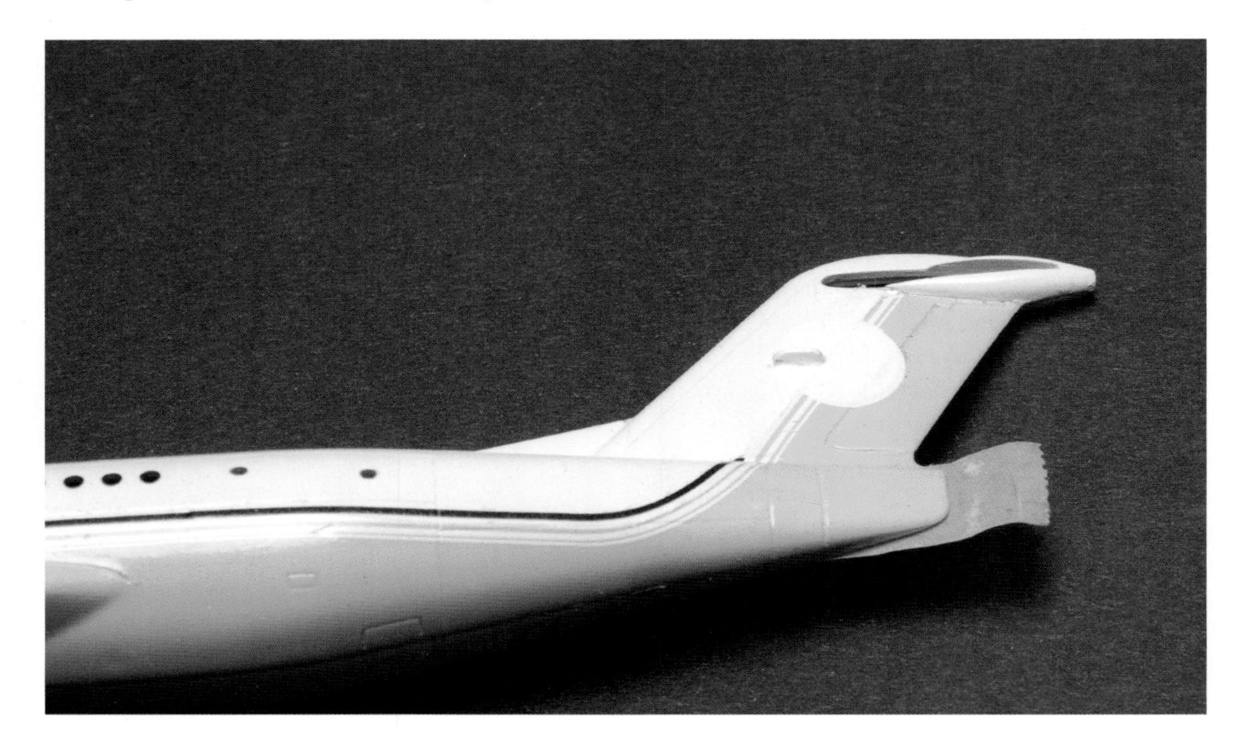

Revell has a large following for this kit and it now attracts quite high prices on the auction sites: hopefully Revell have it in mind for a re-release.

This is a very fast build and, at some point, I will do another as I did buy another set of RBA decals. These scarcer decal sheets have a habit of disappearing very fast and then reappearing later on the popular Internet auction sites at very high prices! There are some areas that I'd want to do more justice to: for instance, in my impatience to get this model finished I totally forgot the wingtip navigation lights! But if you want to start a simple first airline model kit, then this beautiful little kit would be a great place to start!

Despite the omission of the wingtip lights, my own airline career is slowly being represented in model form and that theme will continue in the next few chapters. But for the next chapter we stay with Revell and have a look at their superb kit of the Airbus A319. We'll also look at one area of 'modern' airline liveries that is certainly a trend at this time, with many airlines adopting 'retro' schemes on modern aircraft types.

CHAPTER 21

LET'S GO RETRO!

REVELL 1/144TH AIRBUS A319

I'm going to start off with an apology to anyone who is not a fan of Airbus, as the next few pages are almost solely dedicated to the European manufacturer. This particular chapter, though having an Airbus A319 as the main subject, takes a look at an area of airline liveries that has really taken hold and, although there are some retro liveries on Boeings: KLM has a B737 and Thai a B747-400 for example, the majority of European flag carriers have a retro Airbus in their fleet.

I am not really sure of the history of this trend, but someone, somewhere had a very good idea and decided that promoting an airline via a retro, or heritage livery was something that the public would like: they were not wrong! The launch of a new 'Retrojet' says something about the airline; to me it says that they are a company with a long and proud heritage and, naturally, this seems to work with the main flag carriers. The trend is also well established in the USA, with many of the larger carriers having an aircraft wearing a heritage livery. I would love to include a full set of photographs of all the retro livery airliners produced, but it's far easier for you to search online, just put 'retro livery' in the search engine. This will not only give any airliner fan hours of entertainment but also inspire some of you towards adding one to your collection.

The main kit manufacturers would probably not risk releasing a kit in retro schemes, but Revell has an established line of the Airbus A319/320/321 and these have been released in many schemes so far, including the Lufthansa heritage livery aircraft, D-AIRX. But it has mostly been left to the aftermarket industry to allow us the chance to create a model wearing a special scheme and in this case, once again it is TwoSix decals that have many such schemes in their catalogue. If you have a look at the TwoSix website, just put 'retro' in the product search field and you'll find many alternatives to the modern, current liveries.

After looking through the liveries available, I eventually chose to model the A319 of Iberia and just a few days later the decal sheet arrived. For me there is something very significant in the Iberia retro livery; it looks more military in its design and certainly depicts Spain's national carrier very well at a time when the country was under the dictatorship of General Franco. After the death of Franco in late 1975, Spain underwent a massive transition from its austere past and the country went into party mood, a party that lasted well into the 1980s! Many symbols of the Franco period were withdrawn and today a number of symbols from that time are banned, such as the coat of arms and the flag bearing the imperial eagle. A more colourful Spain emerged after the new constitution was established and the livery of the

The Revell A319 has been released in a few different boxes, with different liveries included.

national carrier, Iberia, was changed to reflect the country's new mood of 'Sun, Sea and Sangria!'

Revell's range of Airbus airliners includes all of the single-aisle aircraft, with the exception of the A318, but even that diminutive little airliner is a simple conversion from the A319 kit. The company has released the A310, A330-300 and the A340-200, as well as the huge A380. For real Airbus fans the A300-600ST Beluga has also been released, allowing the airline modeller something very different to have on display. The photo below clearly shows the size difference between the fuselages of the Revell kits along with the A300 released by Airfix, which is the fuselage with the open doors. The three models that Revell has released of the single-aisle family, the A319, A320 and A321 are very similar in presentation, but one simple fact should be known to the unwary and I'll mention this later; all I will say is that I should have known better!

The model kit boxing that I had of the A319 shows either, a British Midland International Airways, or a British Airways aircraft in flight and it was the latter kit that I used. However the engines that the British Airways A319s are equipped with, the IAEV2500, are different to those used by Iberia, who use the CFM56: thankfully Revell has provided the two engines in the one kit.

The Revell kit, although nicely detailed, is showing it's age a little with a lot of flash on the parts. This shows the age of the moulds and, although easy to clean up, does sometimes put modellers off, especially those who are used to seeing nice clean sprues of parts. But do not be put off, as the excess plastic is very easy to clean off the kit parts with a sharp scalpel or modelling knife and a sanding stick. I have certainly not experienced any reduction in the quality of parts fitting together where flash is present, so don't be worried when you do see it, just be careful when using the sharp blades to remove it.

Having chosen the livery and identified the correct parts to use, the modelling can now begin. The cabin windows are supplied by TwoSix as decals, so I started this particular build by filling the kit's windows with Tamiya Putty. This is a simple process and a long smear of putty is applied to the inside of the fuselage, then pushed through the window openings carefully and allowed to dry. The result is that on the exterior of the model fuselage you will see little 'sausages' of putty that can be cut off with a scalpel and then sanded smooth. A final thin application of putty to the outside can then be allowed to dry and sanded and polished and in no time at all you'll have blanked all the cabin windows off.

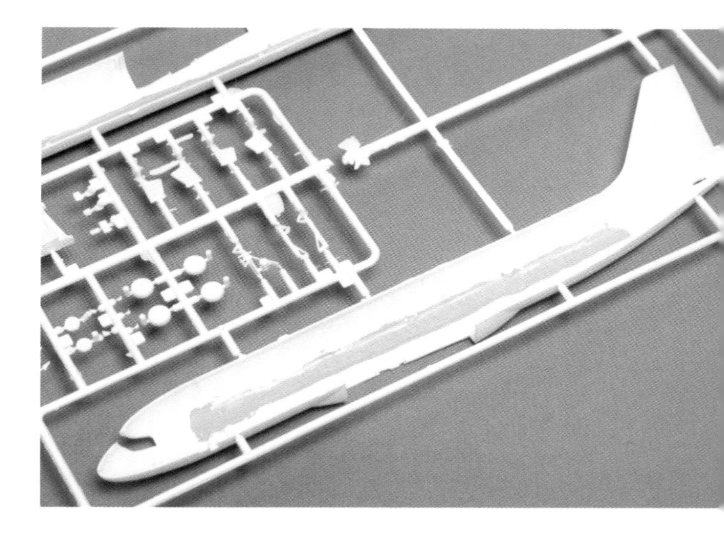

In order to close up the windows, the Tamiya putty is applied and pushed through the openings.

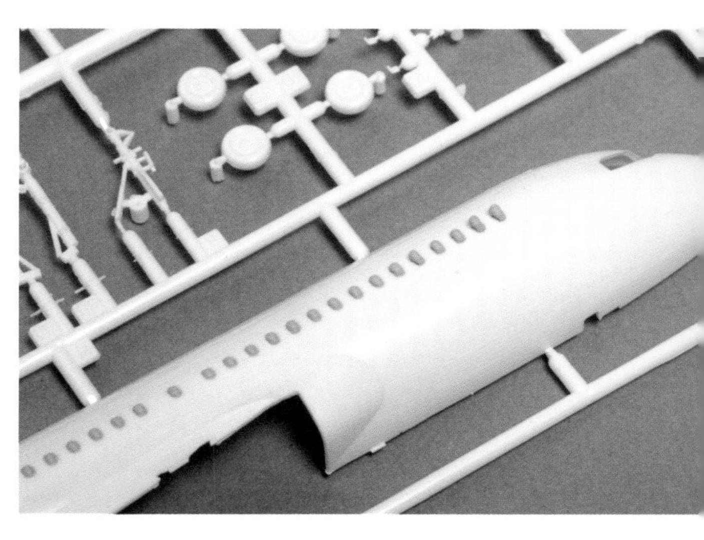

The resulting 'sausages' can be cut off and sanded smooth.

After the finely detailed nose wheel undercarriage and bay have been assembled, they are sandwiched between the two fuselage halves. The putty 'sausages' are then sanded smooth and any areas that need a little extra putty are attended to.

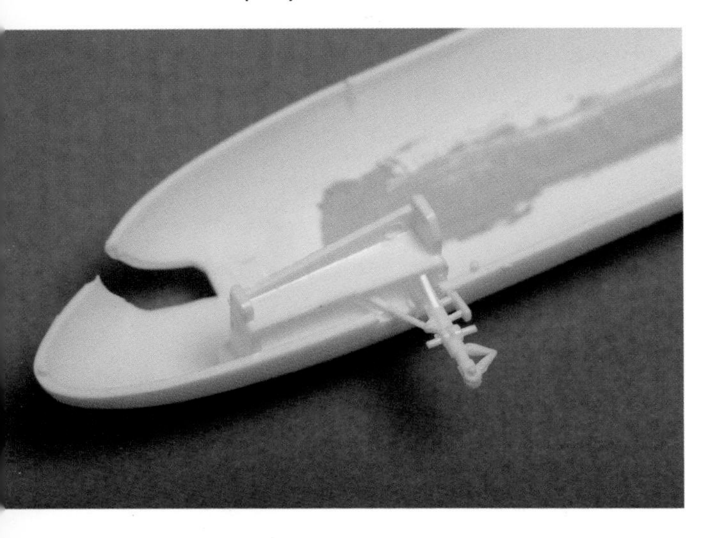

The nose wheel is especially well detailed and accurate.

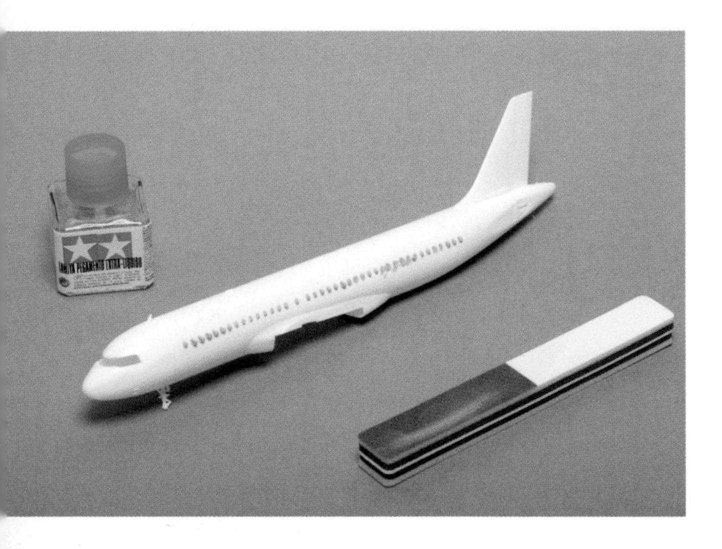

A three-way nail file is used to smooth the putty in the windows, as well as to sand the fuselage seams.

Once again, due to the engineering of the kit, the model is assembled very quickly and, after just a few hours work, the main components are all together and the aircraft looks just as it should, a miniature A319. Well, almost...

Painting is as described in previous chapters, with the usual combination of Tamiya Surface Primer, sanded smooth with fine grade sanding cloths followed by Halfords' Appliance White. The upper surface of the fuselage is masked off and then the lower fuselage, wings and horizontal stabilizer are sprayed grey. I did initially use the Airbus Grey from Xtracolour's range, but this was far too light in my opinion and after comparing the range of paints that I had with photos of the real aircraft, I eventually chose Xtracolour RAF Light Aircraft Grey, X015. This certainly seems to be more in keeping with her military or government livery, although could only be claimed as artistic license on my part!

As described before, after masking the white upper surfaces, another careful application of white paint from the airbrush along the edge of the masking tape seals it and stops the grey paint from bleeding under and spoiling the demarcation line. After that has dried, the grey can be safely painted and the model left aside to dry. At this point it is so tempting to remove the masking but experience has taught me that it is always best to just leave it alone; I have fingerprints all over some of my models to prove it!

Although it takes just a few hours for the grey paint to be dry to the touch, it takes another two days to harden and it is then that the masking is removed to reveal a very neat edge between the two colours.

The model, now basically complete and ready for decaling still does not look quite right and I can't put my finger on the reason. There is something wrong with the way the wings look. Oh well, time for the decals.

As we've seen already, the TwoSix decals are exceptional and really well designed and printed. The decals are applied in the normal way with no need for any decal softening liquids, primarily as the decals are placed on mostly flat surfaces. The livery is relatively minimal and the model itself quite small,

CLOCKWISE FROM TOP LEFT:

The upper surface is masked with Tamiya masking tape, prior to the lower surfaces receiving their coat of RAF Light Aircraft Grey.

The Xtracolor X015 dries quite quickly when used with Xtracolor own brand fast dry thinners.

Looking almost military in her appearance, the A319 is ready for her retro Iberia livery.

therefore the decaling is complete within an hour and the model of Iberia's retro A319, EC-KKS, is almost complete.

Final details include the placement of the horizontal stabilizers, the undercarriage bay doors and despite the photo below, yes; she does have her navigation lights attached! The aerials that were removed from the fuselage at the beginning prior to painting are re-attached and the anti-collision lights placed on the upper and lower fuselages; these are from the resin sets produced by CMK. The building of this particular model, and especially the choice of the retro livery of Iberia, has given me the bug to have a complete collection of retro liveries in the display cabinet, I just need to get a bigger cabinet!

But there is still something not quite right with the way that the wing looks. I found out later exactly what was wrong and that is just part of modelling, but I could have shot myself when I realized! Anyway,

With the decaling complete, the final details can be added.

I'm going to hold you in suspense until the next A319 model build to tell you exactly what the particular problem was. In the meantime I hope that you have enjoyed looking at this simple build; we are now going to have a look at something a bit bigger, a bit more complex and although not too difficult, certainly a little more challenging.

A common site in the Spanish capital, as well as around the Iberia short-haul network.

CHAPTER 22

CUTTING AND SHUTTING

REVELL 1/144TH AIRBUS A330-300 CONVERTED TO A330-200

In 1986 I saw Airbus demonstrate an A300, F-BUAD, with large Fly By Wire (FBW) titles down the side; it was the knowledge of the flight control systems in this development aircraft that was used in the design of the new Airbus wide-bodied family, the A330/340. I thought it was a very bold move to go from conventional flight systems to a dependency on FBW, with little thought as to how my own career path would develop. At that time I had only held my private licence for four years and would soon become a flying instructor on Cessna C152 and Piper PA28 aircraft; I thought that FBW was a thing for the fast jet military aircraft!

At the very outset of an Airliner's development, the manufacturers will be looking at ways to get the very most out of a single design and the fuselage and wing of the A330 and A340 are common components, despite the latter being a four-engined aircraft. The advantage of the common fuselage is obvious when one considers the different configurations that airlines demand, with the longer fuselage carrying more passengers, at the expense of being able to carry less fuel. When an airline demands more range, that would mean the ability to carry more fuel and, due to weight restrictions, normally means fewer passengers in a shorter fuselage. If you now consider the aerodynamic forces over the tailfin and rudder are less, due to the shorter moment resulting from the shorter distance between the vertical axis of the aircraft and the fin, this would normally mean a larger fin to compensate, and to allow the rudder and fin to have the same aerodynamic effect as the smaller fin/rudder on a longer fuselage.

I hope that all sounds simple and relatively easy to understand, but a quick look at Boeing's B747SP, with its extremely short, dumpy fuselage and over-sized fin will quickly illustrate my point.

When Airbus revealed the A330-300, it went around the world on a sales tour in the colours of one of the initial customers, Cathay Pacific. I remember seeing it on the apron in Brunei for the first time and thinking: "That fin looks too small!" Of course, who was I to argue with the designers of the aircraft, but to me eyes it was not as aesthetically pleasing as it could have been.

The A330-300 is essentially based on a stretched A300 fuselage. The new fuselage length is 63.69m (69.65ft), but new wings, stabilizers and fly-by-wire systems are all incorporated. The -300 carries 295 passengers in a standard three-class cabin layout with a range of 10,500km (5,700 nautical miles). The cargo capacity is of note as it is comparable to that of the early Boeing 747s. It was also the first Airbus to be offered with a choice of three engines, the General Electric CF6-80E, Pratt & Whitney PW4000 or Rolls-Royce Trent 700. This makes it important for the modeller to choose the correct airline / engine combination.

My aesthetic view of the A330 was changed when, in 1998, Airbus introduced the A330-200. This is a shortened, longer-range variant, with a typical passenger load of 253 in a three-class layout, but having a range of 13,400 km (7,200 nautical miles}. The shorter moment arm of the -200's shorter fuselage meant that the vertical stabilizer needed to be increased in height and with this increase of 104cm (41in) it certainly now looked right, in my humble opinion at least! But when I look at the dimensions and that lovely long, thin wing I do seriously consider the A330-200 to be one of the most beautiful airliners to grace the skies.

It was not just externally that the -200 differed from its older brother. Internal changes were also incorporated into the design of the -200 with the wing being modified with internal strengthening, allowing the maximum takeoff weight of the aircraft to be increased to around 230 tonnes. Airbus also boosted fuel capacity by using the centre 139,100l fuel tank from the A340. As of December 2011, 572 of the A330-200 had been ordered, 444 of which had been delivered, with 440 aircraft in current operation.

In March 1999, I left the shores of Borneo and my time with Royal Brunei came to an end. I had successfully applied to join Emirates airline in Dubai and was thrilled to be given a start date on a conversion course for the A330-200 fleet; and it is one particularly special aircraft that is the subject of this chapter.

Having spent the previous five years flying the B767, B757 and Fokker 100 for RBA, joining Emirates was a challenge on many levels. Changing company, country and aircraft type in one go meant relatively high stress levels and I found my experience on the Fokker 100, albeit for just eighteen months in Brunei, well worth it as there were similarities between the two European manufacturers in terms of their vocabulary and philosophy. The course went ahead at full speed and just three months later I was fully qualified and ready to fly the A330 on the line, all I needed now was an aircraft to fly. In fact I had to wait another month before the first A330 was delivered to Emirates and, after line training was complete, spent a large amount of time off whilst new pilots were trained up on type. But as the deliveries of new aircraft continued to Dubai and new routes opened, it was not long before I learned never to complain about having too much free time!

By now you should be familiar with the layout of the Revell airliner kits and this larger Airbus is no exception. However, the level of detail is much higher on components such as the undercarriage, and in this chapter we will take a look at how to enhance them further to create more realistic looking landing gear. But, although we will have a look at some extra detailing, this chapter primarily looks at the conversion of the original kit of the A330-300 to the -200 and it is as simple, as they say in the car trade, as a cut and shut!

Another rare kit from Revell that commands high prices on the Internet auction sites and, hopefully, one that will be re-released in the future.

Revell's Airbus A330-300 kit is actually very scarce these days and has been long deleted from their catalogue, but as mentioned earlier, the company has also released the A340-200 and this is easily converted to an A330 with the appropriate after-market engines, stabilizers and tailfin. It's certainly cheaper doing that than paying some of the auction prices that the A330 kits go for – when you can find one that is! The A340 kits seem to be relatively easy to find and the parts that are common to both kits are included; such as the blanking panel to cover the wheel bay of the A340's centre gear leg. But regardless of which kit that you start with, to complete the conversion to a -200 you will need the parts from Bra.Z which include: the taller tail fin, horizontal stabilizers and, in the case of the Emirates aircraft that I wanted to represent, a set of their Rolls-Royce Trent 700 engines. Decals came from the Brazil Decals sheet, BD144-14, which I have had in my stock of decals ever since they first came out.

All the parts are washed and cleaned up before the first part of the building process begins, which is to cut the fuselage up in to pieces! There are a few resources available on the Internet as to exactly where to cut, but you will see from the photographs shown here, the segments of the fuselage that need to be removed. The fuselage is first taped together and then masking tape wrapped around the position of the relevant cuts.

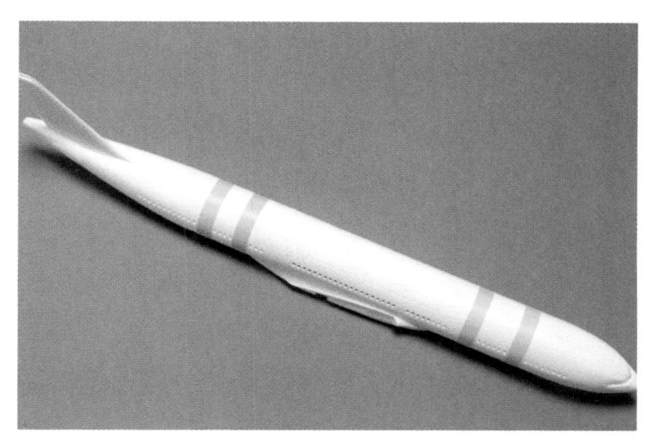

It is best to assemble the fuselage halves with tape and make a single cut through both halves, following the masking tape line carefully.

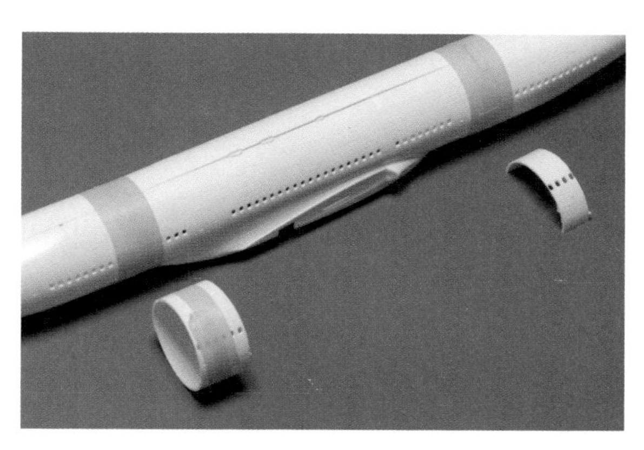

The removed sections and shortened fuselage.

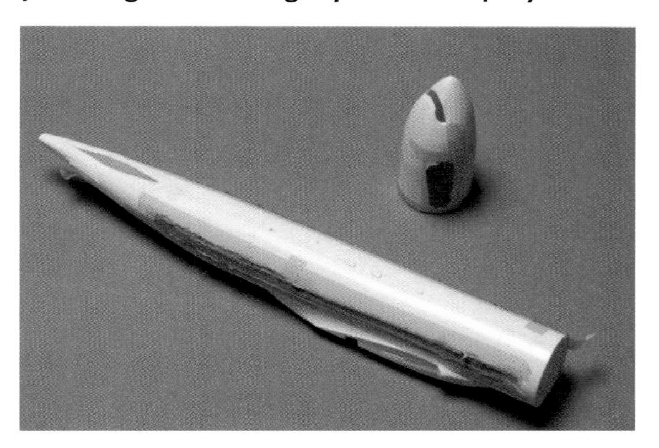

All windows are filled with Tamiya putty.

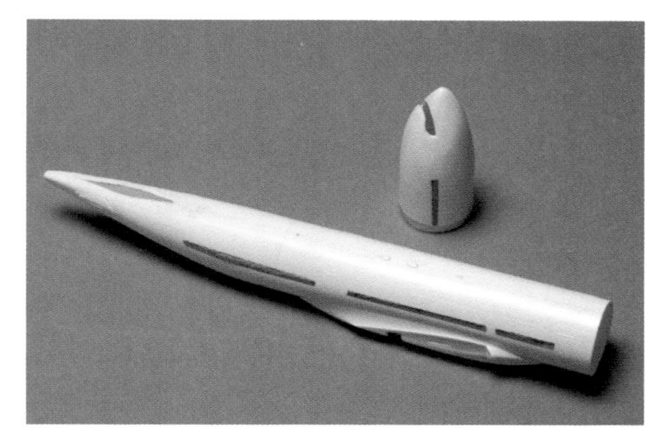

The masking tape is carefully removed to reveal how much sanding is required.

Cutting the parts is done by carefully following the masking tape with a razor saw and, once the cuts are completed, a quick check is made to ensure that the remaining parts of the fuselage fit together without any problems. A quick dry-fit ensures none are found and so it is now on to filling all the cabin windows as, once again, these are supplied as decals.

The same method in filling the windows is used here as in the A319 chapter earlier, and the two halves of the fuselage are taped above and below the cabin windows in order not to let too much putty cover the fuselage. This time the windows are filled from the outside and, when the putty has dried, the tape is removed to leave two thin lines of putty down the side where the windows are which will need to be sanded back and polished smooth.

In the photo above you can also see that the nose section has been adhered together and a very thin sheet of plasticard has been glued to the inside of the nose section. This plugs in very neatly to the centre section of the fuselage and gives a strong join and you can see that the rear tail section has already been assembled with the fin cut off ready for the resin replacement.

Normally the kit requires that the nose landing gear be installed prior to joining together the fuselage halves. But as I had cut the nose off, this left the area inside the nose accessible so that the nose gear could be worked on now and then installed just prior to the nose being joined to the fuselage.

The nose gear itself is very well moulded with some lovely detail, but the bay is rather simplified and

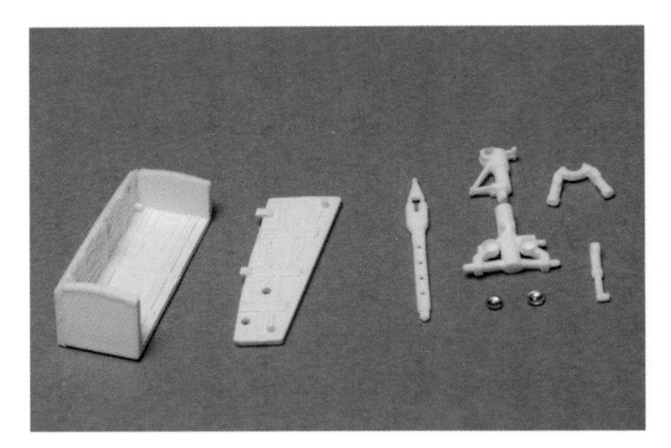

Once again, Revell provides a very detailed undercarriage.

Although nicely detailed, the undercarriage could have some extra work done on it to enhance it further.

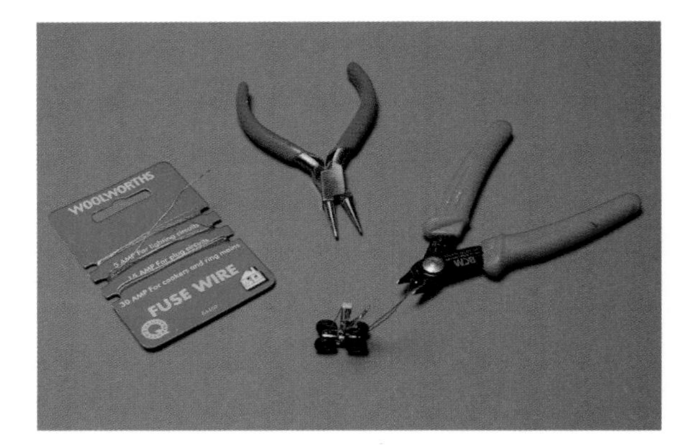

Fuse wire, cutters and round nosed pliers help to detail the undercarriage leg.

With the hydraulic brake lines added and painted, the main undercarriage legs look far better now.

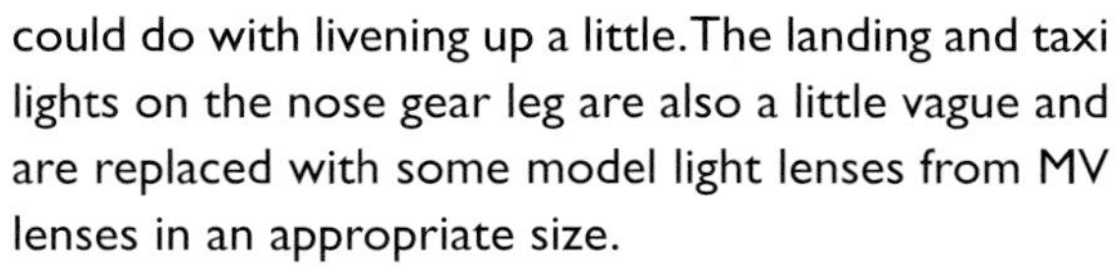

could do with livening up a little. The landing and taxi lights on the nose gear leg are also a little vague and are replaced with some model light lenses from MV lenses in an appropriate size.

While working on the nose gear I also begin putting together the main landing gear: this really needs some extra work to get the best out of the already nice parts from Revell. For this I just follow the finely moulded lines on the kit parts and replace them with more realistically sized piping in the form of fuse wire.

On a full sized aircraft, you will see prominent pipes between the main wheels and these are the hydraulic fluid lines that supply the high-pressure hydraulics to the brake calipers. They are normally steel pipes until the area just above the oleo strut, or shock absorber, where the pipes are flexible braided hose. This flexible area is often either blue or black braiding and being blue on the A330-200 it adds some colour and interest to an otherwise plain area. The pipes are created from fuse wire and bent to the approximate shape around the gear axles, secured in place with superglue.

The flexible sections are painted blue prior to the addition of the wheels, which are painted dark matt grey with white hubs. A red creep mark can be seen painted across the tyre and hub and is a simple indicator to show whether the tyre is moving around the hub at all. This is recreated by a simple application of red paint with a fine brush.

Finally, on the main gear legs, a couple of small placards from a generic placard sheet are used to represent the placards on the real thing.

This was a really enjoyable build and, given the extra detail being put onto the gear and wheel bays, was proving very rewarding. Modelling can be as expensive as you want to make it, especially with the resin and etched-metal after market sets that are available, so it really feels good when you can add a major enhancement to the model using just your own vision, a bit of patience and a few pieces of fuse wire!

The main undercarriage parts are put safely aside, whilst the nose gear is kept on the bench as work continues on the fuselage. The nose gear is adhered in place in the nose section prior to joining it together with the centre fuselage section. The resulting join line around the fuselage sections is masked either side and a thin line of filler applied around the circumference.

At this stage the new resin vertical fin can be attached but, a word of warning here to the unwary: when selecting the tailfin from the replacements available, it should be noted that there were two types fitted to the A330-200 and it is quite easy to get this right as Bra.Z supply both. The earlier type, used here, was fitted to all A330-200 aircraft prior to Manufacturer's Serial Number, MSN, 555. There are plenty of resources on line to show which MSN went to which airline, so just research the particular aircraft and choose the correct fin.

The fin itself is a simple butt fit and needs to be joined using a gel-type superglue to allow for some movement prior to the adhesive setting, as well as being useful as a filler.

Inevitably, there is also the need to apply some filler around the join but, being cellulose based, this will also add strength to the assembly as it eats into the plastic when applied, just like the plastic adhesive does. Once it has dried the whole assembly is very rigid and will survive the handling that it has to endure over the next few days.

The last job prior to sanding the fuselage is to attach the horizontal stabilizers, again by Bra.Z, which are nicely cast along, with separate elevators.

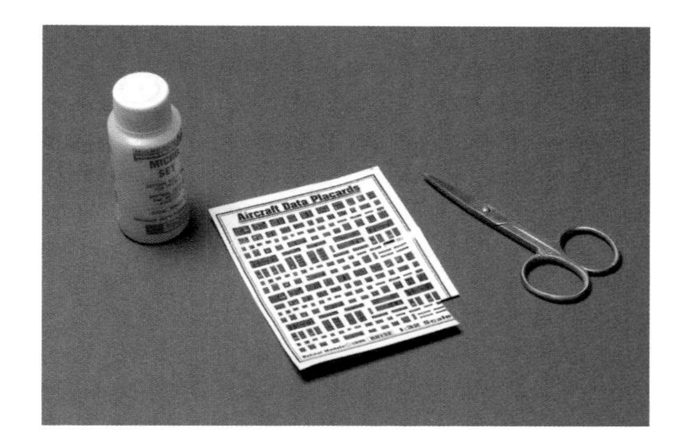

Generic placards are sourced from an old, 1/32nd scale Reheat Models' decal sheet.

The nose wheel bay also receives further detailing with the aid of fuse wire.

The Bra.Z replacement resin tailfin, for an early A330-200.

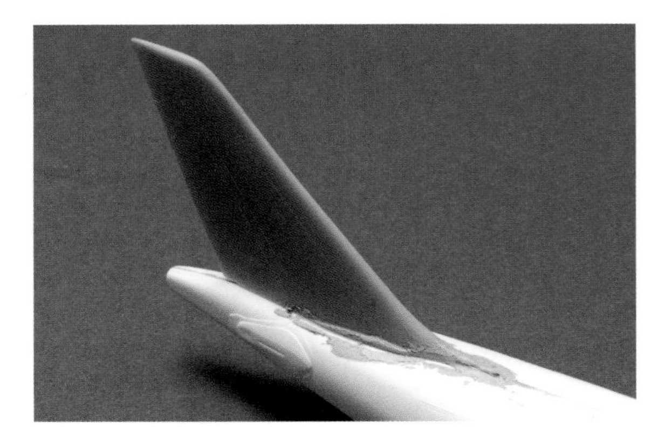

After securing in place with CA, the tailfin needs some filling around the joint.

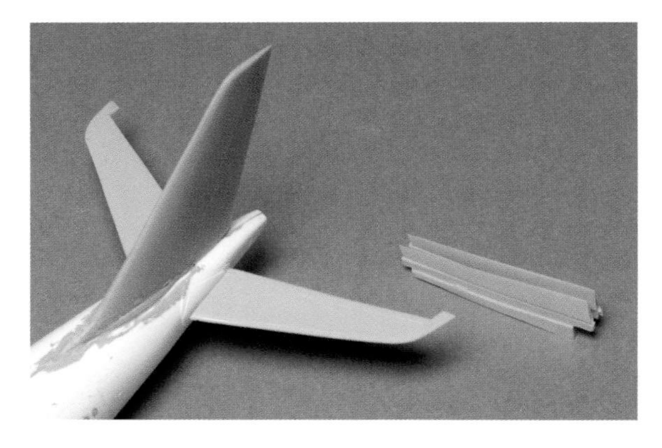

Bra.Z also provide the accurate horizontal stabilizers with separate elevators.

The airframe is soon looking like an A330-200, but there is still much more work to do.

It is very common to see the military modellers depict their aircraft as they would be seen on the ground, with elevators drooping and maybe the ailerons displaced. Model airliners are not often seen like this, yet careful study of photos shows that, in many cases, the elevators do drop as the hydraulic pressure drops on engine shutdown.

In time that it took to get to this stage, I could have finished one of Revell's A319s! All I had to show for days of work was the undercarriage and a rather messy fuselage, covered in filler! But that all changes very quickly as, armed with increasing grades of sanding cloth, the filler is sanded back to a smooth finish. There a many ranges of sanding sheets, but for a job like this I always use the Tamiya sanding sheets, sanding with water to reduce the amount of dust that is created; this is followed by polishing the model further with progressively increasing grades of sanding cloth from Micro Mesh.

After carefully looking at areas that might need another application of filler, the model is sprayed with a light coat of primer to highlight the areas that need attention; slowly the model begins to take on a neater appearance as the putty is sanded and polished. Any areas that do need going over again are given another application of filler, which is allowed to dry then primed, sanded and polished again. Now if you think this all seems like hard work, just wait until the A340-600 coming up, this is just a practice run compared to the work involved in the next model Airbus!

Gradually the fuselage is closer to being finished and, prior to painting, there is one important detail that needs to be added to the fuselage. Modern aircraft have many aerials along the fuselage and most of these are for radio and navigation purposes and are supplied in the kit. But many modern airliners also rely on satellite navigation and Bra.Z have released a set of generic satellite receiver housings that are invaluable when constructing a modern airliner.

Photographs will help when placing these correctly onto your own models and they certainly help to create a more accurate replica. Being made from polyurethane resin, they are attached to the upper fuselage with cyano acrylate. The cockpit glazing is

After priming the model, various areas are brought to light that need further filling and sanding.

The rear windows are seen here with a further application of filler.

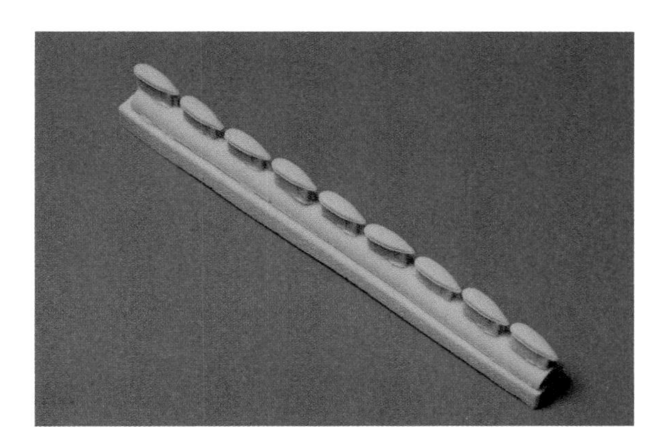

Bra.Z has many accessories for the model airliner fan, including these generic satellite receiver housings.

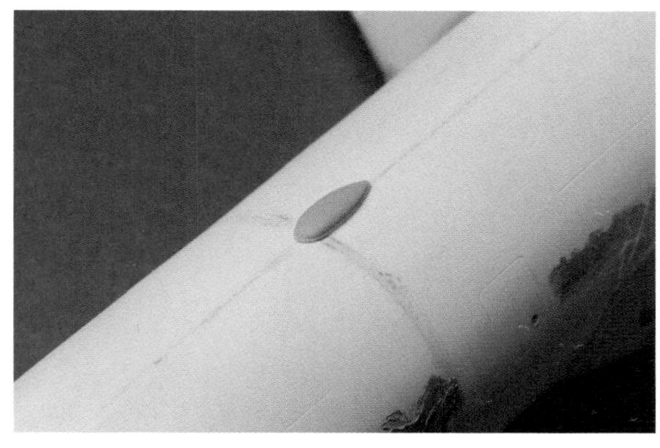

Reference photographs will ensure you place them correctly.

Finally the wings are firmly attached to the fuselage and the seam is filled.

The windscreen is attached and the joints filled and sanded.

also attached and, once again, a decal will eventually be applied to represent the windscreen, so the plastic part is filled along the edges and sanded smooth.

The lower and upper halves of the wings are joined together and then attached to the fuselage. The resulting join has a very fine gap along the length of the wing root so is masked off and Tamiya's putty applied; finally the separate winglets are added to the tip of each wing. These had the navigation lights moulded in and, as I wanted to represent these more realistically, are filled to the correct shape of the light housing. The lights themselves will be created from small coloured resin pieces from the CMK set that I've used in earlier chapters.

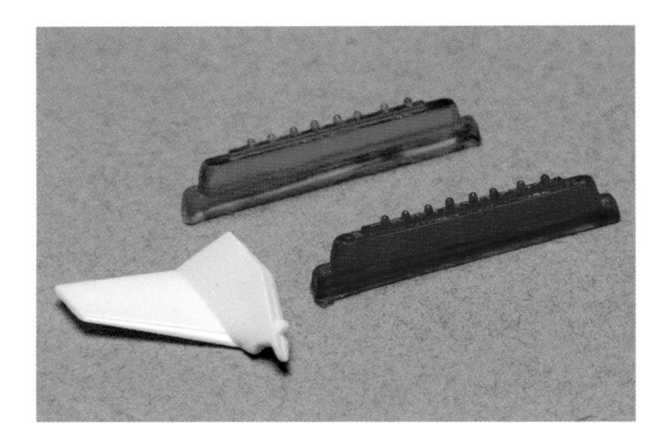

CMK Resin navigation lights are used to replicate the lights in each wingtip.

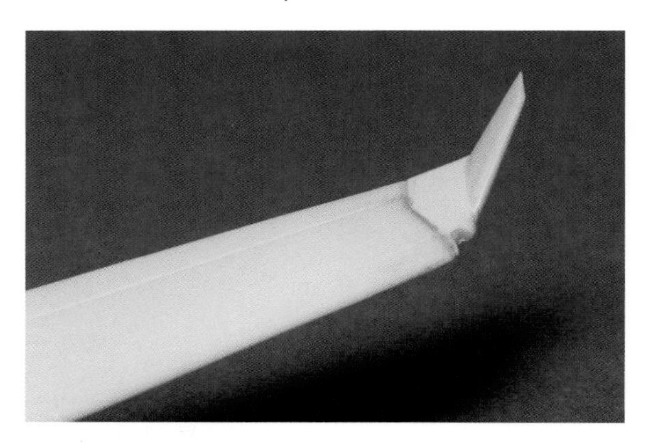

The winglets fit nicely in place on the wing tips, but do require a small amount of filler to blend them in smoothly.

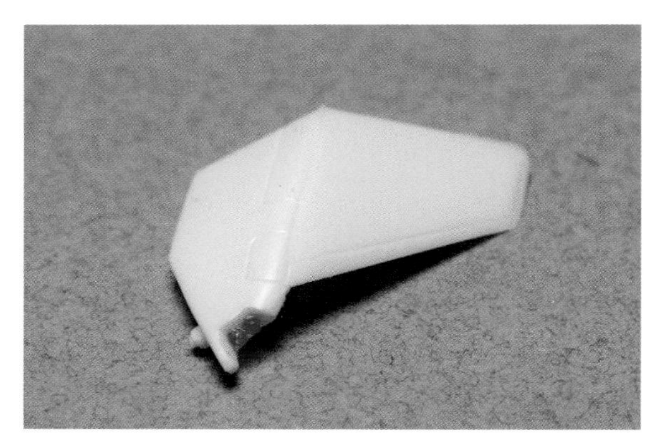

Two tiny resin pieces are encased in superglue, which is sanded and polished to a clear finish.

Jumping ahead a little, but whilst we are looking at the winglets, here's a quick explanation of how I do this, using a couple of winglets from the A340 kit. As mentioned earlier, the area that the navigation light is seen in is actually moulded as part of the solid and needs to be removed. Then using two of the tiny dome shaped clear resin pieces, not forgetting the correct colours for each side: red is on the port or left, green on the starboard or right, the miniscule resin lights are adhered in place using superglue.

To finish them off, the resin pieces are covered with thick, gel-type superglue that is left to harden before being sanded and polished to a very clear finish.

Of course, the extreme close-up photograph of the lights shows up some air bubbles in the super-

The completed port navigation light unit.

glue, but at life-size and viewed from a normal distance, these are totally invisible. In fact I did not notice them until the macro lens gave them away! But they do look far more realistic than just painting the lights on later.

So back to the aircraft itself and with the wings attached, all joins are now sanded and polished smooth and the whole airframe is given a few coats of Tamiya Surface Primer, which shows that all the work in preparing the model has been worth it. The next items to be dealt with are the engines: for the A330-200, Emirates Airline chose the Rolls Royce Trent 700s to power the fleet and these are not included in any of the A330 kits released. So it is back to the aftermarket companies and Bra.Z produce the required pair of engines. These capture the lovely aerodynamic shape of the cowl and the subtle flat bottom of the lower cowl very well indeed. The engines come in two halves, with the main body being one piece and the fan and front cowl being another. The pouring blocks are cut off with a razor saw and then cleaned up before simply butting together and adhering using cyano acrylate. The joint between front and rear has a fine gap and once this has been filled, the engines are primed and sanded.

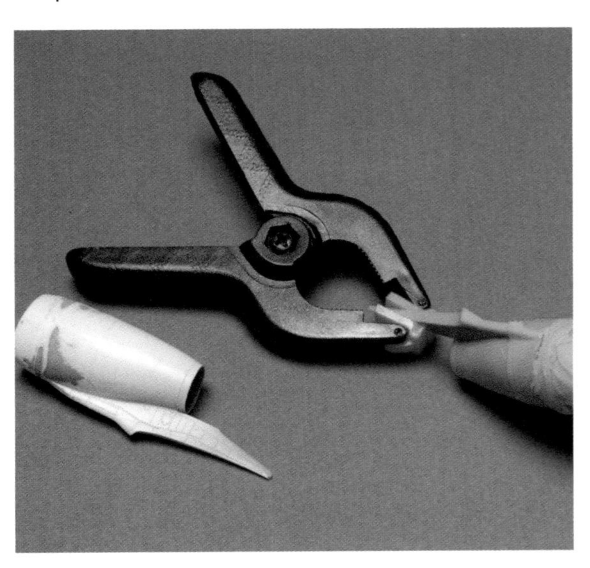

Bra.Z has many replacement engines in their range, including the Rolls Royce Trent applicable to this model.

Impatience got the better of me and I could not resist tacking the engines in place to see how the model would look and I have to say that I was very pleased with the results so far.

With the engines temporarily tacked in place, the model is once again sprayed with Tamiya White Surface Primer.

The wings and horizontal stabilizers, along with their elevators, are spayed Xtracolour Airbus Grey, allowed to dry and then the wings are masked off ready for the spraying of the fuselage.

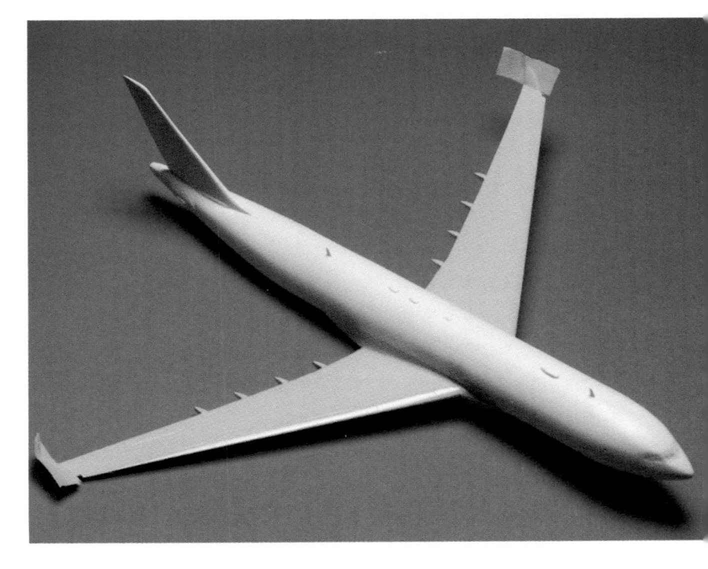

Airbus Grey is available from the Xtracolor range and is used here.

The wings are masked prior to the fuselage being sprayed.

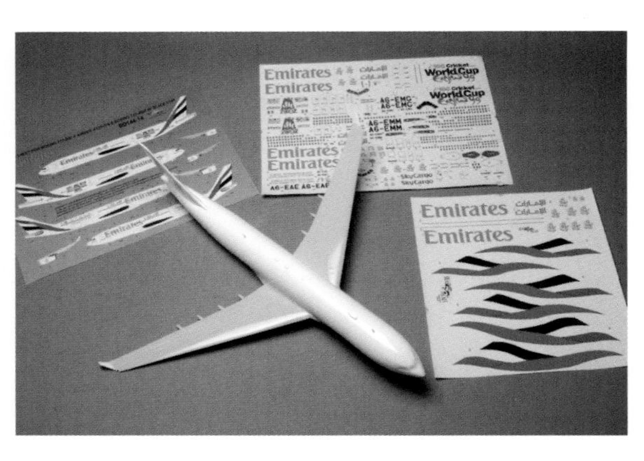

The decals are amazing and include many of the 'special' schemes applied to the Emirates A330 fleet.

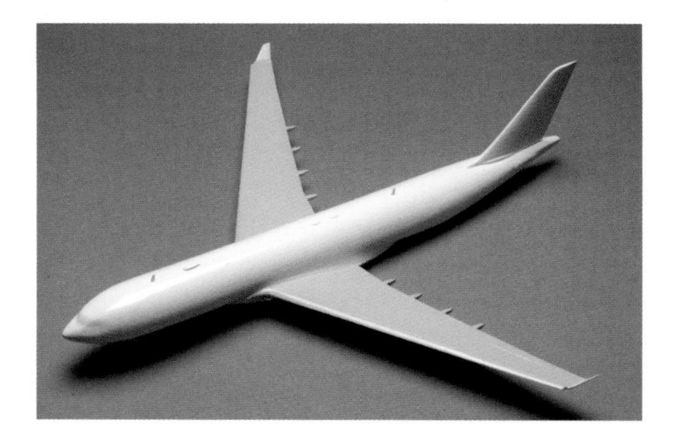

The Halfords spray paints really do give a superb finish to airliner models.

A simple but appealing scheme.

Having spent a few days drying, the fuselage is now ready for the decals: these are extremely well printed with dense colours and are applied bit-by-bit, over the following few days. Allow them to dry and try not to handle the model too much: you do not want to ruin the finish of this kit at the last hurdle and so care and patience are in order.

After the main titles are applied the smaller decals gradually bring the plain white fuselage to life!

After the fuselage has been completed, the whole model is given a sealing coat of Johnson's Future and this protects the decals from the work to come on the wings. I had hoped to get some decals for the Corogard finish on the upper wing surfaces, but decided instead

There is no excuse for not guessing what aircraft type this is!

The Corogard areas are masked off and sprayed using Xtracolor's enamel paint.

This particular model has pride of place in the display cabinet!

to paint them and after masking the relevant areas, the Corogard finish is sprayed using the relevant paint from Xtracolour. I was certainly glad I'd sealed in the decals as a wayward piece of masking tape will pull any unprotected decal clean off!

The last few decals are now applied, the engines attached as well as the undercarriage. Final details include the upper and lower anti-collision beacons, from the CMK resin set.

It seemed a daunting task to cut down the original kit of the A330-300 to create the shorter A330-200 but, with a little patience, any airliner model can be reduced in length to create another version within the family; just make sure that you research the subject fully and ensure the correct areas are removed. But the model was a relatively simple conversion and sits proudly at the top of the display cabinet; another model of an aircraft that I flew during my own career.

I think that I'm going to go back to a simpler project before attempting the sanding and filling that I know will be required for the next conversion, so let's revisit the Airbus A319 to find out what it is about that wing that looks wrong. Have your sunglasses ready, as we'll also take a look at a very bright A320 indeed!

CHAPTER 23

LOW COST WITH CARE AND CONVENIENCE

DETAILING REVELL'S 1/144TH AIRBUS A319

Ask anyone to name a British airline and I can guarantee that easyJet will be one of the airlines that most people will recall. So many people have now chosen to go on holiday with the British low cost carrier and the branding is certainly bright! The distinctive orange tailfins dominate London's Gatwick and Luton airports and the company now has nineteen bases across the United Kingdom and Europe. With over 200 aircraft in the fleet, the company is certainly much larger than many flag carriers now and the orange tailfins have become such a familiar sight at airports throughout not only Europe, but the western edge of the Middle East too.

The company started operations with the Boeing B737-300 and had a long relationship with the American manufacturer, lasting from the company's start until 2011, when the last B737, a -700 series, flew easyJet's last Boeing flight. Since the last Boeing left, the airline is now solely Airbus, with both the A319 and A320 in service.

It was a telephone call to TwoSix decals asking them whether they would be releasing the easyJet livery that resulted in an interesting few months. It seemed that the company had wanted to do a set but to print the decals, TwoSix had to have approval from the brand owner, in this case the easy Group, which 'leases' the brand to easyJet Airline Ltd. It all got a bit complicated but the result of lots of phone calls and a meeting with senior management was that TwoSix were given the approval and were officially licenced to print the easyJet decals.

The wait was worth it and what a great sheet it is! Not only does the sheet include the standard livery and the specific names of some of the aircraft that were given especially to them, but it also includes the 200th Airbus delivered to easyJet in a very bright, reverse scheme of an overall orange fuselage with white titles. Just like easyJet's famous orange hangar headquarters at Luton Airport, the orange A320 can be seen from miles away! So it was decided that to complete my own flying career history in model form, I just had to do an A319 and the special 200th Airbus, an A320.

TwoSix decals were the first to release properly licenced decals for the easyJet Airbus fleet.

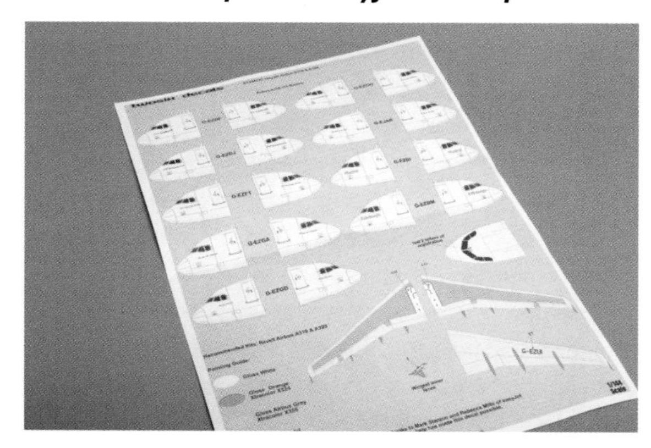

This sheet includes everything you need to make every single Airbus operated by the Luton-based airline.

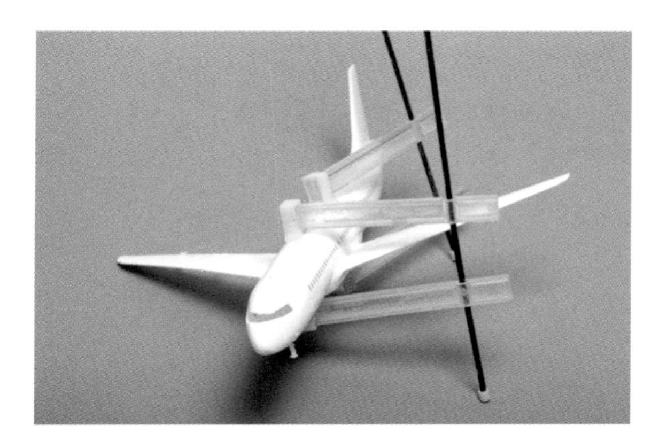

The Berna clamps in action once again, this time holding the wing section in place as the adhesive dries.

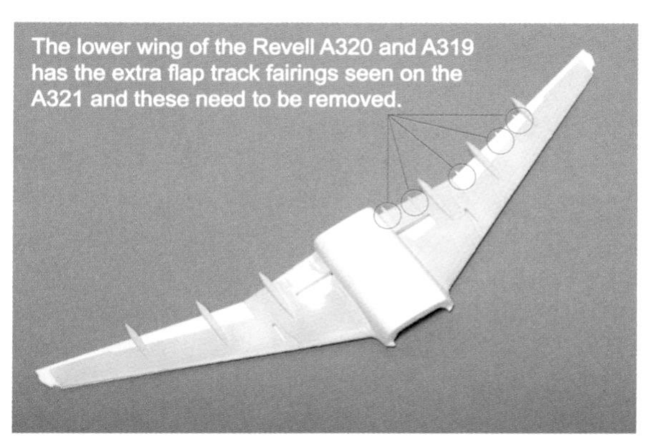

This picture clearly shows the parts that need to be removed.

From the earlier chapter, you will already be very familiar with Revell's A319 kit and the A320 is no different, just having a longer fuselage. I have become very familiar with the kit myself by now and in no time at all the whole airframe comes together.

But what about that wing and the fact that it did not look right? Well, I did laugh when I realized what it was and I really should have known better! The Airbus single aisle jets in Revell's range share many common components and the wing is the same in each of the three different kits. But the full size A321 wing is different to its smaller siblings and has five extra, small flap track fairings along the trailing edge of the wing. These are clearly shown on the photo below and if you are modelling an A319 or A320, then they do need to be removed. A simple cut with a scalpel blade and a clean up with some fine sand-paper is all that it took to convert the wing to the right configuration.

As seen in the previous chapter, the undercarriage can quite easily be detailed over and above that provided in the kit and this is done once again with some fuse wire, painted as before. The navigation lights are also detailed and as Revell supply these as very small clear parts, they are drilled out slightly from behind with a very fine drill bit. Be careful not to drill right through as all you want is a small hole that can be filled with the appropriate colour of clear paint. I use Tamiya X-25 clear green and X-27 clear red for this

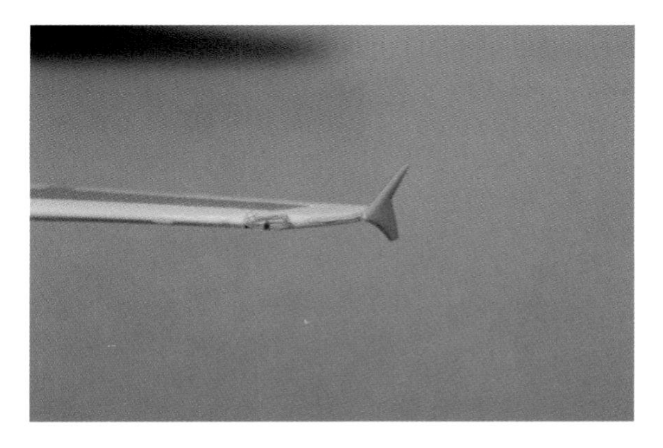

The rear of each clear light lens is drilled into and a small drop of either transparent red, or transparent green paint, from the Tamiya acrylic range is applied.

The result is a very nice representation of the wingtip navigation light unit.

purpose and, being acrylics, they dry quite quickly. Once the paint has dried these can be set aside and stuck in place when the model has been completed.

The assembly and painting of the two Airbuses is completed over a few days, allowing the orange paint to really harden prior to the model being handled again. The white is, once again, the Appliance White from Halfords whilst the orange is available in the Xtracolour range, number X324. The wings are painted Airbus Industrie Grey and the Corogard panel is sprayed as well. Prior to spraying though, the landing gear bays are plugged with small pieces of sponge to mask them off.

It was not too long ago that even the military modellers had to mix their own shades to get a good approximation of the colour that they wanted. Nowadays we are so lucky to have many shades already premixed and available from the model paint manufacturers. Who would have thought a few years ago that easyJet orange would be available in a tinlet? But thankfully it is and completing projects like this is so much easier for it.

The models are left for quite a few days and are now ready for the decals to be applied, prior to applying the main livery. The decals from the kits are used as the sheet includes a huge number of stencils, doors and other safety markings, such as the escape area on the upper surface of the wing. The kit's supplied decals are by DACO and are of excellent quality and there are so many small ones that it took a whole afternoon to apply them all.

We've seen a few models here that have been decorated with TwoSix decals and I was looking forward to seeing the new easyJet decals on these two Airbuses. I had already chosen to reproduce the A319 with Madrid as its title; this aircraft is registered G-EZBI and the decals are flawless in their application. Even though I worried that the white decals would not be dense enough over the orange, they looked perfect; I just needed to be patient enough to let that gloss orange paint fully harden!

With the two models basically finished and drying off out of the way of careless hands, we can now have a look at ways of further detailing the kits to get more out of them. There are a host of improvements

The removed masking reveals nice, clean paint lines.

Xtracolor come to the rescue with the correct shade of paint.

The kit decals are used for the various data placards and stencilling.

that you can do with some basic scratch building; here are a few ideas:

The hydraulic brake hoses can be replicated with fuse wire and there are now after-market detail sets available of etched metal for airliners, with one company, Extra Tech from the Czech Republic, seemingly adopting the genre as their own. Extra Tech have released many 1/144th scale detail sets for airliner kits, as well as a set to produce the baggage carts seen around airliners whilst they are being loaded and unloaded. The set for the A319 contains replacement parts for the undercarriage doors, engine fans, wheel hubs and the blade aerials that are all a little over scale on the plastic kit. Even a tiny pair of windscreen wipers is included on the small sheet of etched brass.

When you look at the front of an airliner's engine, the large fans will have a spinner at the centre and this often has a spiral pattern painted around it. This spiral is a visual clue to ground crew as to how fast the engine fan is turning and some reports also say that it has a beneficial effect scaring birds away. The former is certainly valid as an airport apron is a busy and noisy place and many ground crew working around a stationary aircraft will have hearing defenders on. A jet engine is a very high-powered vacuum cleaner and it is important that they stay well clear of any operating engine.

The latter, that of scaring birds, is something that I have often read but must admit to being very skeptical as to its effectiveness. To reproduce these spirals you need a very steady hand and a very fine brush, or you could simply use decals. The decals used here were found on the Skyline decals sheet for the B737-300 and carefully applied with a sharpened toothpick helping to position them. They are tiny and the process of getting them to settle down around the spinner is quite frustrating, but with some decal softening solution they wrap around the cone nicely and are left to fully dry before I touch them again for fear that I might dislodge their position!

If you take a close look at the trailing edge of the wings, elevators and rudder of every aircraft, you'll see that there are fine aerial-like protrusions, which are actually static electricity dischargers. These dissipate

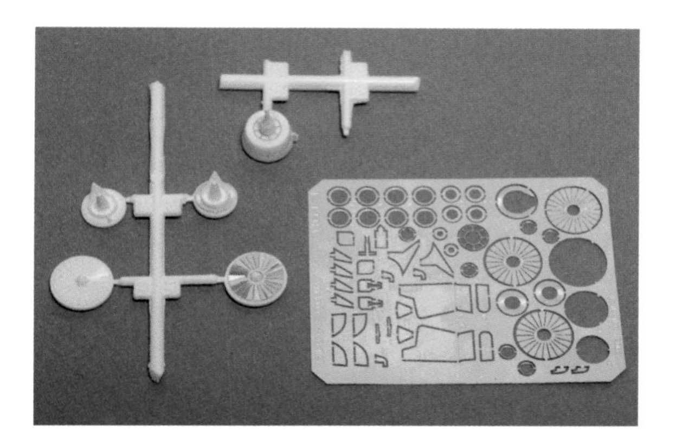

There are more and more manufacturers making after-market sets for airliner modellers.

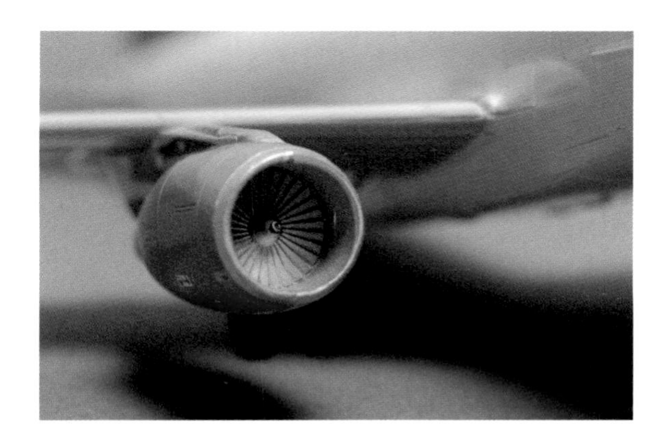

This takes the record as the most frustrating of decals to apply!

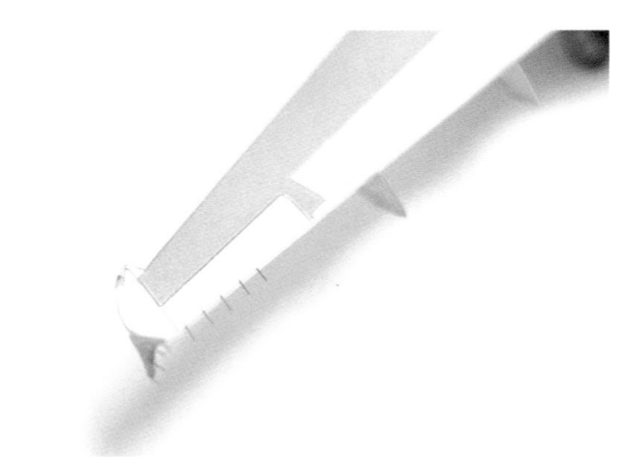

Fine lengths of stretched black sprue represent the static dischargers on the flying surface's trailing edges.

static electricity that builds up on the airframe as it flies through the air and are quite prominent on the Airbus A319 and A320. These are really very easy to replicate and it just takes some patience and, as with all fine detail work, a steady hand. But I think that the extra detail really livens up the model. I always have a huge stock of plastic runners and sprue in various colours left over from previous models as they always come in handy when super-detailing a project. In this case, I have used some black vinyl plastic that came, I think, with a Hasegawa Spitfire kit. The flexible vinyl sprue held some small vinyl propeller retaining caps and this material is perfect for creating static dischargers. You just apply a little heat; use a tea light candle and stretch the vinyl sprue until you get a nice continuous fine length of the material. A little of this goes an incredibly long way as you only need about 3mm of it to attach to the trailing edge of the flying surfaces to create nicely replicated static dischargers.

Research the aircraft type carefully and using photographs you can position the little static wicks correctly, which will really enhance the final model.

Further enhancements to the kit can be achieved with some basic scratch-building techniques and some plasticard. The cargo doors can quite easily be opened using a drill bit to chain drill the opening before cutting the door out.

You will, of course, need a second kit to supply the doors, as it is difficult to open up any door opening without damaging the door itself. Once the door

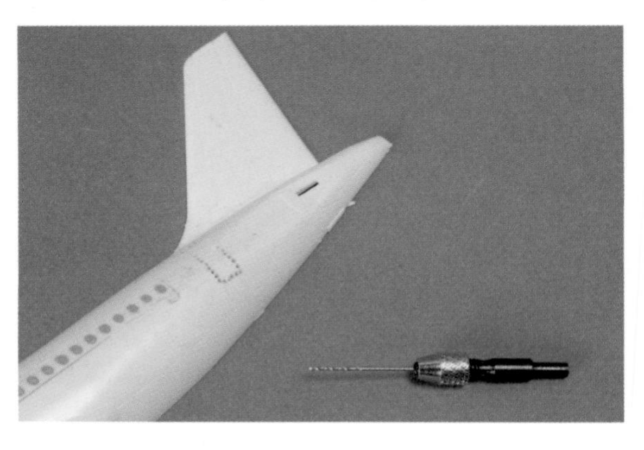

If you do want to open a door, it is best to go around the edge and chain drill holes that make the door much easier to cut out.

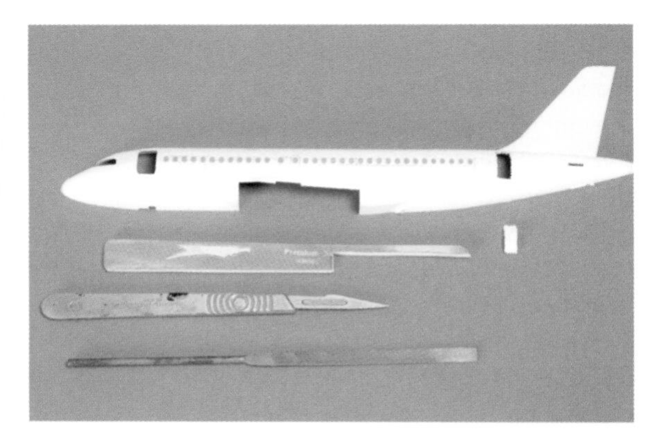

The resulting opening can be sanded smooth with files and sanding sticks.

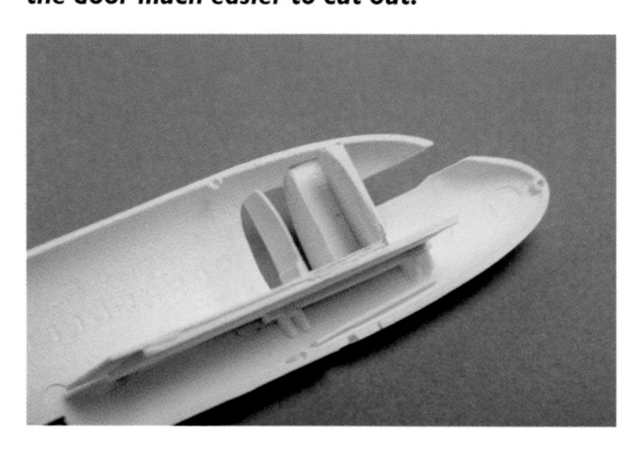

The bulkheads and floor are exceptionally simple to make.

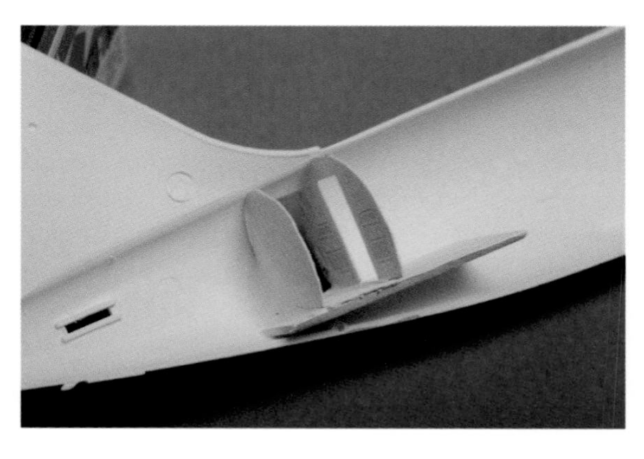

This is the rear galley area, made up from the Airwaves etched metal A320 interior detail set.

openings have been cleaned up, the interior can be built up using some plastic sheet for the floor area and interior bulkheads. There is an interior detail set for the A319 from Airwaves and this is in etched brass, providing some interior detail in the galley areas.

Surprisingly in 1/144th, Revell's kit of the A340 actually has a basic representation of the cockpit and as the Airbus cockpits are very similar, this can be cut and sanded to fit inside the nose of the A319. The screens are represented by simply painting some small pieces of masking tape, tacked into place on the instrument panel. You can do as much or as little as you dare when detailing something like the flight deck in 1/144th scale, the only limitations being your imagination and patience!

With respect to the cargo bay, this can be built up using plasticard. The bulkheads are cut from the plastic sheet after the interior of the fuselage has been correctly measured with a counter gauge. The resulting shape is then transferred to the plastic sheet and cut out.

The walls of the cargo bay are installed, along with the floor, and the assembly can then be painted and detailed as you wish. Airliner cargo bays normally have canvas or nylon webbing nets to retain the cases in place and these can quite easily be made from thin strips of masking tape woven together.

Airliner models are typically shown as they would appear on the apron but it is possible to show them in a more dynamic configuration. One manufacturer of after-market resin accessories, Contrails Models, has released sets for the Airbus A319 that include engines with the thrust reversers deployed, as well as a full wing set with separate flaps and speed brakes, so that you can show the aircraft as it would look just after touchdown! The resin sets are simple replacements of the kit parts.

So that's a brief look at further enhancing the kit and some, or all, of these tips can be incorporated into your own projects. If you need inspiration as to what can be achieved, a trip to Telford for the annual IPMS (UK) Scale ModelWorld show is certainly worthwhile: there you can find the Airliner Special Interest Group displaying their skills. It really is worth making the time to go; apart from tempting you to spend more money on kits and accessories, in many cases direct from the manufacturers, the show gives any modeller as much inspiration as they need!

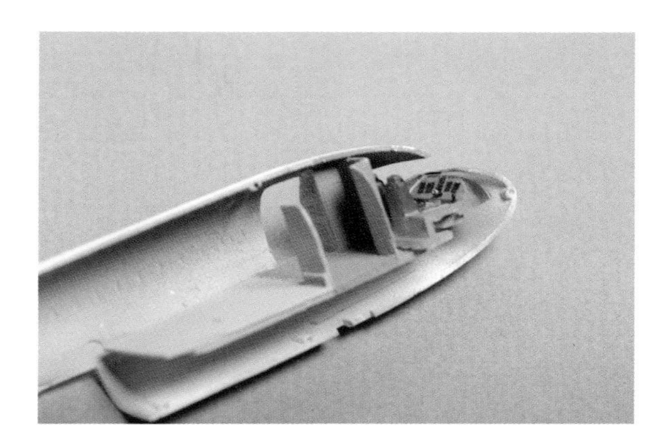

Why not scratch-build your own cockpit?

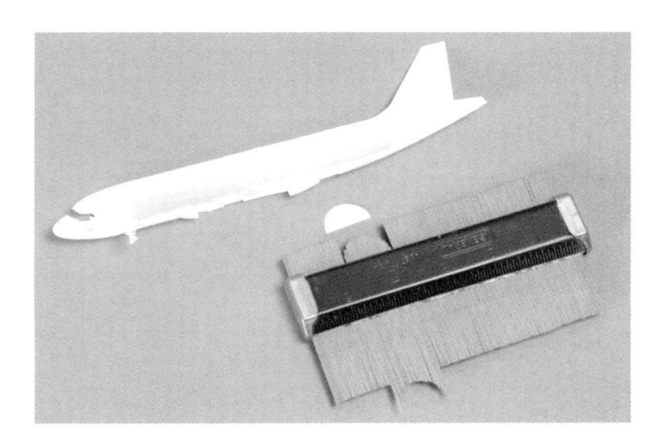

A counter gauge is a good investment to cut out interior bulkheads correctly.

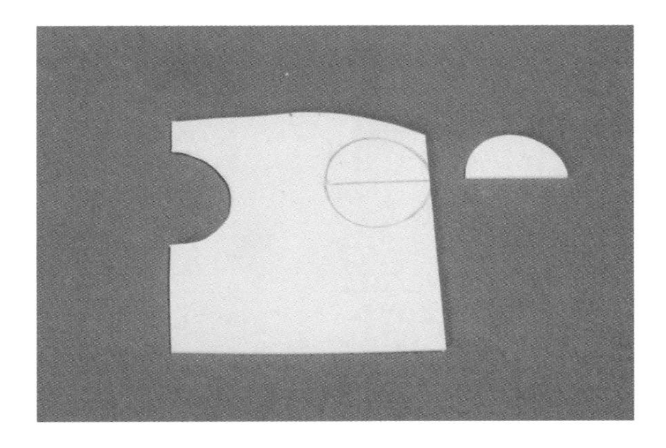

The resulting interior curve can be measured and traced onto plasticard.

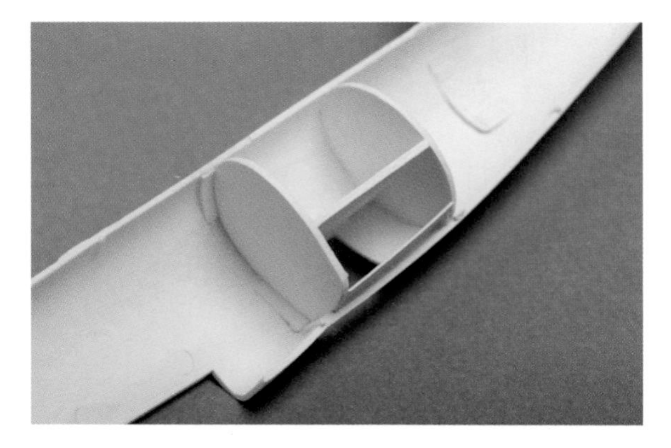

Cargo bays can also be scratch-built.

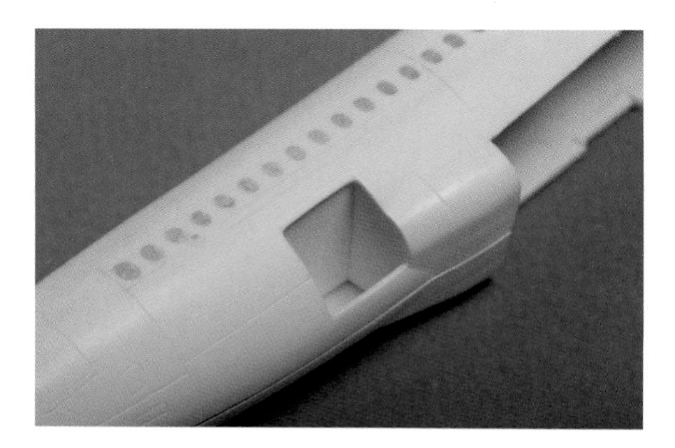

The doors have to be sourced from a second kit though.

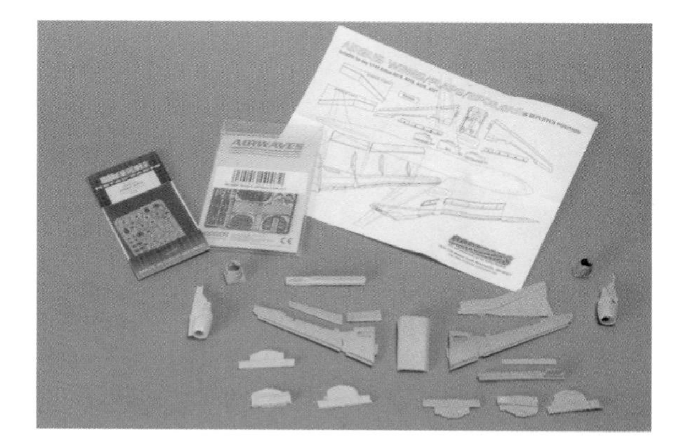

Contrails Models have released detailing sets that include extended flaps and thrust reversers.

Now that the Airbus duo has fully dried, the decals are applied gradually, building up the distinctive livery of easyJet. First the smaller details are added and these come from the excellent DACO designed sheet supplied with the kits.

The completed duo really did lend a splash of colour to the workbench, as they got closer to being completed. With the final decals applied I took them over to the photography area and placed them on a the simple paper backing sheet that I used for the majority of photographs in this book and then I had an idea…

My modelling ideas normally mean I end up taking much more time on the hobby and this idea was no exception. As a young boy, I always wanted to build a large model railway layout and was so impressed with the scenery created by the modellers of that genre. So with a hint of indulgence I set about creating a little piece of an airport on which to display and photograph the easyJet pair. The grass areas are simply made using the paper-backed model grass available from model railway stores; the remainder of the base is just painted and shows a segment of taxiway joining the runway. A bit of fun and yes, certainly an indulgence, but it brings the models to life and gave me the bug to start a model railway layout again. Maybe one day! Anyway, that brings me to the end of this chapter and in the following chapter we are going to have another look at converting a model kit to another variant; just make sure you have plenty of sandpaper and a dust mask to hand. A serious amount of elbow grease is also employed! But in the meantime, I hope that you enjoy looking over the photographs of the easyJet duo, as they embark with excited holidaymakers to sunnier shores.

Now the paint has fully cured, it's decal time!

Incorporating some basic model railway layout skills, and a huge helping of imagination, the two models really do come to life in a basic diorama setting.

CHAPTER 24

LONGER, LARGER, FARTHER, FASTER, HIGHER, QUIETER, SMOOTHER...

CONVERTING REVELL'S 1/144TH AIRBUS A340-300 TO THE -600

When I first saw the A340-600 airborne, it was at the 2003 Paris Air Show and was adorned with the fuselage titling 'Longer, Larger, Farther, Faster, Higher, Quieter, Smoother...' Airbus were not shy of expressing their new aircraft's attributes, and what attributes they are! I was astounded at the sheer length of the aircraft. From the tip of the nosecone to the trailing edge of the rudder, it is 75.3m, (247ft) in length. That is almost two and a half Boeing 737-300s! The aircraft is so long that when it turns, you almost expect it to bend like a train going round a bend on a track. When the aircraft was first launched she was the longest commercial aircraft in operation and has only just been overtaken with the introduction of the Boeing 747-8.

The aircraft has a range of 7,500 nautical miles and carries 379 passengers in a typical three-class layout. Designed as a direct competitor to the earlier Boeing B747s, the A40-600 certainly has the range and passenger load, but considering that the aircraft carries 25 per cent more cargo and with lower operating costs, I would have expected Airbus to have sold many more than they have. But then the manufacturer was in the process of designing the A380 and maybe a lot of airlines were hanging out for that model? But airline economics is a subject for a different book; all I wanted to do was to have this particular Airbus in my own collection.

When Airbus re-designed the A340 to produce the two new models, the -500 and -600, the new aircraft had a brand new wing, different engines and the two-wheel centre undercarriage gave way to a four-wheel unit. With the only model of the A340 in 1/144th being Revell's A340-300, it seemed a huge task to even consider converting this to one of the larger variants.

But on a trip to the IPMS show at Telford, I was talking to Ivo at Bra.Z's stand and he smiled as I talked of the A340-500 and -600. From below the

The Revell release of the A340-300 (this one being the Wiener Philharmoniker version) can be converted to any of the A340 family with the help of Bra.Z, some filler and a lot of sandpaper!

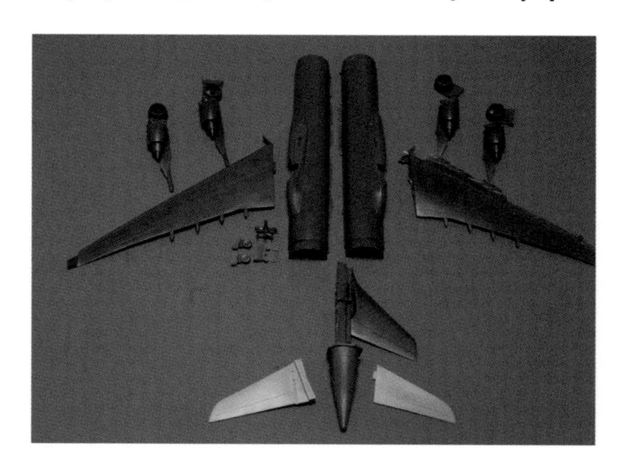

The Bra.Z resin conversion set for the A340-600.

counter he showed me a plastic bag containing some of the largest pieces of cast resin I have ever seen! In my hands were the centre fuselage section, replacement wings and engines, correct tailfin and horizontal stabilizers, a new tailcone section and all the parts needed to make a correct four-wheel centre undercarriage unit for a -600! Incredibly Bra.Z have produced a conversion set and I was as close to airliner modelling nirvana as I would ever be! It is this set, along with the Revell A340-300 kit, which is the subject of this final chapter.

The BraZ conversion set is available in a few different liveries and it was the red and pearly grey finish of Virgin Atlantic that caught my eye. A quick run over to Hannants' stand provided me with the correct paint colours, as the pearl finish is available as a grey undercoat, with a mica varnish applied on top of the grey. The paint is from Xtracolour and coded X367 Virgin Atlantic Grey and X368 Mica and my initial thoughts were that this could possibly end up looking a little 'toy-like'.

So where do we start on a project as large as this? Well, cleaning up the resin parts will take some time as there is quite a bit of flash on the wing leading edges and the fuselage parts have prominent pouring stubs that will need cleaning up. This project is going to need a lot of sanding and polishing and I have found that nail files and sanding sticks are an economical alternative to those found in the hobby shops. I have used various styles and types of sanding cloths and sticks on this model and you'll be able to see a few of these in the photographs, a few eyebrows were certainly raised, though, as I left the chemist with a whole bagful!

The resin is soft and very easy to work with and, in fact, the cleaning up of all the parts only takes a couple of hours with a scalpel blade and some sanding sticks. All the parts of the kit itself are then washed in warm soapy water, rinsed off and allowed to dry before I start to get to grips with the sequence of construction for this model.

I decided to tackle the fuselage and I had read that the centre section has shrunk slightly, resulting in a narrower diameter than the kit's fuselage sections. Not a huge problem, but certainly something to con-

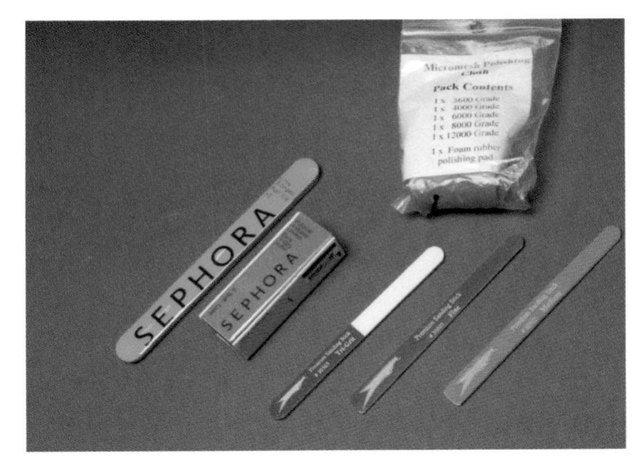

This is going to require a lot of sanding: in addition to the various grades of sanding sheets, various nail polishers are also employed...

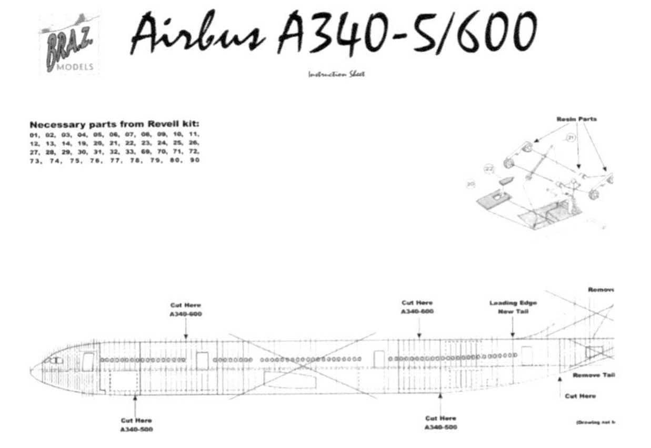

The Bra.Z instruction sheet shows clearly where the kit fuselage needs to be cut.

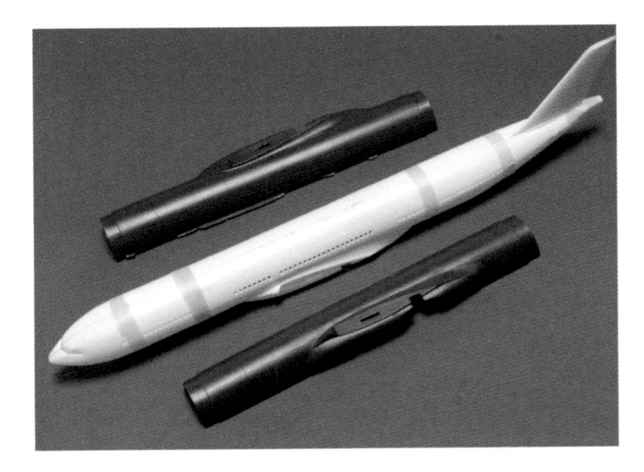

The new fuselage insert is huge and heavy!

sider rectifying. Studying the Bra.Z instructions for the conversion showed me exactly where to cut the Revell fuselage and is done in exactly the same way as the Airbus A330 conversion, by taping the fuselage together and marking the exact place to cut with masking tape.

You can see from the photographs that the resin centre section extends the Revell kit enormously. I now started to have reservations regarding display or storage space!

With the nose and tail sections now separated from the original centre section and taped together, the new resin section, again with both halves taped together, is presented to the Revell parts. Why I was surprised that it all fitted together I don't know; the fit is excellent for such large conversion parts and, although there is evidence of shrinkage and a little warping, this can easily be rectified.

With resin parts, if there is any warping, letting the part soak in hot water will return the part to its original shape, but remember to let it cool before handling. The large gaps will need to be filled but that can be incorporated into the cleaning process.

So, knowing what lay ahead I set to work filling the cabin windows of the original kit parts and joining the respective halves together. These are left to fully set while the two resin fuselage halves are stuck together with epoxy resin adhesive. This has the advantage that it does form a very strong join when cured but, as it sets relatively slowly compared to cyano acrylate, it gives more freedom to move the parts around until they are correctly positioned. This is certainly important here, as time is needed to get the four sections of the fuselage straight and in line. After working slowly and carefully, each section is adhered to the next with the epoxy adhesive and, once the parts are all in line, the whole assembly is left to set.

Copious amounts of filler are then used on all the seams, especially the large seam along the top of the fuselage which is first filled with gel-type cyano acrylate followed by a spray of accelerator. This makes the cyano acrylate harden immediately and gives a good backing for the filler to go onto, rather than falling through into the hollow fuselage. Once

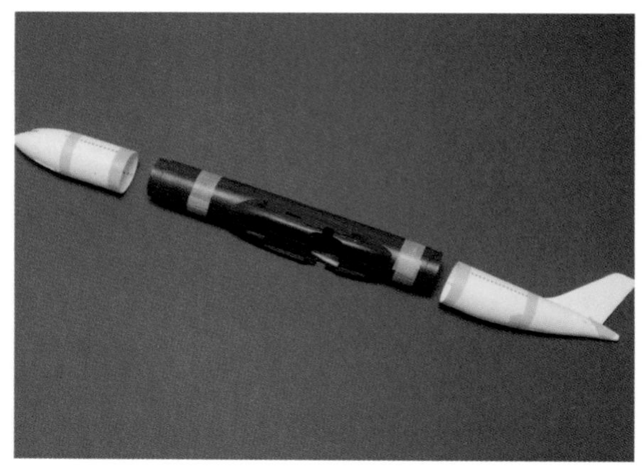

After the cuts have been made, the only parts of the kit fuselage that are needed are the nose and tail...

...although most of the tail area is also discarded! Here she sits next to the A330-200 fuselage from earlier.

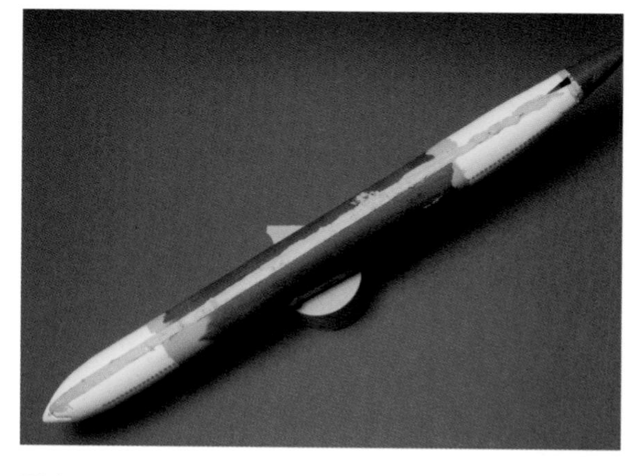

This project is going to need a lot of filler!

the whole fuselage has dried, the real work begins! It takes more repeated filling and sanding than I think I have done in my whole modelling lifetime, but the work slowly shows worthwhile results.

However, those rumours of shrinkage turn out to be true and the fuselage has a subtle coke bottle shape to it. So there is nothing else to be done other than build up the entire centre section carefully with more filler.

This now needs to be allowed to fully harden; leave the model for around a week before attempting to sand the whole fuselage again. At this stage the wings are also attached; the wing to fuselage seam will also require filling and sanding so may as well all be tackled in one go.

The model is then carefully sanded using Tamiya's sanding sheets, under a running tap to ensure that the resin and filler dust is trapped and not allowed into the air. A dust mask should be worn during the whole process and hands washed carefully after each session. Slowly but surely the model starts to look less of a mess and definite progress can be seen, but I will not downplay the time spent on filling and sanding: it is hard work, but the quite gorgeous resin conversion really does deserve it.

The fuselage is given a light spray of primer to highlight any areas that need attention: there are, naturally, many and so filling and sanding begin again, followed by another primer coat, more filling, sanding and so on.

At this stage, the fin is also attached and the base filled. Gradually the model really starts to look as if it is going to be finished, which is a relief as I have just exhausted my supply of filler!

Taking a break from the filling and sanding of the fuselage I had a look at the resin replacement engines. The beautiful replicas of the Rolls-Royce Trent 500s are each supplied as two halves, the front fan section and the rear. The resin pouring stubs are cut off each part and then the two halves stuck together with cyano acrylate. The seam does require a small application of filler and this is then sanded smooth with the nail polishing sticks. The engines are dry fitted to the wing to ensure their fit, which is perfect, before the entire airframe is given a final coat of Tamiya surface primer.

After the filler has dried, sanding commences.

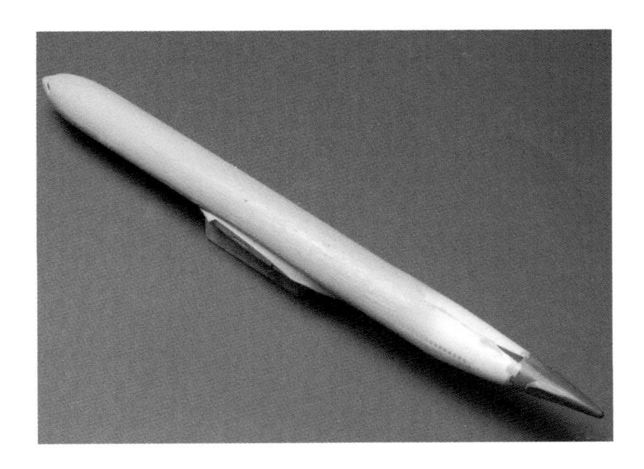

The fuselage insert is slightly smaller in diameter than the kit and needs building up with filler – a lot of filler!

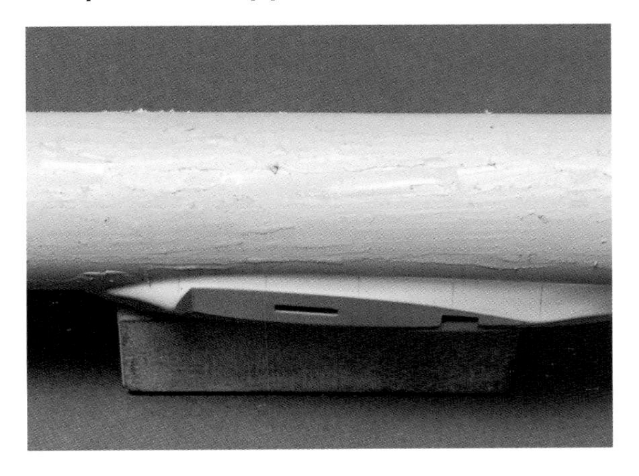

Slowly but surely, the filler builds up and is sanded progressively smoother until...

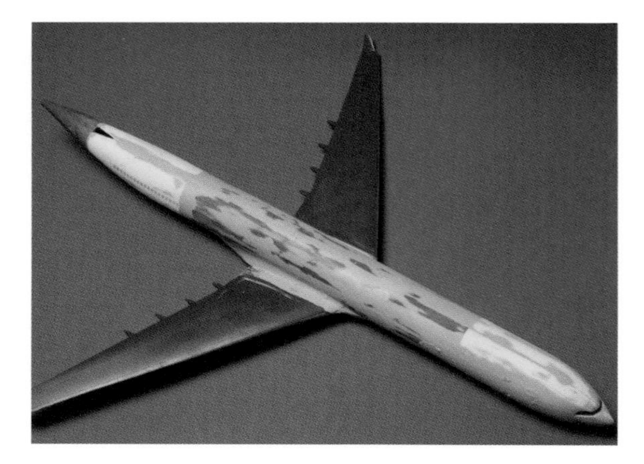

The amount of filler used is evident here.

But the effort is rewarded when the first coats of primer are applied.

There are a few areas that need attention, but this seems like child's play now!

There are still some areas that need further filling: it is sometimes not until you get a good primer coat on the model that areas that need work show up. A little extra filling and sanding is not a problem, but I could do with a little respite from the fuselage and so turn my attention to the smaller details; starting with those Trents.

Each engine is primed and then the cowling lips sprayed aluminium, as well as the front fan blades in a contrasting, slightly darker shade. The rear sections of the engines are also sprayed in darker metallic shades, with the exhaust cone having a mix of brown and aluminium applied to match the colours seen on the real aircraft. After the metallic colours have dried, they are masked off before the cowls are sprayed red using Tamiya acrylic paint. The exact shade is actually the matt red, XF-7, which dries very quickly and under a gloss varnish topcoat looks to be the correct shade of Virgin's red livery.

The undercarriage of the A340 is essentially the same as that of the A330, apart from the addition of a third main undercarriage bogie under the centre fuselage. The A340-300 Revell kit supplies the two-wheeled unit seen on the

-300 and these wheels are used, along with the pair supplied by Bra.Z, to make up the four-wheel bogie seen on the -500 and -600. Once again these are detailed with fuse wire to represent the hydraulic brake lines.

After all the undercarriage units have been assembled it is time to go back to the fuselage and further practice my sanding skills! The windscreen has already been attached, filled and sanded and, apart from some minor flaws in the finish that need attending to, the main airframe is ready. Finally the last coat of primer can be applied, after which the model is allowed to dry for a few days before receiving a final sanding with Micromesh sanding and polishing cloths. These are excellent for getting an exceptionally smooth surface as they are very finely graded. With the primed surface ready, it is time to spray the wings Airbus Grey; the model is then left well alone to allow the paint to dry before handling again. It takes a few days for the grey enamel to harden, after which the wings are masked off and the fuselage is ready for the final colour.

CLOCKWISE FROM TOP LEFT:

The Bra.Z engines are dry-fitted and tacked in place to reveal the full size of this model.

The whole airframe is given a further light dusting of primer to reveal any imperfections.

The Bra.Z resin Trent 500s are initially primed white and then the metallic areas sprayed.

Finally the first coat of red! Tamiya's XF-7 matt red is used and, although a matt finish initially, is brought vividly to life under a coat of Johnson's Future.

The centre undercarriage on the -500 and -600 versions of the A340 have a four-wheel bogie, which has brake units on all four wheels. The hydraulic lines are once again made up from fuse wire.

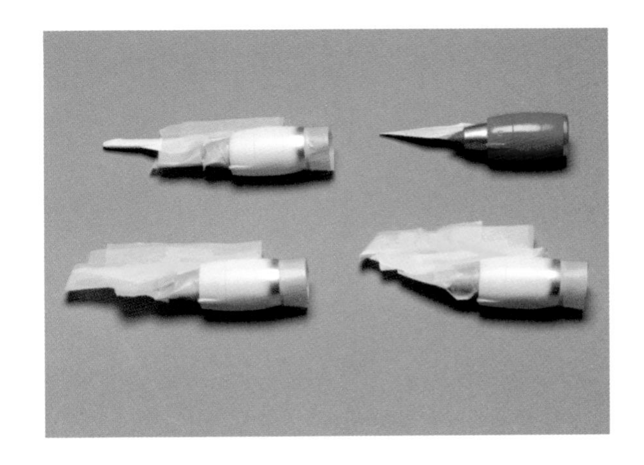

Masking the wings prior to the fuselage being sprayed with the first coat.

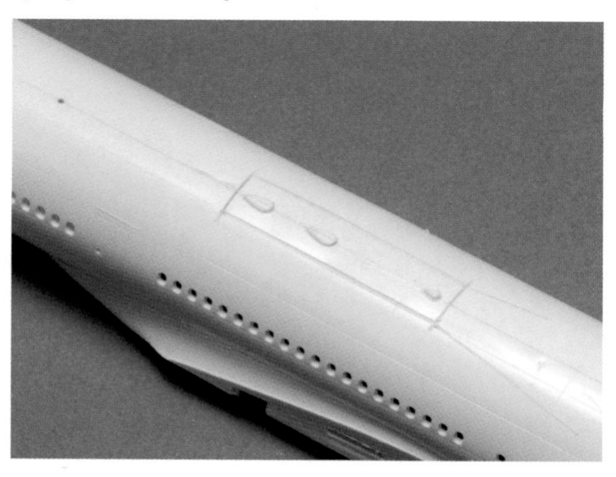

The small dome aerials on the fuselage top are sourced from the removed section of the original kit.

The two-part application of paint really does give a fantastic finish!

At this point I have spotted a small mistake: the two small dome aerials on the upper fuselage are missing. These are simply sourced from the original kit, as they are present on the Revell kit but not with the Bra.Z resin parts. There is no problem in removing the parts from the Revell fuselage: first attach the two halves of the plastic fuselage together, before cutting the section out of the fuselage top and then sanding the parts down until the aerials are free. These are then glued separately in place on the resin fuselage and given a coat of primer before the main task of spraying the final colour.

Xtracolor's X367 Virgin Atlantic Grey is carefully applied first, using the airbrush. Gradually build up the coats on the fuselage, leaving about fifteen minutes in between each coat, will give a smooth and uniform finish although it does look a little military being just plain grey. But after the enamel paint has hardened, again after leaving the model well alone for a few days, the X368 Mica topcoat is applied and my fears of it looking like a toy are totally unfounded. The finish is superb and the fine metallic flakes in the mica varnish really do give the model a beautiful pearly lustre. I just hope that the photographs do the finish justice; otherwise you will just have to take my word for it that Xtracolor have produced a superb finish with these paints.

The masking is removed from the wings and the tail masked and then sprayed red, once again using the Tamiya acrylic paint. Once the paint has fully dried, the whole model is given first a dust coat of Johnson's Future, before building the gloss finish up carefully, making sure that not too much is applied as there is a danger of runs forming. Once again the substantial model is left aside to dry before the next job can begin, that of applying the decals.

The tail fin is tackled first, followed by the fuselage after the wings have had their Corogard sections applied. The decals are superb and although, as with the easyJet decals, I was worried about the density of the white as it was applied to the bright red surface, there is no need to worry as the classic Virgin titling looks superb against the red tail. The leading edge of the fin has another decal applied that gives the effect of the red having a gradient to it and this decal proves to be very effective in getting the right look.

The next job on the list is to mask off the Corogard areas and then spray these with the Corogard paint from Xtracolour. These have fine walkway lines around them and the fine black lines are sourced from the Revell decal sheet, as are many of the generic stencils.

The majority of the painting is now complete and the decaling continues with the main fuselage titles, as well as the windows, doors, registration codes and smaller stencil decals. The winglet Union Jacks certainly give the model a splash of colour at the end of those huge wings!

With the decals all in place, it just remains for the undercarriage to be attached, as well as the horizontal stabilizers, followed by the final details such as the blade aerials and anti-collision beacons.

I have no idea how many hours I spent on this superb conversion from Bra.Z, but this gave me more hours per pound spent than any other project I have completed so far. With the end of this chapter also comes the end of our modelling journey through the history of commercial aviation.

There are many more aircraft that I would have liked to complete for this book and I apologize if your favourite subjects have not been covered. But the principles are the same with building most airliner kits; the future for our hobby is also secure with new products coming onto the market all the time. Of course, the history of commercial aviation continues with the manufacturers releasing new model airliners, as well as newer versions of existing models, and the model kit manufacturers are now not far behind. Zvezda of Russia has released a kit of Boeing's 787 Dreamliner and Revell have the huge Airbus A380 in their catalogue now too. As this book was finished, Zvezda announced the release of their new model kit of the Boeing 747-8. And if you thought the A340-600 was long...!

In the meantime, I hope that this book has proved useful in improving your skills, or introducing you to the subject of airline modeling. After months in progress, here is the A340-600, finally finished and now sitting in pride of place amongst my own collection.

The tailfin is masked and Tamiya XF-7 sprayed on.

With the bright red engines attached I'm really quite pleased with the progress so far. The Corogard areas are now masked off prior to them being sprayed.

The smaller parts now receive attention – quite a time-consuming job on such a large model.

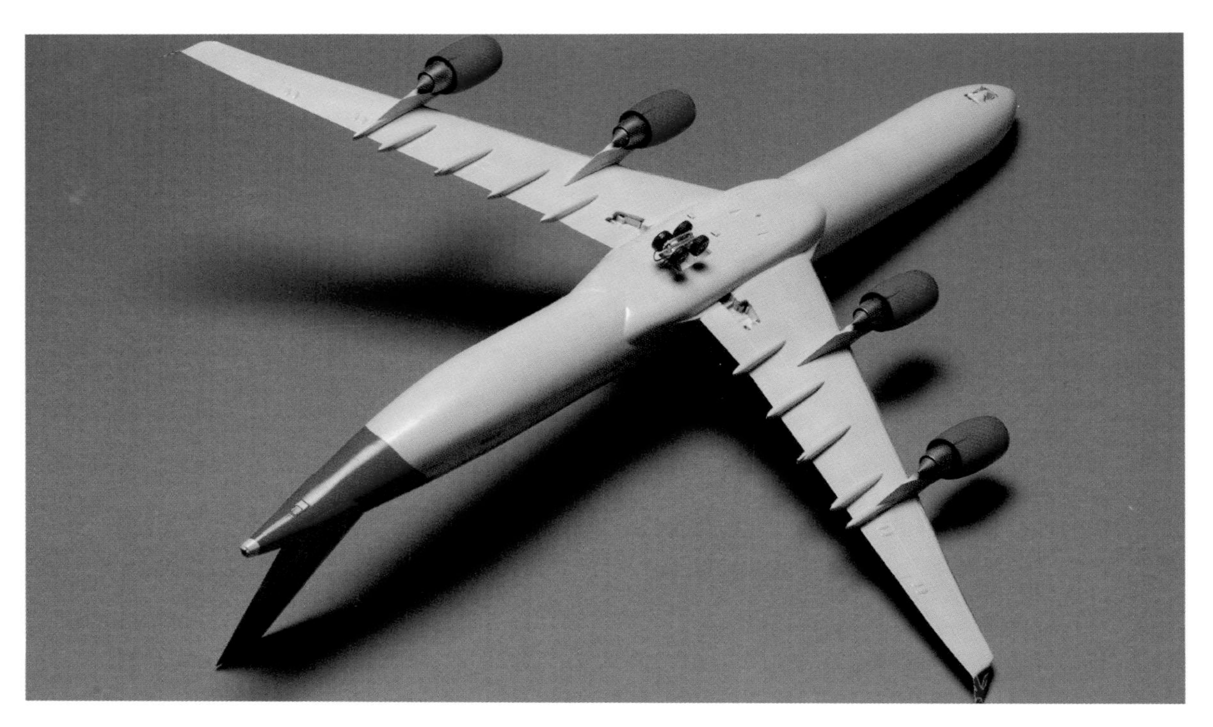

ABOVE: ***A view of the underside: with the centre undercarriage in place and the vibrant red engines really standing out.***
BELOW: ***After a seemingly endless amount of time and effort, I am very proud to present, quite possibly, the most satisfying model I have ever built!***

CHAPTER 25

IT'S ALL IN THE DETAILS

A PICTORIAL WALK AROUND THE AIRBUS A319

The Internet is an incredible source of photographs to help with reference when you are building your models. However, there is a lack of detailed photographs that show areas of the aircraft not normally seen; so I'd just like to share some photographs of the Airbus A319, which I hope will help when detailing your own models, or indeed when applying washes and streaks of paint to weather the finish realistically.

The wing to fuselage join on the A319.

Many details, such as the static pressure sensors, are depicted as decals on model aircraft.

The nose wheel, showing the take-off and taxi lights.

The metallic areas of jet engines display numerous shades.

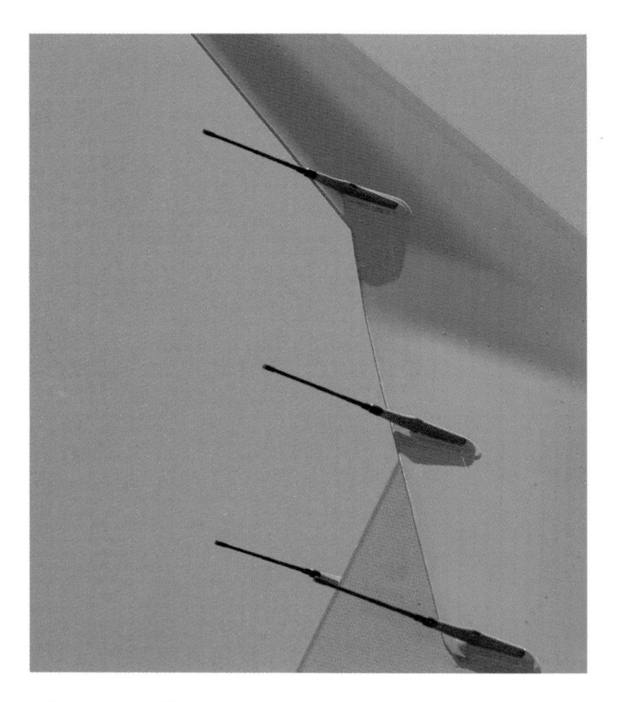

The static dischargers are quite prominent on the wing tip fences and trailing edges of the wings, elevators and rudder.

A detail view of the engine inlet and front fan of the CFM-56, which powers the Airbus A319 in service with easyJet.

The main undercarriage leg and door: this area can get very dirty.

The reverse thrust doors open, showing the green/yellow interior colour.

The interior of most panel doors is red.

The starboard main landing gear, viewed from the rear.

The interior of the main landing gear bay, showing how dirty this area gets.

A view from the rear of the engine, into the area behind the front fan.

The main landing gear bay has a lot of pipework that is often missing in an aircraft model kit.

The engine pylon is constructed of various materials and is a patchwork of different metallic shades.

The rear fuselage, unless straight out of the cleaning bay, is normally covered with fluid streaks.

The area immediately behind the nose landing gear also gets quite dirty.

Detail shot of the open cargo door, showing the hydraulic ramps at the top.

The ground handlers control the opening of the cargo door from behind this panel: the panel is normally seen open during passenger boarding.

CHAPTER 26

HEALTH AND SAFETY – LOOK AFTER YOURSELF!

This final chapter is reproduced with the kind permission of Rob Plas, a Dutch modeller who has extensive knowledge, through his work in the chemical industry, of many of the products that we use in our hobby. It is therefore with thanks and gratitude that I am able to include this particularly important part of our hobby, written from the viewpoint of someone far more qualified than I. Without trying to scare modellers away from their hobby, this chapter tries to teach us all a little about some of the health risks which are present when building scale models, therefore, do please heed Rob's advice. Without further ado, I would now like to hand over to Rob Plas:

As most of you will probably know well, the hobby of building scale models; from trucks, tanks, aeroplanes and ships, has taken an enormous jump forward over the last ten years. New techniques, as well as new materials have created a whole new era in making replicas of the subjects we admire for one reason or another. With all these new materials, new chemicals have also been introduced to the hobby. Think about glues, paints and plastics; many of these materials can, and do, present a risk to your health.

Firstly, I should say that I work in a chemical plant and have received a lot of training about the dangers of certain chemicals, such as solvents and I feel that I should share this information with other modellers. Secondly, the risks are present and, if care is not taken, then serious health issues can develop. In our own Model Club a member was hospitalized for around ten days after working with cast resin parts after suffering severe respiratory problems and nose bleeds.

The dangers involved with modelling can be divided into two main kinds of risks: the short-term and the long-term risks. So let's have a quick look at the differences between them.

Short-term risks include the obvious injuries to hands and eyes from cutting, grinding and the use of other mechanical tools. Other short-term risks include: eye injuries through contact with chemicals and injuries caused by fire.

Long-term risks are a little harder to define, as they are less obvious and immediate. But these include: allergic reactions to certain chemicals, problems associated with the respiratory system due to over exposure to chemicals, and brain damage caused by over exposure to solvents.

SHORT-TERM RISKS

INJURIES TO HANDS AND EYES

When working with sharp knives it is almost inevitable that you will cut your fingers once in a while. Usually these are tiny cuts with razor sharp scalpels, so always keep a few plasters handy! But every now and then on some of the Internet forums, messages appear regarding serious wounds modellers have sustained after accidents with scalpel and X-Acto blades, or other sharp tools. There are some basic rules to prevent you from receiving a really bad cut and I apologize if these appear to be simple, almost childish rules, but they are worth repeating.

Never work towards yourself, always cut away from your body. If the knife slips away you won't cut yourself badly on either your hand or fingers. A more serious problem, though, is the fact that splinters, sawdust and other tiny bits can come into contact with your eye whilst cutting. Electrical tools can also let drill bit shrapnel fly all around your modelling space. Avoid injuries by wearing safety glasses and, if an injury is sustained, do not rub your eyes! Ask for help to rinse your eyes with some clean water and see a doctor if your eyes keep hurting.

Eye injuries sustained through contact with chemicals

By contact, I mean contamination of your eyes with fumes from superglue, thinners, solvents and paints: if you are splashed in the eye by any of these do not rub your eyes; it is important to firstly rinse with water and then go and see a doctor. If you do get any superglue, or cyano acrylate glue in your eyes go directly to a doctor, do not attempt to open the affected eye yourself as you might damage the surface of the eye which is irreversible!

FIRE

Some of the methods used in our hobby require the heating of plastics on an open flame, as well as the use of soldering irons and heat-treating, photo etched metal sets. Often this is done on a workbench loaded with other hobby gear.

Take a look around your own bench and what do you see? A bottle of thinner? Some turpentine and alcohol based products too? Perhaps an open jar containing thinner for cleaning brushes? Polystyrene glue? All these chemicals are highly flammable; therefore be very careful with heat and open flames. An accident can occur before you even realize it and let's be honest, do you have a fire extinguisher to hand on your workbench?

All of the above are risks associated with immediate dangers, but the long-term risks are possibly more dangerous, due to the fact that the threats are not immediate and often not always very clear.

LONG-TERM RISKS

These are basically allergic reactions to certain chemicals and problems associated with the respiratory system, due to over exposure to chemicals. To realize what dangers we are talking about here, you first need to know some basic information. Allergic reactions occur when we come into contact with materials our body cannot really cope with. An allergic reaction can display itself on the surface of the skin, in the form of red spots or even wounds in the long term, or by associated problems with the respiratory system. We probably all know people who are allergic to cats and dogs, whilst the symptoms shown by hay fever sufferers are also typical of an allergic reaction.

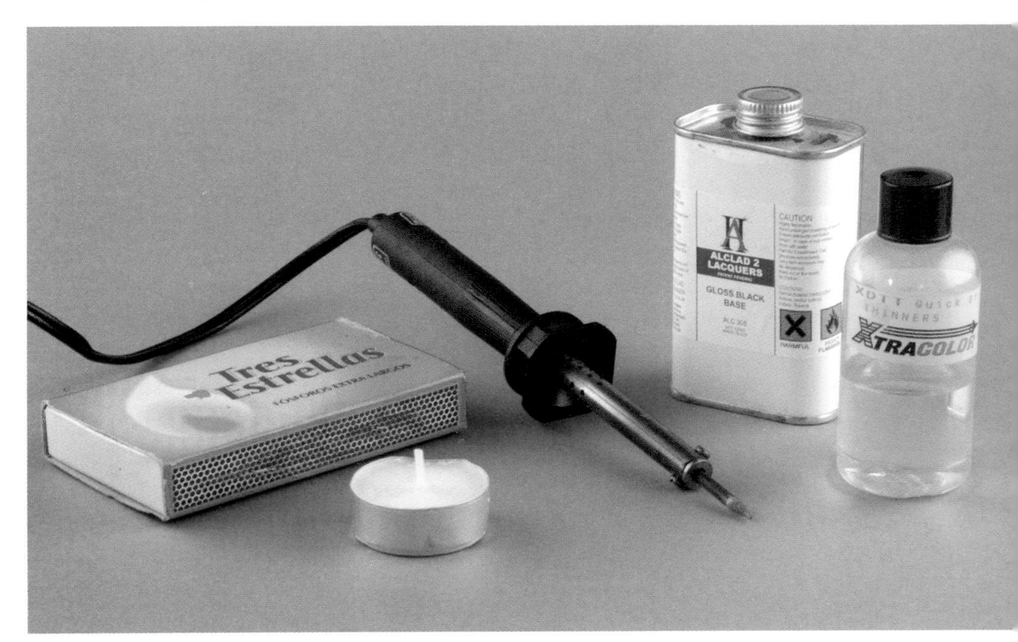

Heat sources and solvents should always be kept far apart.

It is a fact that you can usually withstand a lot of contact with a material you are, in fact, allergic to, without having any trouble at all. But, when you finally reach a point where your body starts 'over-reacting' to contact with a substance it will hardly ever go away.

You can develop an allergy to solvents and thinners and also resin, more precisely Polyurethane Resin, which is a chemical that can give very strong allergic reactions. So, when working with Polyurethane Resin it is essential that you try to minimize the amount of dust you inhale when sanding, sawing and cutting plastics. The easiest way to do this is to wear a safety mask, use wet sandpaper and clean up the work-bench as often as possible. Also, be sure not to eat, drink or smoke while working with these plastics.

BRAIN DAMAGE CAUSED BY OVER EXPOSURE TO SOLVENTS

This may sound very dramatic but it doesn't have to be. More and more literature is being published about a disease called OPS; it is now clear that this disease is caused by minute brain damage due to years and years of working with solvents. In Holland the disease is called 'Painters' Disease', because this is one of the groups of workers that frequently show symptoms of this disease. These include: sudden mood changes, loss of concentration and feeling tired and numb. Although most modellers don't use the large amounts of thinners and solvents that may inflict injury upon people, they do often work in ill-ventilated areas with these substances very close to their faces; in fact usually they are sitting right above the fumes and vapours, almost with their noses in the bottles! These solvents are to be found in many paints, thinners, glues and fillers.

Some solvents are also possible carcinogens, which means they may increase the risk of developing cancer. Here is a short list of chemicals commonly used by many modellers, with the associated risks to your health:

- **Acetone:** Used for gluing and cleaning airbrushes and brushes; a solvent associated with OPS.

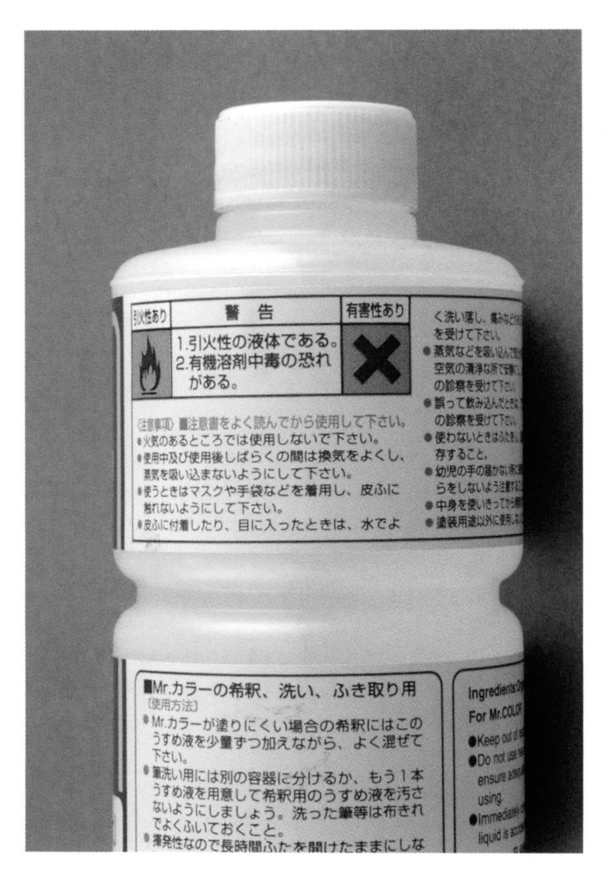

Regardless of the language on the label, the hazard labels themselves are internationally recognizable.

- **Cyano acrylate or superglue:** Suspected harmful fumes and also dangerous for the eyes, well known for gluing flesh together.

- **Acrylic Paints:** The safest paint to use, low in fumes and solvents, often alcohol-based.

- **Benzene:** Used for cleaning airbrushes, a solvent and a risk for OPS as well as being a carcinogen. Not normally available in hobby stores as it is not very nice at all.

- **Caustic Soda:** Sometimes used for stripping paint off models, can give you severe burns and can cause blindness when the solution is too strong.

Some hazards are obvious, others less so. Always read the hazard warning labels to see what risks are present.

- **Enamel Paints:** Paints based on oils, their thinners are the most risky components.
- **Epoxy Puttys such as Zimm-it-rite and Miliput:** Can cause skin and eye irritation, harmful when swallowed.
- **MEK:** This is a strong solvent that is widely used for cleaning airbrushes and gluing plastics; dangers include OPS and it is also a suspected carcinogen.
- **Pigments in paint:** Some of the pigments in paints are based on oxidized metals like Cadmium and Titanium. A Dutch beer brewery had to destroy all of their yellow crates a few years ago because of the Cadmium Yellow pigments in the plastics.
- **Polystyrene glue:** Often Toluene based, it is a solvent with an associated OPS risk and suspected of being a carcinogen.
- **Polyurethane Resin:** The dust is the most dangerous element because it can enter your respiratory system.
- **Polyester:** Very harmful vapours occur during the curing process.
- **Primer paints:** Often from a spray can, lots of unhealthy vapours and pigments.

- **Silicone Rubber Compounds:** Can cause skin and eye irritation.

- **Soldering lead:** The fumes are not very healthy and, of course, lead is very poisonous.

PROTECTION

So, now that you are sufficiently enlightened to the dangers associated with our hobby, and before you decide to stop modelling and get another hobby, protecting yourself from these risks is really quite easy and not expensive to do.

For most solvents and fumes a respiratory mask will do, but certainly obtain a type with changeable filters, this will be cheaper in the long term. A good mask will cost you about £20 or €25 and it will last for ages. There are also a few rules to follow which will reduce the hazards:

- Ventilate the room when working.
- Do not lick your brushes.
- Wash your hands after finishing the job and don't eat, drink or smoke during your modelling session.
- Use a dust mask when sanding plastics and always try to use wet paper; apart from the health advantages you will get a smoother finish too!
- When working with resin, do not use your Dremel or other electrical tool; the dust generated by these tools is enormous.
- Work in good light conditions so that you don't accidentally cut your fingers.
- Try to wear safety glasses when working with your Dremel or other electrical tools.
- Be very careful when building your own compressor. A well-known story in modelling circles is of the gentleman who built his own compressor from an old refrigerator compressor and a gas tank. He blew up his shed because he forgot to turn the thing off and failed to incorporate any pressure safety devices!
- Be very careful with pressurized gas containers; I have seen postings of people wanting to use Nitrogen gas, Carbon Dioxide and other industrial gases as a propellant for their airbrushes. Do not do this; a (silent) compressor is still the best option.

Many thanks to Rob Plas for allowing me to reproduce here what was first published in the magazine of the Dutch chapter of the IPMS. Ruud

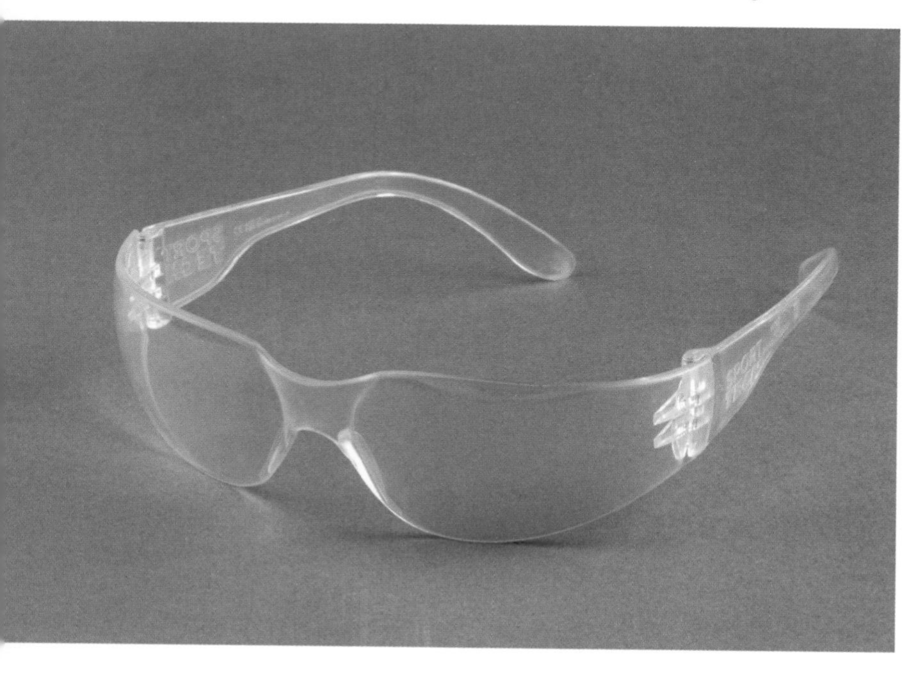

A pair of safety goggles is a cheap and effective way to protect your eyes from flying parts.

A good quality facemask will protect you from breathing in harmful vapours and fumes.

Pronk, Product Manager, Filters and Masks at Dräger Nederland, has written a sequel and I am very happy to reproduce it here. This article is a partial repeat of the above, but with his professional knowledge and association with the devices that protect us from many of the dangers present in our hobby, it is well worth reading!

When looking at our hobby from the perspective of my professional background I have to state that, while modelling, people often use many potentially dangerous chemicals that can be harmful to their health.

Many of these chemicals are used in industry, where the people that need to deal with these substances have the right and the duty to use protective clothing and devices: something that is regulated by law. In this situation the employer is responsible for providing the best possible solutions to prevent health hazards to the people that work for them.

But working with these chemicals as a hobbyist, these laws will not protect you and it is therefore of great importance that you understand the risks and consequences.

HAZARDOUS CHEMICALS

When we talk about dangerous substances we are talking about the following risks:

- Flammable and combustible substances.
- Poisonous and/or harmful substances.
- Aggressive and/or irritating substances.
- Substances harmful to the environment.

When dealing with poisonous chemicals you have to consider that there are three ways you can be affected:

1. Swallowing.

2. Absorption through the skin.
3. Inhalation through breathing.

Swallowing is, in many cases, a simple matter of hygiene. When you are dealing with poisons you need to wash your hands, face and arms from time to time. Eating, drinking and/or smoking are well known contamination sources so that's a no go!

Swallowing poisons is normally a matter of personal discipline, and the willingness to follow that discipline is often a matter of knowledge about the chemicals we work with.

Many dangerous substances are absorbed through the human skin. This can become a critical situation if a large amount of it is spilled when accidentally turning a bottle over on the worktop.

Instant poisoning needs immediate action, but do you know which actions to take for the different chemicals you work with? For every dangerous substance you can find a safety sheet (Material Safety and Data Sheet or MSDS) that contains the most important data about the chemical it concerns. In Dutch and other European laws a compact version of this sheet is obliged to be visible on the packaging of the chemical. (Certainly the UK, by law, carries full details on the packaging and labels of solvents, adhesives and paints.) On the Internet you can also find these sheets; just type the name of the chemical and MSDS into the search engine of your browser and you will normally find what you are looking for. Be aware that many companies use commercial names for their products, but by checking the labels you must be able to find the substances used in their products.

A different kind of poisoning is repeated contamination with small doses of chemicals that, in isolation, are not a danger. But many of these chemicals tend to build up in the body and will only display their harmful effects after many years; because of this, it is often very hard to find the cause of an illness. These problems are often summarized as 'Professional Diseases' in Europe.

Poisoning through the respiratory system is the most common and well-known cause and will be recognized by many as the primary cause of poisoning. The symptoms of this type of exposure are often:

- Headaches.
- Nausea.
- Skin rash.
- Affection of internal organs such as the kidneys and liver.
- Affection of the nervous system, brain and reproductive organs.
- Congenital defects.
- Orientation problems.
- Mood changes.
- Allergic reactions.
- Digestion problems.

We can find these substances in the following areas:

- Gas.
- Vapours (This is a gas that can condense into small droplets).
- Liquids.
- Solids.
- Fog/Mist (A combination of gas with small droplets of a liquid, also known as aerosols).

PROTECTING YOUR RESPIRATORY SYSTEM

Facial hair like moustaches and beards do negatively influence the effectiveness of all types of protective devices. Everything that sits between the bare skin and the edges of a mask will cause leaks, thus allowing the fumes to bypass the filters that are used to absorb the dangerous substances. It helps to read the manual that is usually supplied with the filter of your choice; it normally describes how to check for leaks.

Breathing protection is roughly divided into two classes: **Independent and Dependent.**

- **Independent** protection means you can breathe independently from the surrounding environment, normally we are talking about scuba gear or the pressurized air tanks and masks used in industry and/or the fire department.
- **Dependent** means you breathe the surrounding air, but filter the dangerous gasses and vapours from it. This is the class most often used.

Different types of masks

The first type of mask is one that partially covers the face, with an exchangeable filter cartridge with different types of filters.

1. Dust filter: It's all in the name; this type of cartridge only filters dust from the air that you are breathing. They will not protect you from gases and/or vapours.
2. Gas filters: These filters will protect you from harmful chemical vapours and gases.
3. Combined filters, simply a combination of the two filters mentioned above.

Full-face masks also protect the eyes and skin of the face, whilst half-face masks are intended for the protection of the respiratory system only. These masks can also be sub-divided into the following different types: namely durable, re-usable masks, and masks for one-time use only, which must be disposed of after use. Disposable masks are not as effective as the masks that can be re-used. The main problem is to get a good, tight fit on the face. Often these masks leak air between the edges and the skin so, even if the mask itself is made of quality materials, the air will by-pass the mask and you will still breathe in harmful substances. These disposable masks are only usable when the exposure to dust is slight and not for too long a time. They are not really suitable as personal protection for most of the chemicals already named here. A good quality disposable mask can be recognized by its classification marks and these masks follow the EN143 classification:

- FFP1: This has the lowest filtering capability and will only stop particles with a value of 10mg/M3 (think about sand grains here).
- FFP2: This mask will filter any medium sized dust with a value of 0,1 to 10 mg/3.
- FFP3: These are the masks with the highest classification and they will filter particles that are smaller then 0,1 mg/M3, such as asbestos and quartz.

Other markings that you can find according to these EN standards are:

- S = Solid, or solid particles.
- L= Liquid, suitable for filtering droplets and mists.
- V = Valve, a valve for the outgoing air is added (this prevents the air from going trough the filtering layers twice, so the filter will last longer).

When using a filter you will feel a resistance in the airflow. This is quite normal, and the better the filters the higher the resistance will be. When using a very fine FFP3 filter use one with a valve, thus reducing the resistance when breathing out. You won't find these filters in a DIY shop and they are a lot more expensive then masks without a valve. Therefore, for modelling use at least a FFP2 mask.

How long should my mask last?

This depends on a number of factors:

- How much pollution is on the mask after use?
- Blockage of the airflow due to saturation of the filter medium.
- Moisture from exhaling will cause the particles to stick to the mask.
- By handling the mask with dirty hands it will get dirty very easily.
- Air leaks will cause the edges to get dirty very easily.
- Leaving the mask at the work desk will cause it to get dirty very easily.

Gas filters

Gas filters do their work by binding gasses and vapours by active carbon. This can work in two ways, depending upon the chemicals used; the molecules bind physically to the carbon or can be bound chemically. Dependent upon the filter and chemicals, one of either process takes place and the choice of filter should always be made with the pollution level taken into consideration.

Always use a certified filter (EN141); you can recognize it by its markings:

- A = Brown stripe, usable for organic vapours with a boiling temperature >65 degrees Celsius.
- B = Grey stripe, usable for acid gasses, formaldehyde.

- E = Yellow stripe, for Sculpture Dioxide.
- K = Green strip for Ammonia.
- AX = Organic vapours with a boiling temperature <65 degrees Celsius.
- P = White stripe for dust, because a good one also filters out dust particles.

On each filter that is made following official standards there is also an indication for its capacity, divided into three classes: Class three has the highest capacity, classes one and two are normally used with masks that only cover the mouth and nose.

How long should a filter last?

How long a filter will last depends on several different factors:

- The nature of the gasses and vapours: some chemicals do not bind as easily to the active carbon.
- A combination of different chemicals: due to differences in reaction capacity, some chemicals tend to slip through the filter because others bind much more quickly to the carbon. This can even result in exchanging chemicals that were already bonded by the carbon, to let go again in favour of the new chemical.
- Temperature and humidity: as a rule the higher they get, the worse they affect the capacity of the filter used.
- The amount of air and the concentration of the pollution in that airflow.
- A filter that has been used before will contain chemicals that can be released during the next use.
- When a filter is stored between uses it will continue to absorb water and chemicals from the surrounding air, so lock it tight in a plastic bag or something similar.
- If the air contains droplets or a mist of chemicals (airbrushing!) it will result in a very high contamination rate. Using a P-filter will prevent this, thus keeping the filter in better shape.
- Mechanical blockage of the filter by high concentrations of dust particles.

To give some direction the industrial researchers have come up with the following guidelines:

- Maximum time for using a filter is eight hours in total, over a three-month period, providing that the filter is stored in an airtight seal in between uses.
- If you smell the chemical through the mask it's a clear sign that the filter is saturated and needs to be replaced immediately.
- On a good quality mask you will be able to find a production date and, when stored in the appropriate way, it can be used for four years after production. A good way to store your mask is in a dry, sealed bag at room temperature.

These figures follow standard safety rules, but you will probably find out that your filter mask will last a little longer, mostly due to the low exposure rates normally involved with the smaller amounts used in our hobby. It makes a big difference if you are working with a small bottle of thinner, compared with a truckload of it!

To summarize in a few sentences: you can follow these simple guidelines to work in a safe way with the chemicals used in our hobby. Use at least a filter mask that covers your breathing organs (nose and mouth) to keep safe and healthy. After studying the different chemicals used in our hobby I came to the conclusion that an A2-P2 mask is the best and safest possible solution, with the best cost/effect ratio. There are special filters for working with chemicals like Acetone, with a bigger absorbing capacity. The filter I advise will provide you with the same absorbing quality, but will last a shorter time. Even when taking this into consideration, the A2-P2 filter is still the best and cheapest possible solution, even though it has a shorter lifespan.

Ruud Pronk, Dräger, The Netherlands

Rob Plas continues:

I'd like to finish this article by stating that I don't want to tell you how to do your modelling, this article is purely intended to make people aware of some of the risks involved with working with the substances we use. Maybe some newcomers to the hobby are not aware of these risks and will be more careful now.

I would like to thank you for taking the time to read through this chapter, as it really does provide much more detail on the health aspects of modelling, regardless of the genre, than I could ever hope to be able to provide you with myself. So it is with thanks to both Rob and Ruud for providing me with this excellent information. Finally, with respect to buying a good quality mask, a good source are shops that sell car paints and specialized safety articles; no doubt you will be able to find one or two near you and the investment is certainly worth it!

Finally, ladies and gentlemen, we are at the end of our journey. That now concludes our look at modelling commercial aviation and I hope that you have had a comfortable and enjoyable read. On behalf of myself, and all of the crew, thank you once again for choosing to buy your modelling book from The Crowood Press. Please have safe and pleasant onward modelling and we all hope to see you again soon, reading the pages of one of our modelling books!

APPENDIX

CONTACTS AND SUPPLIERS

MODEL KIT MANUFACTURERS

Airfix:
www.airfix.com

Authentic Airliners:
authentic-airliners.de

Minicraft:
www.minicraftmodels.com/index.htm

Revell:
www.revell.com

Hasegawa:
www.hasegawa-model.co.jp/e-w/E-index.htm

Welsh Models:
www.welshmodels.co.uk

Zvezda:
www.zvezda.org.ru

DETAIL AND ADDITIONAL PARTS

Bra.Z Models:
www.brazmodels.com

Contrail:
www.contrailsmodels.com

Extratech:
www.twosixdecals.co.uk

DECAL SHEET MANUFACTURERS

TwoSix Decals:
www.twosixdecals.co.uk

Flightpath Decals:
www.greatmodels.com

Liveries Unlimited:
www.airline-hobby.com/shop/index.cfm?action=ViewCategory&Category=68

Draw Decals:
www.drawdecal.com

Brazil Decals:
www.airlinercafe.com/photosearch.php?man=174

SUNDRIES AND MATERIALS

Alclad II metallic paints:
www.alclad2.com

Swann-Morton Scalpels:
www.swann-morton.com

Winsor and Newton:
www.winsornewton.com

Xtracolour Paints:
www.hannants.co.uk

Xuron Cutters:
www.xuron.com

HOBBY SHOPS, DISTRIBUTORS AND SUPPLIERS

Airline Hobby Supplies:
www.airline-hobby.com

Amerang Ltd:
www.amerang-group.com

The Aviation Hobby Shop:
www.tahs.com

Hannants:
www.hannants.co.uk

Heritage Aviation:
www.heritageaviationmodelsltd.com

Relish Models:
www.relishmodels.co.uk

INDEX

RELATED TITLES FROM CROWOOD

ADVANCED AVIATION MODELLING

JOHN McILLMURRAY

Advanced Aviation Modelling
Jon McIlmurray
ISBN 978 1 86126 753 5
160pp, 330 illustrations

SCALE AIRCRAFT MODELLING

MARK STANTON

Scale Aircraft Modelling
Mark Stanton
ISBN 978 1 86126 445 9
160pp, 250 illustrations

SCALE CAR MODELLING

MAT IRVINE

Scale Car Modelling
Mat Irvine
ISBN 978 1 84797 291 0
176pp, 360 illustrations

SCALE SPACECRAFT MODELLING

MAT IRVINE

Scale Spacecraft Modelling
Mat Irvine
ISBN 978 1 86126 386 5
208pp, 350 illustrations

In case of difficulty ordering, contact the Sales Office:
The Crowood Press, Ramsbury, Wiltshire SN8 2HR UK
Tel: 44 (0) 1672 520320 enquiries@crowood.com www.crowood.com